L et us be among the first to congratulate you on the purchase of your new home. AmeriSpec is proud to have been able to advise on the condition of the house and its various systems.

Over the years our highly trained, certified inspectors have examined more houses than any other home inspection company in North America. In the process, we've come to know a great deal about the benefits of conscientious house maintenance and about the kinds of problems that tend to crop up in even the best-maintained homes. We've now combined all our experience and now present what we've learned in the pages of this book.

Use this book in conjunction with your AmeriSpec report. The report clearly indicates any areas of the house that need immediate attention, and the book can help you decide whether to make the necessary fixes yourself or hire a professional. In the years to come, keep the book nearby for year-round advice on seasonal maintenance and for quick instructions on everything from freeing clogged drains to replacing damaged exterior siding.

We hope you'll take great pleasure in your new home.

AMERISPEC®
HOME INSPECTION SERVICE

contents

taking care of your new home

This book will help you diagnose and solve many common household ailments that can be repaired by a determined homeowner. You may not be able to work as quickly as a professional carpenter, plumber, or electrician on some projects, but many minor repairs are just as quick to perform yourself. Even if you do decide to hire a pro, understanding the causes of problems and knowing your repair options will enable you to save money by avoiding unnecessary work and to ensure an effective job.

You may face an emergency that requires you to shut off the supply of water, gas, or electricity to all or part of your home. The illustrations at right give a quick overview of these shutoffs. See pages 8–9 for more specific information on how to locate and use them. In this chapter you'll also find tips for making your home safer, as well as effective methods for handling specific emergencies, from a sudden grease fire to an overflowing toilet. Finally, a seasonal maintenance chart will help you keep track of routine measures that can prevent major repairs later on.

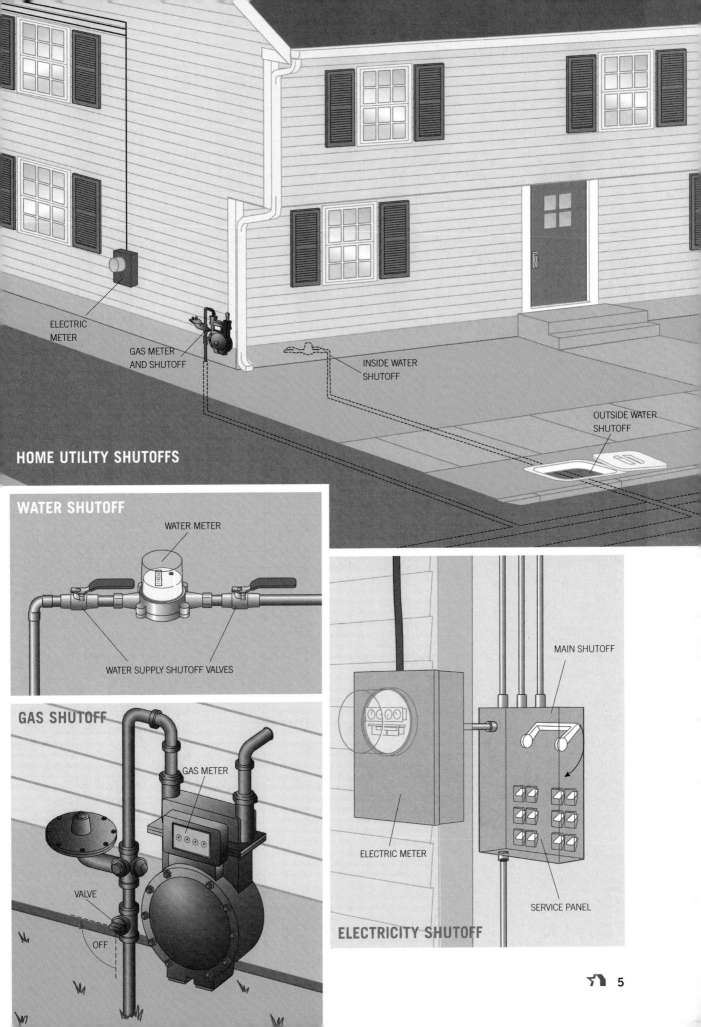

ELECTRIC
METER

GAS METER
AND SHUTOFF

INSIDE WATER
SHUTOFF

OUTSIDE WATER
SHUTOFF

HOME UTILITY SHUTOFFS

WATER SHUTOFF

WATER METER

WATER SUPPLY SHUTOFF VALVES

GAS SHUTOFF

GAS METER

VALVE

OFF

ELECTRICITY SHUTOFF

MAIN SHUTOFF

ELECTRIC METER

SERVICE PANEL

the responsibilities of homeownership

A home inspection report will give you plenty of essential information about the structural integrity and safety of your home. It's important to spend some time studying the report both to get to know your home and to learn ways to minimize problems in the future. Ask your AmeriSpec home inspector questions if you are unsure of any part of the report. Be aware, however, that an inspection does not guarantee that everything in your home will work for years. You may have problems inside your walls that are not visible to the inspector, and new problems can always arise after the inspection. This book will help you deal with most of them.

REPAIR COSTS

While many repairs can be accomplished by a homeowner for a small cost, others need to be done by a professional and can be very expensive. To avoid home repair sticker shock, it's a good idea to set up a savings account for future repairs. To prepare for a new roof or another major project, some experts suggest that homeowners deposit 1 to 2 percent of the house's value every year into such an account. An older or run-down home may need more than 2 percent. If your inspection report indicates that you will need, for instance, a new roof or exterior painting in the next five years, start saving now.

SHUTTING OFF UTILITIES

Every adult family member and older child should know how to:
■ Shut off water to individual faucets and fixtures, and to the entire house.
■ Shut off the gas to the house.
■ Turn off electricity to individual circuits and to the entire house.

The following pages show you how, and subsequent chapters on plumbing and wiring provide additional information.

BUILDING CODES AND INSPECTORS

Your local building department has codes covering every aspect of your home, including wiring, plumbing, structural elements, insulation, and safety. Inspectors enforce those rules. Building codes may seem confusing and heavy-handed at times, but they exist to ensure your safety and the continued stability of your house.

In general, codes and inspectors come into play whenever you install something new and substantial. If you are replacing an existing fixture or appliance—such as an overhead light, a toilet or sink, a water heater, or a window or door—you most likely do not need to go through the inspection process. The same is true if you are building a structure that is not permanent and/or attached to the house, such as a playhouse without a foundation. However, anytime you install a fixture where there was none before, or anytime you build a substantial structure that is attached to the house, you will need to pull a permit and schedule inspections. You will certainly need an inspection when you run new electrical cable or plumbing pipes. A patio laid in sand may or may not need an inspection; a concrete slab probably will.

Codes change over time, and they generally become more strict. In most cases, existing structures are not required to meet contemporary code, though any additions must meet the new requirements. However, if an inspector sees an unsafe existing installation, he or she may demand that it be fixed.

Local codes are based on national standards, but they can vary greatly from town to town. Even adjacent towns may have very different requirements. For some jobs, codes may require that a licensed contractor do the work or at least supervise it.

By law, it is your responsibility to learn and follow codes, and it is definitely contrary to your interests to violate codes. Not only is out-of-code work potentially dangerous to you and your family, but an inspector who sees such work can make you re-do it. And you may not be allowed to sell your home until you have fixed a violation.

So find out ahead of time what your town's requirements are, get your plans approved, and schedule inspections. Be sure that all of the required work is done before the inspector shows up, and don't cover up anything that the inspector needs to see (for example, by drywalling over wiring or plumbing that has not been inspected).

ZONING AND SETBACK REQUIREMENTS

You may have a survey or official property map that shows your property lines. Take the time to locate them as precisely as possible. Local regulations likely have setback requirements, which state that certain structures must not be too close to the boundaries.

Your town may also have requirements for the exterior appearance of your home. Many towns are lax

PREVENTING DAMAGE TO UTILITY LINES

Know where your utility lines run and how they connect to your home. Never dig a hole in your yard unless you are sure you will not damage a water, gas, or electrical line. If you are at all unsure, contact the appropriate utility company, which should send out a service person for free.

about this, while others get surprisingly specific. Make sure any changes in siding, windows, doors, roofing, and even paint color will not violate these rules.

WHEN TO HIRE A PRO

Before you plunge into a project yourself, make an honest assessment of your abilities and your time. If you do need to hire a pro, choose carefully and take the time to write a good contract.

DO YOU HAVE THE TIME? If a repair must be made immediately to protect people or property, such as fixing a broken step or unclogging a backed-up toilet, call a professional if you can't do it right away.

When timing is not critical, consider the size and scope of the work. A project that might take a professional a day or two could take you weeks of working in your spare time—if you can find it. Weigh the inconvenience of living with a repair in progress against the cost of having the work finished quickly.

TOOLS AND EQUIPMENT Consider the cost of buying or renting any special tools required for a job, particularly if you don't expect to use them again. To repair your roof, for example, you must have safety equipment. Clearing a clogged main drain calls for a power auger. A pro has already invested in special tools and calculates the expense in his fee.

YOUR SKILLS Be realistic about your knowledge and abilities. If you aren't sure how to make a particular repair after reading about it, or if you feel unsafe tackling the job, it probably makes sense to have it done professionally. When appear-

ance counts, such as with finish carpentry or repointing bricks, it may also pay to call in an expert if you have no woodworking or masonry experience.

CHOOSING A PROFESSIONAL The best way to find a competent professional is to ask friends or neighbors for recommendations. You can also seek referrals from a hardware store, a home center, or a community college. The phone book lists professional repair services under specific categories, such as "Electrical Contractors," "Glass," or "Roofing Contractors." Be sure that a plumber or electrician is licensed and insured.

THE CONTRACT You can arrange for a small job by hiring a handyman on an hourly basis, but for a substantial job—especially one that calls for wiring, plumbing, structural work, or roofing—it's a good idea to write a contract. It should be very specific about which materials will be used. Drawings may be attached showing the shape and dimensions of a project. Installation methods should be described in detail. There should be assurances that your property will not be damaged while work is in progress. The contractor should have insurance to cover any accidents that may occur; make sure you will not be responsible for such an incident. The timetable for the work should be laid out clearly. It is often reasonable to pay a deposit before work begins, especially if the contractor must buy materials. However, structure the remaining payments so that the contractor has plenty of incentive to do a good job and do it on time.

plumbing, gas, and electrical emergencies

Here are some tips for dealing quickly with sudden problems. For more solutions, see the plumbing and wiring chapters.

PLUMBING PROBLEMS

In a plumbing emergency, you'll need to stop the flow of water quickly before it seeps into floors and walls. To do this, you and your family need to know the location of the shutoff valve for every fixture and appliance, as well as the main valve for the house. Practice using them so you know how they operate.

If the emergency involves a specific fixture or appliance, look for its shutoff (often called a stop valve) and turn it clockwise to close it. The valve is usually underneath a fixture such as a sink or toilet, or behind an appliance such as a clothes washer, at the point where water supply pipes connect to it. For a tub or shower, the shutoff may be behind an access panel on the opposite side of the wall in an adjacent room or closet.

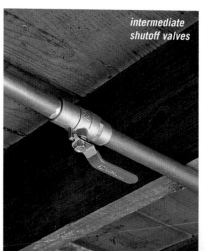

stop valve

If the problem is not with a particular fixture or appliance, or if there is no shutoff valve for the appliance or fixture, there may be a pair of intermediate shutoff valves (for hot and cold water) that control flow to one or more rooms. Turn them clockwise to test which water outlets they control.

If there are no intermediate shutoffs, you will need to turn off water to the entire house. You'll find the main valve on either the inside or the outside of your house where the main supply pipe enters.

main shutoff valve

Often there is a main shutoff or two near the water meter. Turn the valve clockwise to close it. If the valve requires a wrench, keep one nearby so it's always handy.

Often there is another way to shut off water to your house, with an underground valve located outside. The valve is likely encased inside a housing that is sometimes called a Buffalo box. The cover may be obscured by plants. Once you remove the cover, you may find a valve that can be turned by hand, or you may need a special tool, often called a key.

buffalo box

PLUMBING EMERGENCIES

LEAKING OR BURST PIPE If a pipe leaks, turn off the intermediate or main shutoff valve and open a nearby faucet to drain the pipe. Make temporary repairs to stop the leak (see page 154).

OVERFLOWING TOILET If your toilet bowl is overflowing, don't panic. Lift off the cover of the tank, reach inside (this water is clean), and push the tank stopper down into the valve seat. Turn off the water at the fixture shutoff valve. If there is no valve there, turn off an intermediate valve or the main shutoff. Unclog the toilet using a plunger or an auger (see page 148).

STOPPED-UP SINK Shut off any faucet or appliance that's draining into the sink. Unclog the sink using a plunger or auger (see pages 144–145). Do not use a chemical drain cleaner if the blockage is total.

A FAUCET WON'T SHUT OFF Immediately turn off the water at the shutoff valve under the sink, at an intermediate valve, or at the main shutoff. Repair or replace the faucet (see pages 134–141).

intermediate shutoff valves

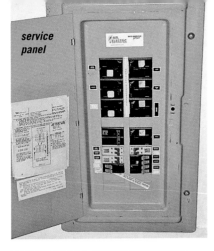

service panel

ELECTRICAL EMERGENCIES

You and other adult family members should learn how to turn off the house's electrical power during an emergency, as well as when you need to make electrical repairs. Never work on a live circuit of any fixture, appliance, receptacle, or switch. Shut off power to the circuit or to the house first and test the circuit carefully with a voltage tester to be sure it's not live. See pages 174–175 for more information.

Keep the area around the service panel clear so that it can be reached easily at all times. Keep the door closed. If the panel is in a place where children can reach it, you may choose to padlock the door. Have a flashlight with extra batteries as well as candles and matches handy in case of an electrical emergency or an outage.

POWER FAILURE If the electricity fails suddenly, first determine whether it's just in your house or throughout the neighborhood. If the outage affects the neighborhood, notify the utility company. To prevent food spoilage, avoid opening the refrigerator or freezer during the outage. If the problem is just in your home, check for tripped circuit breakers or blown fuses. (If your service panel does not have an index indicating which electrical users are controlled by which circuit, see page 177 for instructions

on making such an index.) Replace any blown fuses or reset any tripped breakers and test for a short circuit or overload (see page 175). Once the problem has been corrected, restore the power.

A SMOKING OR SPARKING APPLIANCE Immediately unplug the appliance or shut off the wall switch that controls it. Do not touch the appliance itself. Turn off the power to the circuit if you can't unplug the appliance. When the appliance cools off, take it to a repair shop or arrange for a service representative to come to your home and make any needed repairs. If the appliance catches fire, get everyone out of the house and call the fire department from a neighbor's house or a cell phone. Do not use water on an electrical fire. If the fire is small, you may attempt to put it out using an extinguisher with a Type C rating.

A SMOKING OR SPARKING APPLIANCE PLUG At the service panel, cut off the power to the receptacle. Unplug the appliance by the cord and allow the plug to cool off. Check the plug and cord for signs of damage and replace them if they're defective (see pages 180–181). Once the plug is repaired, check for and replace any blown fuse or reset a tripped circuit breaker. If the cord and plug are in good condition, the

fuse box

receptacle may be faulty. See pages 184–185 if you need to replace it.

GAS LEAKS
If you ever smell gas anywhere in your house, take the following precautions:

■ Get everyone outside the house immediately.

■ Use a neighbor's phone or a cell phone to call your gas company or the fire department.

■ Do not light a match and do not turn any electrical switch on or off. The danger of fire or explosion is severe. Leave as many windows and doors open as possible to help clear the gas from the house.

Once everyone is safely out of the house, turn off the gas supply at the main valve, or wait for the utility company to do it. The shutoff is usually on the inlet pipe next to the gas meter. To close the valve, use an adjustable wrench or a large pair of pliers to turn it 90 degrees in either direction so that the valve head is perpendicular to the pipe, as shown in the illustration at right.

main gas shutoff

OFF   ON

Do not turn the gas back on until you've discovered the source of the problem and have corrected it.

In a natural disaster, you may have to turn off the gas supply yourself. Make sure all family members know the location of the shutoff valve and how to operate it. To identify the valve, attach a tie-on tag and label it. Leave a wrench in an accessible location so it will be close at hand in an emergency.

home safety

The following pages help you minimize hazards in your home and show you how to deal with common emergencies. Every family member should know the steps to take in a fire, and everyone should be familiar with the switches and valves that control the flow of water, electricity, and gas. If a special wrench is required to turn a valve, keep one close by.

In a natural disaster, you may need to shut off the gas, electricity, and possibly the water. It's an excellent idea to have some basic emergency supplies on hand at all times. Your kit should include bottled water, nonperishable food, a portable radio, a flashlight with extra batteries, and a first-aid kit with instructions.

FIRE SAFETY

There are three elements to a fire safety strategy:
■ Plan an exit strategy in case of a house fire.
■ Install smoke detectors and fire extinguishers.
■ Learn how to extinguish minor fires yourself.

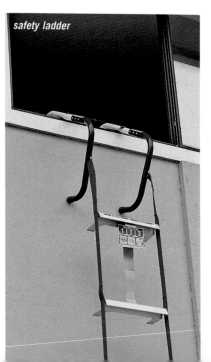
safety ladder

AN EXIT STRATEGY In the event of a large fire in your home, immediately take the following steps:
■ Get everyone out of the house.
■ Call the fire department from a neighbor's house or from a cell phone.

Develop a household fire exit plan. It's even a good idea to have a fire drill now and then. With your family, map escape routes from the house, particularly from bedrooms, and designate a central meeting area outside the home so that

smoke detector

everyone can be accounted for quickly. If your home is more than one story high, make sure you have safety ladders near windows. If any windows are barred, ensure that the emergency releases are fully functional. If you have a double-keyed lock on any exterior doors, be sure a key is nearby so anyone can open the door quickly.

SMOKE DETECTORS These provide excellent early warning of fire. They are your first line of defense against fires that break out at night. Install one or more detectors on every floor of your house, near exits, and adjacent to bedrooms. Install them near the center of a room or hallway.

A photoelectric smoke detector sounds when its internal light beam senses smoke or steam.

fire extinguisher

An ionization detector can sense the presence of fire even when there is little smoke. Both types work well. Battery-operated smoke detectors can be screwed to the ceiling, so you can mount them yourself. A hardwired detector should be installed by a professional electrician. It should have a battery backup so it can work when a fire damages wiring.

Check your detectors every month by pushing the test buttons. Replace batteries yearly, even if they test OK.

FIRE EXTINGUISHERS Keep a fire extinguisher handy in a kitchen, garage, workshop, and any other location where a small fire may occur. Extinguishers are labeled according to the type of fire they can put out. Type A can extinguish ordinary fires involving wood, cloth, and paper. Type B is for fires fueled by gasoline, oil, kitchen grease, solvents, and other combustible liquids. Type C can handle electrical fires. The higher the UL number, the larger the fire the unit can put out. An extinguisher with a rating of 1 for A fires and 10 for B and C fires will take care of most minor blazes.

HOW TO PUT OUT A FIRE

First, get everyone else out of the house. Then grab a fire extinguisher and follow the **PASS** method:

P Pull the safety pin.

A Aim the extinguisher at the base of the flame.

S Squeeze the handle.

S Sweep the nozzle from side to side to cover the entire base of the fire.

In addition to following these general instructions, be aware of the peculiarities of various types of fires:

KITCHEN GREASE If the fire is in a pan, turn off the heat and cover the pan with a lid. Pouring water on a grease or oil fire will cause the fire to spread.

OVEN Turn off the heat and let the fire burn itself out. Do not open the oven door. This will let in more air, feeding the fire and causing it to grow.

CHIMNEY A chimney fire occurs when soot and creosote deposits inside the flue ignite, making a loud roaring noise and causing flames and sparks to shoot out of the chimney. The sparks may ignite the roof as well. Get everyone out of the house and call the fire department. Do not try to put it out. To prevent a chimney fire, keep the chimney clean and install a spark arrester at the top (see pages 98–99).

ELECTRICAL If a fire is caused by a light or appliance cord, pull out the plug or shut off the power at the wall switch or the service panel. Use a C or ABC extinguisher. Never use water, which can cause the fire to spread and can also cause electrical shock. If you don't have an extinguisher, cover the fire with a nonflammable cloth. If the fire continues, get out of the house and call the fire department immediately.

DRYER If a fire occurs inside a clothes dryer, keep the dryer door closed. Shut off the gas or electricity. If the fire continues, get out of the house and call the fire department immediately.

Check an extinguisher's gauge monthly to be sure the unit is fully charged. Some models can be recharged, while others should be replaced.

SECURITY AGAINST INTRUDERS

Certain precautions can greatly reduce the chances that a burglar will break into your home.

■ Exterior doors should be solid wood or metal. Install high-quality deadbolts with 1-inch throws. The strike plate (the socket where the throw inserts) should be installed with 3-inch or longer screws that penetrate the house's framing, not just the jamb. See page 76 for more information.

■ Windows should be locked. See page 58 for locking options. If you have jalousie windows (with open horizontal glass slats), replace them with windows that can be locked.

■ Provide ample lighting with motion sensors outside your home. Intruders will be surprised by bright light that comes on when they approach the house.

■ A dog—the louder, the better—is an excellent deterrent against most intrusions.

■ An alarm system is the ultimate measure of protection. Most systems have a network of sensors that sound an alarm when a door or window is opened, controlled by a keypad that allows you to turn the system on and off. The alarm may sound a siren and/or alert the local police. If you choose this option, shop for a reputable dealer. There will probably be an installation charge, plus a monthly fee if you want the system monitored.

CHILDPROOFING

Here are some simple ways to make a home safer for small children:

■ Keep hazardous materials—such as cleaning products, paints, and solvents—locked away, tightly sealed, and on high shelves.

■ Move small appliances to where children cannot get at them, and keep them unplugged when they are not in use. Keep sharp knives out of reach as well.

childproof receptacle covers

- Cook on back burners when possible and keep children well away.
- Make sure large pieces of furniture and appliances—especially televisions—are placed so they will not tip. Hang mirrors and large pictures securely.

Childproofing products address other potential hazards. Here are just a few:

- Cabinet door safety latches install quickly and keep children out.
- Sharp table corners can be dangerous. Cushioned protectors take the edge off.
- Children like to turn knobs. Install safety covers on your stove's burner controls.
- Safety gates keep small children from falling down stairs or entering unsafe rooms. Accordion-style gates work only if you install them tightly. Gates with parts that screw to stair railings or walls work better.
- If a child licks an electrical receptacle or pokes it with a wet hand, a dangerous shock could result. Cover unused receptacles with safety plugs. Also install covers so kids can't get at cord plugs.

AIR AND WATER QUALITY

You may decide to hire another company to test whether the water and air in your house are safe. If they are not, find out how serious the problem is and how much it will cost to fix it. The major issues are carbon monoxide, lead in water and paint, radon, asbestos, and mold.

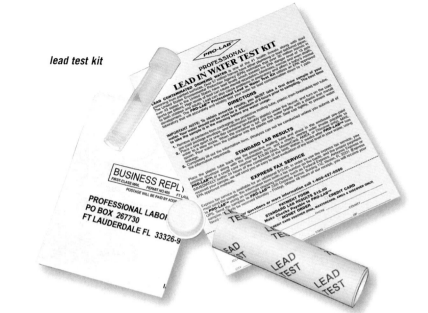

lead test kit

CARBON MONOXIDE This gas, often referred to as CO, results from the incomplete burning of gas or other combustibles. In a home, it is usually caused by the improper ventilation of a gas water heater, heat system burner, or stove, or by a wood-burning stove or fireplace.

CO is colorless and odorless, but it's very dangerous. Low levels cause headaches, drowsiness, and nausea. Higher levels can lead to an oxygen deficiency that causes respiratory problems and even death. Very young and old people are most at risk.

Install a CO detector in the same room as a gas burner or water heater—the likeliest culprits. Also install at least one near sleeping areas. A good detector will have a peak level memory, which tells you the highest readings attained over a given period. Keep the detector equipped with a battery, as you would a smoke detector.

If you get a high CO reading, call your gas company for a free inspection. In many cases, the solution will be to mend or reconfigure a flue so that all fumes are sucked out of the house.

LEAD The two main sources of lead are drinking water and old paint. Lead paint was commonly used prior to 1950, and was sometimes used up to the 1970s. If you suspect it, especially in an area where children may come into contact with paint chips, you can use a home testing kit to find out for sure. Lead paint on walls is usually not a danger as long as it does not chip or peel off. But paint on windows and doors, where two surfaces rub against each other, will cause a dust that can be harmful. If you have lead paint, covering it with a good primer and new paint will certainly help. To get rid of it completely, contact a certified lead paint removal contractor.

Some older municipalities and homes have lead pipes. Your building department can tell you if the pipe leading from the street to your house is lead. Prior to 1986, many copper water supply pipes were joined with a solder that contained lead. To deal with these sources of lead, many municipalities add a tiny amount of phosphate to the water to coat the pipes and keep lead from leaching into the water supply. If a test reveals that you have lead in

CO detector

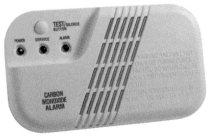

your water, you may want to install a purifier for your drinking water. Contact your local health department or water supplier for more information.

RADON This is another odorless gas, caused by natural radioactivity in many soils. It is harmless outdoors, but it can create a hazard indoors. Breathing high levels of radon for 10 to 15 years increases the risk of lung cancer and other serious ailments.

Test for radon when windows have been kept closed. This is when levels are highest. A long-term test is best, since radon levels can vary greatly from week to week. In addition to having a test performed during your house inspection, you can purchase a home testing kit or hire a company to test for you. If you get your water from a well, test the water for radon.

Solutions to high radon levels are often low tech. Seal all the places where radon enters your house, including water pipes, cracks in basement floors, gaps in siding, and around a sump pump. Also increase your home's ventilation. If these measures do not solve the problem, call in a professional who specializes in radon abatement.

ASBESTOS Asbestos was often used in home construction—especially for pipe insulation—before the late 1960s. Inhaled asbestos fibers, even if microscopic, can cause various types of cancer and respiratory problems.

If you have old pipes or a furnace wrapped in insulation that is covered in cloth, it may be asbestos. Asbestos is light gray and looks like corrugated cardboard. Loose insulation in an attic may contain asbestos. It will appear fluffy and light gray in color. Textured "cottage cheese" ceilings

installed before 1970 may contain asbestos. Older acoustic ceiling tiles also may contain asbestos.

What to do about it? Opinions vary and have changed over the years. Many experts feel that most asbestos should be tightly wrapped in tape or otherwise encapsulated. Others believe that the best solution is to hire an asbestos removal company. The latter option will cost quite a bit. Contact your local health department to learn the method it recommends.

MOLD Mold is not a problem in small quantities; in fact, it is all around us. However, there is increasing evidence that large quantities of mold in homes may

asbestos pipe insulation

cause asthma attacks in some people. Mold can also irritate the eyes, skin, nose, throat, and lungs.

In most cases, mold is an isolated problem that you can solve by cleaning the area and then keeping it dry. If a moldy area is less than 10 square feet, you can handle it yourself. Consult the health department or hire a contractor if you have larger areas of mold. Wearing gloves, an N-95 respirator (available in many hardware stores or over the Internet), goggles, and

protective clothing, scrape away as much mold as you can. Often mold can be effectively removed by washing with a solution of bleach, vinegar, or Borax and water. You can also try aiming a hair dryer at the mold until it dries out. If those strategies don't work, remove and replace surfaces (such as drywall) where mold has attached itself.

Then ensure that the area will remain dry. You may need to remove nearby shrubs, seal exterior holes with caulk, or repair a roof leak, for instance. Wait a week or so before finishing the area to make sure the mold does not regrow.

If you suspect that mold may be present in your heating or air-conditioning system, do not run the

heater or air conditioner. Consult a professional, who may recommend cleaning the ducts.

Very rarely, large amounts of mold develop inside walls. (This may happen in a home that is tightly sealed with insulation and house wrap but is not properly ventilated.) If family members suffer from persistent asthma-like symptoms, or if you see or smell mold in places that are not wet, contact your building department or a mold abatement specialist.

seasonal maintenance

Preventive maintenance is the best way to keep your home in good repair and to avoid expensive problems in years to come. The chart below lists common procedures, but they are merely a starting point. If you notice a problem developing, take care of it immediately.

The repairs indicated are discussed throughout the book. Appliances vary in design, so the final authority should be the owner's manual.

CAUTION *Before inspecting or working on the electrical system or on any device connected to it, shut off the power and use a voltage tester to make sure power is off, or unplug the appliance. For maintenance of or repairs to plumbing fixtures or water-using appliances, you may need to shut off the water (see page 8). To turn off the gas, see page 9.*

When	Where to Check	What to Do
Every Month	Fire extinguisher	Check that it's fully charged; recharge or replace if needed.
	Smoke detector	Test batteries and replace if needed.
	Sink and tub stoppers and drain holes	Clean out debris.
	Garbage disposer	Flush with hot water and baking soda.
	Water-heating system	Check pressure gauge and drain expansion tank if needed.
	Forced-air heating system	Clean or replace air filter; vacuum registers.
	Heat pump	Clean or replace air filter; clean condenser or evaporator coils and condensate drain; remove snow and/or debris from outdoor portion of unit.
	Air conditioner	Clean or replace filter; clean condenser and evaporator coils and condensate drain.
Every 2 Months	Oil burner	Inspect and clean.
	Wall furnace	Clean grills.
	Range hood	Clean grease filter.
Every 3 Months	Faucet	Clean aerator.
	Tub drain assembly	Clean out debris; inspect rubber seal and replace if needed.
	Floor and outdoor drain grates	Clean out debris.
Every 6 Months	Basement and foundation	Check for cracks and moisture and repair as needed.
	Toilet	Check for leaks and water run-on.
	Interior caulking	Inspect caulking around tubs, showers, and sinks; replace any if it is deteriorating.
	Water heater	Drain water until it is clear of sediment; inspect flue assembly (gas heater).
	Garbage disposer	Tighten drain connections and fasteners.
	Clothes washer	Clean water inlet filters; check hoses and replace them if they are leaking.
	Clothes dryer	Vacuum lint from ducts and surrounding areas.
	Wiring	Check for frayed cords and wires; repair or replace them as needed.
	Range hood	Wash fan blades and housing.

When	Where to Check	What to Do
Every Spring	Roof	Inspect roof surface, flashing, eaves, and soffits; repair as needed.
	Gutters and downspouts	Clean them out or install no-clean versions. Inspect and repair weak areas; check for proper drainage and make repairs if needed.
	Siding	Inspect and clean siding and repair if needed.
	Exterior caulking	Inspect caulking and replace any that is deteriorating.
	Windowsills, door sills, thresholds	Fill cracks, caulk edges, repaint; replace if needed.
	Window and door screens	Clean screening and repair or replace if needed; tighten or repair any loose or damaged frames and repaint if needed; replace broken, worn, or missing hardware; tighten and lubricate door hinges and closers.
	Water-heating system	Lubricate circulating pump and motor.
	Heat pump	Lubricate blower motor.
	Air conditioner	Lubricate blower motor.
	Whole-house or attic fan	Clean unit; check belt tension and adjust if needed; replace a cracked or worn belt; tighten screws and bolts; lubricate motor.
Every Fall	Roof	Inspect roof surface, flashing, eaves, and soffits; repair if needed.
	Gutters and downspouts	Clean out; inspect and repair weak points; check for proper drainage and repair if needed.
	Chimney or stovepipe	Clean flue (more frequently if needed); repair any cracks in flue or any loose or crumbling mortar.
	Siding	Inspect and clean siding and repair if needed.
	Exterior caulking	Inspect caulking and replace any that is deteriorating.
	Storm windows and doors	Replace any cracked or broken glass; tighten or repair any loose or damaged frames and repaint if needed; replace damaged hardware; tighten and lubricate door hinges and closers.
	Window and door weather stripping	Inspect and repair or replace if it is deteriorating or if it does not seal.
	Water-heating system	Lubricate pump and motor; bleed air from radiators or convectors.
	Forced-air heating system	Vacuum heat exchanger surfaces; clean and lubricate blower blades and motor; check fan belt tension and adjust if needed; replace cracked or worn belt; check for duct leaks and repair if needed.
	Gas burner	Clean burners and ports.
	Oil burner	Have it professionally serviced.
	Thermostat	Clean heat sensor, contact points, and contacts; check accuracy and replace the thermostat if it is not functioning properly.
Annually	Septic tank	Have a professional check the tank (watch for back-up throughout the year). In many areas, it is recommended that the tank be pumped every year.
	Water heater	Test temperature pressure relief valve and replace if needed; clean burner and ports (gas heater). Replace the thermocouple.

walls and ceilings

Most homes built before 1940 have plaster walls. The plaster is usually attached to horizontal strips of wood lath that have gaps between them. The rough coat of plaster seeps into the gaps to create a strong attachment, and a smooth finish coat is applied over the rough coat. Often there are three coats, including a middle coat for extra strength. Lath is generally $\frac{3}{8}$ inch thick, while the plaster itself may be anywhere from $\frac{3}{8}$ to $\frac{3}{4}$ inch thick. Sometimes a thick wire mesh, called metal lath, is used instead of wood.

Since the 1940s, most homes have been finished with sheets of drywall, also called wallboard (brand name Sheetrock®). Drywall has a gypsum core that is covered with paper on both sides. It is usually $\frac{1}{2}$ inch thick, but thinner and thicker versions are not uncommon. Drywall is attached to wall studs and ceiling joists with nails or screws. The joints between sheets are sealed with a paper or fiberglass mesh tape and covered with several layers of joint compound, which can be textured or sanded smooth. In some areas, it is common for drywall ceilings to be coated with a texture that looks like popcorn or cottage cheese.

⚡ AMERISPEC® TIP — WATCH FOR CABLES, PIPES, AND DUCTS

Most walls have electrical cables running through them, and many have plumbing pipes or metal ducts as well. Always be cautious when cutting into a wall, because cutting into these lines can be dangerous and can cause serious damage to your home. Unless you are certain the cavity is empty, use a small hand saw rather than a power saw. Open a small area and peer inside with a flashlight or explore with a thin board before making a larger cut.

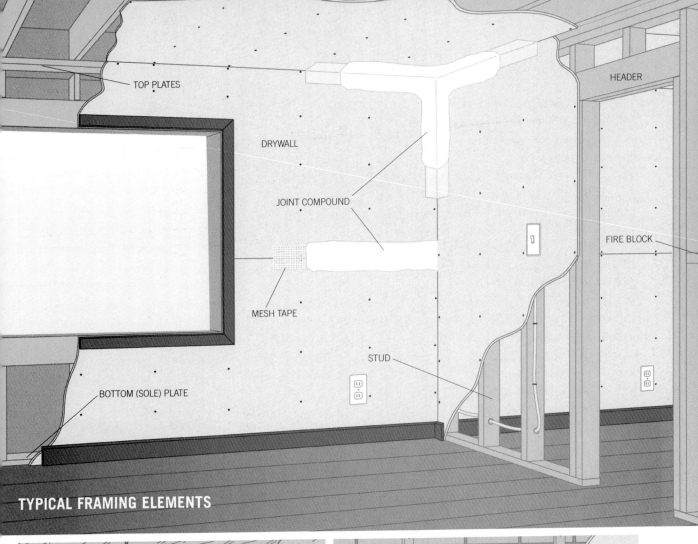

TOP PLATES

HEADER

DRYWALL

JOINT COMPOUND

FIRE BLOCK

MESH TAPE

STUD

BOTTOM (SOLE) PLATE

TYPICAL FRAMING ELEMENTS

ROUGH COAT   FINISH COAT

PLASTER WALL

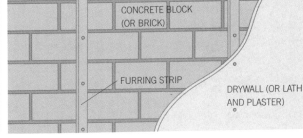

CONCRETE BLOCK (OR BRICK)

FURRING STRIP

DRYWALL (OR LATH AND PLASTER)

FINISHED MASONRY WALL

The large illustration above shows typical framing elements that underlie a drywall or plaster wall. Walls are built of studs, which are typically 2 by 4s or 2 by 6s. Ceilings are framed with joists, which are 2-by-6 or wider boards. Framing members are usually spaced 16 inches apart, but in some homes (especially those with plaster) the spacing may not be regular. You'll likely find fairly wide headers above every door and window. Most walls have top and bottom plates, and often the top plate is a double thickness of 2-by-4 wood. In some prewar homes with "balloon framing," however, there are no top and bottom plates. A masonry wall is likely framed with vertical 1-by-2 boards called furring strips, which are nailed or screwed to the bricks or blocks. Lath and plaster or drywall is nailed or screwed to the 1-by-2s.

repairs to plaster

Plaster is commonly applied over wood lath (see page 17), but it may also be applied over metal lath, over a special wallboard similar to drywall, or directly onto a masonry surface. These pages show repairs to small areas. Fine cracks, nail holes, and small gouges in plaster can be repaired with spackling compound. Larger areas can be finished with setting-type joint compound (which comes in bags of dry mix) or with patching plaster, as shown on these pages. If you use joint compound, you'll need to apply fiberglass mesh tape to the joints between the patch and the surrounding wall.

REPAIRS TO LARGE SECTIONS If a very large area is damaged, you may choose to remove the plaster between studs or joists and then install drywall, as shown on page 21. Purchase drywall that is the same thickness as your plaster and lath, attach it, and tape the joints between the new drywall and the old plaster, as shown on page 23.

FINISHING THE PATCH The patch should match the texture of the surrounding wall. For a smooth surface, apply several coats of joint compound, sanding each, until you achieve a finish that looks and feels smooth. To match a textured surface, use a paint brush, stippling brush, sponge, whisk broom, or trowel—whatever will give you the desired finish. Daub or swirl the joint compound to create the desired pattern.

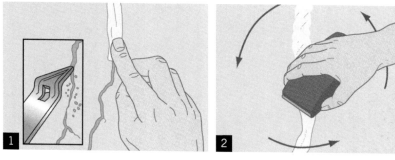

Patching fine cracks

1 Widen the crack to about ¼ inch with the tip of a lever-type can opener (inset). Blow out dust and debris. With your finger or a putty knife, fill the crack with spackle.

2 Sand the spackle once it's dry. Use a block wrapped with fine-grade sandpaper and work in a circular motion. Prime the patch, then paint it.

Repairing a small hole

1 Gently tap out any loose plaster with a cold chisel. Clean out the plaster from the lath to create a surface that the patching plaster can adhere to. Brush the area clean and dampen with a sponge.

If the hole is smaller than 2 inches across (but larger than a fine crack, nail hole, or small gouge), fill it with patching plaster and finish. For larger holes, apply a first layer using a 6-inch taping knife.

2 Score the patch with a nail, then allow the surface to dry. Moisten the patch and then apply a second layer of patching plaster, coming to within ⅛ to 1/16 inch of the surface. Score the patch and let it dry.

3 Apply the final coat, feathering the edges an inch or so beyond the edges of the hole. Scrape a wide taping knife across the wet finish coat to remove any excess material. When the patch is dry, sand smooth.

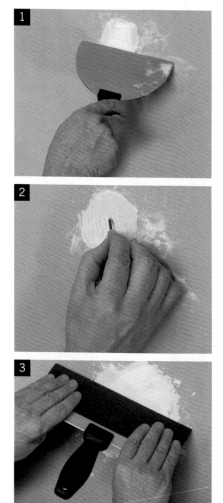

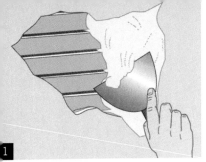

Patching a larger hole

1 Chisel the edges, tap out loose plaster, and dampen the lath with a sponge. Using a 6-inch taping knife, fill a little more than half the hole's depth with patching plaster. Force it through the gaps in the lath. When the plaster is firm, score it with a nail and let it dry.

2 Dampen the patch again and apply a second layer of plaster to within ⅛ to ¹⁄₁₆ inch of the surface.

Score the plaster, let it dry, and apply a third coat. Feather the edges of the plaster an inch or more beyond the edges of the patch.

3 Use a wide taping knife to remove excess plaster. For a smooth finish, dip a metal float in water and, holding the float nearly flat against the wall, draw it down from top to bottom. When the plaster is dry, sand and prime it.

🦊 AMERISPEC® TIP   PLASTER THAT'S COMING LOOSE

If a wall or ceiling feels spongy when you press on it, the plaster has come loose from the lath. You can fix a small area of loose plaster by driving plaster screws, available at some hardware stores. On a ceiling, where this problem is most common, you can attach sheets of drywall directly onto the plaster, driving long screws into the joists. This will save you the trouble and mess of removing the old plaster. You can do the same on a wall, but because the drywall increases the wall's thickness, you'll have to remove moldings and build out window and door jambs before reinstalling them.

PATCHING WITH DRYWALL AND JOINT COMPOUND

For a large patch, this method is usually easier than filling the entire area with compound or patching plaster. Chip away the edges of the hole and remove all debris. Cut a piece of drywall the same thickness as the plaster to roughly fit in the hole. Then attach it with 1¼-inch drywall screws driven into the lath and 2-inch screws driven into studs or joists. Fill gaps between the patch and the wall with joint compound, apply fiberglass mesh tape, and spread joint compound over the tape. Allow the compound to dry and then sand it. Repeat until you achieve a smooth patch.

JOINT COMPOUND

SCREW

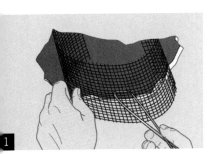
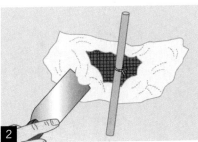

Patching a hole without a base

1 After removing loose plaster from around the hole with a chisel, loop a wire through a piece of metal mesh. Roll the edges of the mesh, insert it into the hole, and flatten the mesh by pulling the wire.

2 Attach the wire to a stick so it holds tight against the wall. Dampen the hole's edges with a sponge. Using a putty knife, fill just over half the hole's depth with patching plaster, forcing it through the mesh.

3 Unwind the wire, then remove it and the stick. When the plaster is firm, score it with a nail. Apply two additional coats of patching plaster and finish the patch.

repairs to drywall

Drywall is composed of a fire-resistant gypsum core between two layers of paper. Greenboard is water resistant for use in damp areas, though it is not as waterproof as cement backerboard. Drywall can be attached with nails, screws, or adhesive. Joints between the sheets are covered with tape and joint compound.

Drywall repairs range from fixing minor dents to replacing an entire panel (see pages 22–23). When a patch is made, finish the section to match the rest of the wall. If the wall is textured, experiment with a trowel, whisk broom, sponge, or other tools until you can achieve a pattern that blends with its surroundings. It is sometimes necessary to paint the whole wall to ensure the repair blends in fully.

Dents, small holes, popped nails, and loosened joint tape all can be easily repaired with spackle or joint compound, as shown below.

For a patch, you will need wood or other backing to provide solid support. Several methods are shown on the next page. When cutting a hole, first score with a utility knife using a straightedge as a guide. Then cut to the inside of the slice line using a drywall saw, making a clean cut that is easier to patch.

At a home center you will find a number of kits that make it easy to patch drywall. One type is shown on the opposite page, lower right.

TAPING AND SANDING This step, the key to blending the repair with the surrounding surface, is done in stages over a period of days. Apply fiberglass mesh tape to the joints (you may choose to use paper tape on inside corners). Use setting-type (dry-mix) joint compound for the first coat, because it is strong. Use ready-mix joint compound (which comes in a bucket) or spackle for subsequent coats, because it is easy to sand. You'll need 6- and 10-inch taping blades and 80- or 100-grit drywall-type sandpaper or sanding screen. Use a drywall-type sanding block, which may be either hand-held or attached to a pole.

To apply joint compound, dip the edge of a clean taping blade into the compound, loading about half the blade. Apply the compound across the joint with the blade held nearly flat to the wall. Then hold the blade at a 45-degree angle to the wall and draw it along to smooth the joint. With practice you will gain proficiency in smoothing.

Once each coat has dried, scrape away any ridges and sand it smooth. Wear a dust mask and protective eyewear when sanding. Avoid sanding the drywall itself, as sanding can damage the drywall's paper. To keep the dust down, use a sanding tool that attaches to a vacuum cleaner.

It will take three or more coats and sandings to achieve a very smooth surface. The compound should both look and feel smooth. Apply a primer, then examine the wall again for imperfections before you paint.

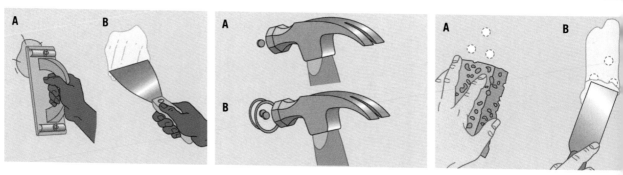

Minor repair

DENT Gently sand the area around the dent (A) to remove any burrs and protrusions, but don't damage the drywall paper. Fill the dent with ready-mix joint compound or spackle (B). Allow each layer to dry before applying the next. When the final layer is dry, sand and prime it.

POPPED NAIL If a nail is loose, pry it out and drive another nail to one side so it hits a stud or joist. If the popped nail is fairly solid, hammer and dimple it (A), then drive another nail just beside it to hold it in (B). Cover the dimples with several coats of joint compound and sand smooth.

SMALL HOLES Brush the holes clean and dampen them with a sponge (A). Use a flexible putty knife to fill the holes with several coats of spackle or ready-mix joint compound (B). When the filler is dry, sand and prime it.

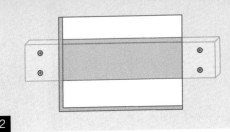

Larger holes

1 For holes or damaged areas larger than 3 inches in diameter, use a framing square and a utility knife to slice through the paper, forming a rectangle around the damage. Then cut out the rectangle using a drywall saw or by cutting repeatedly with the knife.

2 Cut a piece of 1 by 3 about 8 inches longer than the hole and place behind the wall. Hold the wood firmly as you drive 1¼-inch screws on each side of the hole and into the 1 by 3. Dimple the screws below the surface of the drywall but not so deep that they tear the paper.

3 Cut a piece of drywall the same thickness as the wall's drywall to fit the hole, then sand its edges smooth. Set the patch in place and drive screws into the 1 by 3 to secure it. Apply mesh tape to the joints, then spread and sand several coats of joint compound.

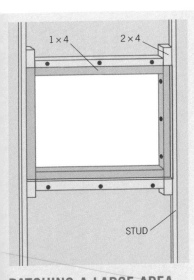

1 × 4   2 × 4

STUD

PATCHING A LARGE AREA

If the damaged area is larger than 12 inches across, install boards all around that you can attach the patch to. Cut a rectangle that spans from stud to stud or joist to joist. Cut 2 by 2s or 2 by 4s a few inches longer than the height of the opening, then screw them to the sides of the studs or joists behind the wall. Also cut pieces of 1 by 4 and drive screws to attach them behind the hole so they can serve as a fastening surface for the patch, as shown. Cut a piece of drywall to fit, tape it, and apply three coats of joint compound.

> **⟆ AMERISPEC® TIP   REPAIRING A CRACK**
>
> A crack—commonly above a door, at the joint between walls, or between the wall and ceiling—can be permanently repaired with fiberglass mesh tape and several coats of joint compound. To avoid the hassle of all those coats and sandings, you could instead apply latex-silicone caulk, though you may need to repeat the application every few years.

Drywall patch kit

1 Purchase a repair kit that includes drywall clips. Cut out the damaged area with a utility knife, then a drywall saw.

2 Slip the clips onto the edges of the hole and screw them into place. Drive the screw heads slightly below the surface of the drywall.

3 Cut a piece of drywall to fit. Drive screws through the patch and into the clips. Apply mesh tape to the joints, then apply and sand three or more coats of joint compound.

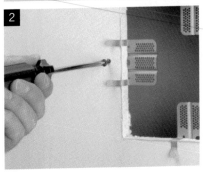

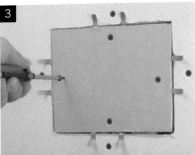

replacing sheets of drywall

When drywall is damaged by water or has large holes or cracks, you may need to remove one or more full sheets and cut new drywall to fit.

REMOVING A DAMAGED SHEET

No matter how your drywall is attached—with nails, screws, or adhesive—the removal procedure is the same.

Sheets may be installed vertically or horizontally. Sometimes it is easy to see the outline of a sheet, but often you can't tell where a sheet ends until you start demolition. Punch through the drywall with a hammer or pry bar and pull off pieces as large as possible. Check for cables or pipes as you work. Use a flat pry bar to tear the panel off the studs. Once you see where a sheet ends, use a utility knife to slice through the taped joints. That will allow you to pull the sheet off cleanly.

When the sheet is removed, use a hammer to pull out nails or screws left in the framing. If the screws are sunk deep into the wood, unscrew them. If the drywall was attached with adhesive, you can leave small pieces of backing paper on the studs.

INSTALLING A NEW SHEET

Measure the opening and, following the directions on the next page, cut a new sheet ¼ inch shorter to accommodate the ragged edges of the cuts. To cut drywall to fit around doors, windows, electrical receptacles and switches, or other openings, measure from the vertical edges of the opening to the edge of the nearest sheet or to a corner.

Then measure from the horizontal edges to the ceiling or the sheet above. Transfer your measurements to the drywall and cut a hole with a drywall saw.

Mark stud locations on the floor and the wall or ceiling above. Position the sheet over the opening, supporting it with a 1 by 4 and a pry bar. Nail or screw the sheet to the studs. Also drive fasteners into the top and bottom plates of the wall framing. Around the perimeter of the drywall sheet, fasteners should be 6 to 8 inches apart and at least ⅜ inch from the panel edges. Along the middle studs, space the fasteners 10 to 12 inches apart. Make sure all fastener heads are dimpled.

Unless the drywall is a backing for paneling, you will need to tape all joints and cover all screw heads with joint compound. This is the most time-consuming part of the job. Sanding joint compound creates a dusty mess, so seal off the room and aim a fan out the window. It will take at least three coats of joint compound—each of which must be sanded—before you achieve a smooth surface.

Hanging a replacement sheet

1 Use a utility knife to slit the taped joints between the damaged sheet and adjacent sheets. Punch through the center with a hammer or pry bar, check for wires or pipes, and pull off pieces. Working from the center, pry the sheet's edges off the studs with a pry bar.

2 Cut the new sheet to fit and support it as shown in the inset. First drive nails or screws into each stud near the top of the panel to hold it. Then space fasteners 6 to 8 inches apart at the perimeter, 10 to 12 inches apart in the middle.

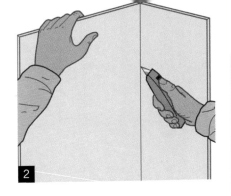

1

2

Cutting drywall

1 Measure the opening and mark the drywall sheet. Hold a drywall square (also called a T square) firmly with your hand at the top and wedge your foot against the bottom, then score a line that cuts through the surface paper.

2 Bend the cut piece back until it snaps. Then cut through the paper on the back side of the sheet. To make a cutout or a notch, use a drywall saw for one or more sides of the cut.

FASTENING DRYWALL

To attach drywall with screws, buy a dimpler attachment for your drill; it will enable you to drive screws to just the right depth so that they are recessed below the surface of the drywall but not so deep that they tear the paper. If you attach the drywall with nails, be sure to dimple the nails by pounding them just below the surface (inset).

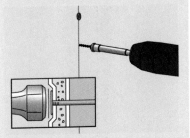

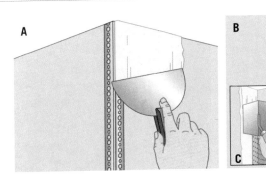

A

B

C

Taping drywall corners

On an outside corner, nail or screw a metal or plastic corner bead, taking care to keep it straight. Use a 6-inch taping blade to apply joint compound across one side and smooth it vertically (A). Repeat on the other side. Apply subsequent coats with a 10- or 12-inch blade.

On an inside corner, apply a layer of joint compound with a 6-inch taping blade. Cut a piece of paper tape to fit, crease it down the middle, and press it into the compound (B). Using a corner tool, press the tape into the compound and add a layer of compound over the tape (C).

FASTENING TO DRYWALL OR PLASTER

The best way to attach something to a wall is by driving a screw into a stud. But if you need to attach at a point where there is no stud, there are a number of wall fasteners that will provide reasonable strength even though they grab onto only the drywall or the plaster. A toggle bolt or a spreading anchor grabs onto the back side of the drywall as you tighten the screw. Tap a plastic anchor into a hole that you drill in the drywall, then drive a screw into it. A drive-screw anchor is the easiest to install. Simply screw it into the wall.

Taping flat seams

At a seam, sand away any burrs or projections. Apply fiberglass mesh tape. Using an 8-inch taping blade,

spread setting-type (dry-mix) joint compound to one side of the joint, then to the other. Feather the compound out on each side. After the compound has dried, sand down the ridge in the middle. Then apply ready-mix compound on each side with a 10- or 12-inch trowel. Sand and repeat until you achieve a smooth joint.

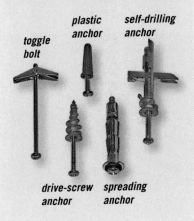

plastic anchor

self-drilling anchor

toggle bolt

drive-screw anchor

spreading anchor

repairing and removing wallpaper and paint

As wallpaper ages, it's subject to loosened edges, tears, bubbles, and other damage—all of which you can repair. Use lap-and-seam adhesive, which is stronger than standard wallpaper adhesive. If you have vinyl wallpaper, use vinyl-to-vinyl adhesive for seams. A seam roller presses the paper smoothly to the wall, but your hand works fine for smoothing small areas.

Take care not to use too much adhesive, as it can soak through and stain the wallpaper. Some thin, paper-only wallpapers are easily marred this way.

You may need a matching piece of wallpaper. If you don't have a remnant it may take a good deal of searching to find a duplicate.

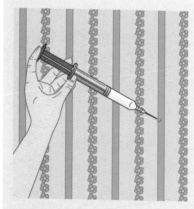

REPAIRING A BUBBLE

Use a sharp knife to cut a small slit in the center of the bubble. Use a hypodermic-needle-like applicator (available at home centers) to squirt a small amount of adhesive into the slit. Aim the applicator in at least two directions. Press the paper to the wall and sponge off the excess adhesive.

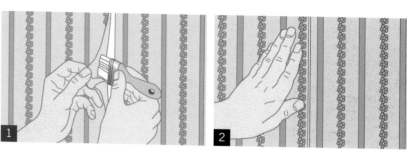

Repairing loose edges and tears

1 Moisten the damaged area and carefully lift the wallpaper away from the wall. Apply a thin layer of adhesive to the back of the paper.

2 Press the wallpaper back into place. Sponge off excess adhesive, taking care not to soak the paper and dilute the adhesive.

Patching a damaged section

1 Cut a piece of matching material 4 inches larger than the damaged area. Align the patch so its pattern exactly matches the damaged area, and attach it with painter's tape.

2 Using a straightedge, cut through both the patch and the wallpaper simultaneously. Don't cut so deep that you damage the drywall. Remove the patch.

3 Score the damaged wallpaper with a series of knife slits, dampen it with a wet sponge, and peel it off. Use a putty knife to scrape away any remaining adhesive. Clean the wall, and let it dry.

4 Apply a thin layer of adhesive to the back of the patch. Position the patch carefully, then smooth it with a clean, damp cloth or a seam roller. Wipe off excess adhesive.

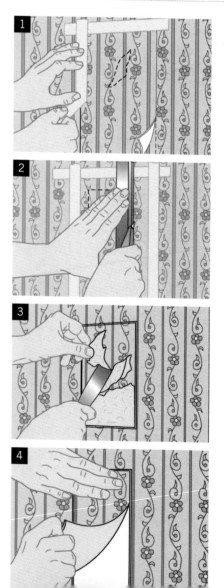

Removing wallpaper

1 Use an inexpensive wallpaper scarifying tool to score a series of shallow lines that go just through the paper but don't damage the underlying wall. If the paper has a vinyl finish, use sandpaper to abrade the surface so moisture can penetrate the paper.

2 Following the manufacturer's instructions, apply a liquid or gel wallpaper remover. Wearing eye protection and long clothing, apply the remover using a pump sprayer, a paintbrush, or a paint roller. For stubborn wallpaper you may need to rent a steamer.

3 Starting near the top of the wall, use a wallpaper scraper or a 6-inch taping blade to remove the paper and the adhesive. Take care not to damage the drywall as you work. If there are multiple layers of paper, remove them one at a time, following all three steps.

PAINT REMOVAL

Paint that has bubbled, cracked, developed "alligator skin," or is unpleasingly built up is difficult if not impossible to repair or patch over. These problems generally occur on painted wood rather than walls. The solution is either to replace the boards or strip the paint. You have several options.

If the area is flat, you can sand the paint off using a power sander. However, do not do this if you suspect that some of the paint may contain lead (see page 12). A belt sander works quickly but is likely to gouge the wood if you are not careful. A vibrating or orbital sander is slower but safer.

You'll find a wide variety of chemical paint removers at a home center. When using a solvent-based stripper, be sure to keep the room well ventilated and wear protective gloves and long clothing. Water-based strippers are less toxic but are also less effective. Gel or paste-type removers generally work best. You can also buy sheets to cover the remover and keep it moist for a day or two so it can work to full effectiveness. Scrape away the remover with a putty knife. Use specially shaped tools to get into nooks and crannies. Then rub the area with steel wool, using a toothbrush to get into tight spots. Finish by washing with mineral spirits or water, as directed by the stripper manufacturer. The residue left over from stripping is actually hazardous waste. Check with your local health department or building department to find the approved method for disposal.

A heat gun (not a hair dryer) generates enough heat to cause most types of paint to bubble up so you can scrape it away. Work carefully and keep your hands away from the heated area. Work systematically in small areas and scrape the paint as soon as it blisters.

CLEANING WALLS

High-quality paint, especially if it is semigloss or gloss, can usually be scrubbed clean with a solution of detergent and water. Experiment on an inconspicuous spot and wait a day to make sure the cleaning product does not dull the finish. To wash painted woodwork, fill a spray bottle with a mild solution of detergent and water, or use oil-based soap. Spray, then wipe with a sponge. Use a soft brush for hard-to-clean areas. If you run into an oily spot, clean it with mineral spirits or turpentine. Or use a commercial stain remover.

Even flat paint on walls can sometimes be washed. Mix a mild solution of TSP (or TSP substitute) and water, or dishwashing detergent and water. Use a sponge mop or a large handheld mop to wash a section, working from top to bottom. Rinse with clean, cold water.

⅄ AMERISPEC® TIP CLEANING WASHABLE WALLPAPER

To remove dirt, grease, and stains from washable wallpaper, thoroughly sponge the soiled area with a solution of dishwashing detergent and cold water. Rinse it with clear, cold water and wipe it dry with a clean, absorbent cloth. To find out whether your wallpaper is indeed washable, test-wash a small section in a spot that is not highly visible. This will show you how much liquid you can apply and how hard you can scrub before damaging the paper.

painting techniques

Applying a fresh coat of paint is a quick way to conceal wall repairs and upgrade a room—making it the most common do-it-yourself project. However, don't take the task lightly. A good paint job requires careful planning, the right materials and tools, and good technique.

THE RIGHT PAINT In most cases, latex paint is the best choice for interior surfaces. Oil- and alkyd-based paints are restricted in many areas. If your walls are painted with oil- or alkyd-based paint, latex paint applied on top will peel or crack unless you first apply a coat of primer. To test for paint type, scrape off a paint chip and bend it. If it flexes a bit before breaking, it is probably latex. If it is brittle, it is likely oil based. If you are unsure, take a chip to a paint dealer.

The glossier the paint, the easier it is to scrub clean. But glossy paint emphasizes imperfections, while flat paint hides them. It is common to use semigloss paint for woodwork and flat paint for walls. Or consider eggshell or satin sheens, which are in between flat and semigloss.

THE IMPORTANCE OF PRIMER Some stains—for example, water stains and tobacco discoloration—may bleed through paint and reappear no matter how many coats you apply. The solution is to use a stain-killing primer before painting. Also apply primer before painting over spackle and joint compound, to seal it and ensure consistent wall color. Primer also enables paint to stick to a surface that is oily or coated with oil-based paint. A paint dealer can tint primer to match the finish paint so you can avoid applying two coats.

THE RIGHT TOOLS Choose high-quality brushes and keep them clean. A good brush will spread a good, complete layer of paint, and may save you from having to apply a second or third coat. A roller with a ½-inch nap will spread a thick coat of paint and will produce a slightly bumpy texture. A ¼-inch nap will produce a smoother surface, but you will probably need to apply two coats.

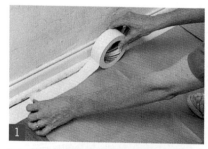

Prepping the room

1 Cover everything in the room with plastic or a drop cloth. Wrap light fixtures with plastic bags and tape. On the floor, run 2-inch-wide masking tape along the edge and then secure a drop cloth to the tape.

2 To mask adjacent surfaces, use 2-inch painter's tape or paper masking strips along the edges. At the baseboard, lay the tape along the upper edge to form a ledge to catch paint drips. Tape plastic sheeting to larger wall surfaces, such as wainscoting.

3 Mask window glass, unless you have a very steady hand. Press masking tape in place with a putty knife to seal the edges. Remove the tape while the paint is still tacky.

4 Whenever possible, remove hardware, fixtures, and electrical cover plates. Painting around obstacles not only leads to a sloppy job but actually takes more time in the long run. When you finish painting, you may choose to install new cover plates anyway.

Loading the roller

PAINT TRAY Pour paint into a paint tray until its reservoir is nearly full. Don't fill the ribbed portion. Dip the roller lightly into the paint and drag it gently across the ribbed part of the tray. Repeat until the roller is evenly loaded with paint.

ROLLER GRID If you are painting from a 5-gallon bucket of paint, this is a quick way to load a roller. Set a metal roller grid into the bucket. Remove excess paint from the roller by running it up and down against the grid.

Cut in the corners first

First paint the edges of the walls, then paint the walls with a roller before painting the trim. When you cut in a corner, position the brush about two brush lengths from a corner and paint toward the corner using long, overlapping strokes.

Rolling a wall

1 Attach an extension to a roller. Load up the roller in the tray or bucket and roll off the excess paint. Starting a few feet from one top corner of the wall, apply the paint in an M or W shape to a section that is 3 to 4 feet square. Work toward the adjacent wall, overlapping the cut-in edge along the corner.

2 Without reloading the roller, roll back over the same section to fill in unpainted spaces. Still without adding fresh paint, make a third pass to even out any marks left by the edge of the roller. Apply more pressure on this third pass. Keep rolling paint on the wall in sections until you have covered the wall.

PAINTING TRIM

Begin about 3 inches from a corner (or end) and brush the paint toward the corner. Reverse direction and, going over the applied paint, brush away from the corner. This will help spread the paint evenly. While the paint is still wet, brush lightly over the painted area again to obscure any brushstrokes. Repeat, beginning a few inches from where you stopped and brushing the paint first into the wet edge and then in the opposite direction.

PAINTING AROUND GLASS

To paint along glass, load the brush lightly. This is the one time you may choose to wipe the paint off one side of the brush. Slowly and steadily draw the brush along the window frame. Let the paint lap slightly onto the glass, to ensure a tight seal against weather.

⤵ AMERISPEC® TIP LOADING A BRUSH

Dip one-third of the length of the bristles into the paint, then lift and dip the brush again two or three times to saturate the bristles. The first time you load the brush, gently stir the paint with it so the bristles spread slightly (do not do this when reloading). Lift the brush straight up, letting excess paint drip into the bucket. Gently slap both sides of the brush against the inside of the bucket two or three times. Do not wipe the brush against the lip of the bucket.

wall tile and grout repairs

When ceramic tiles, especially around a bathtub, come loose from the wall, pull out all the tiles that pry off easily and check the condition of the underlying surface. If the wall is crumbling, remove a section of tiles between studs and repair the greenboard as shown on page 21. Greenboard is only somewhat resistant to moisture, so you may want to install cement backerboard, which resists rot much better. Clean the tiles of grout and adhesive, reinstall them, and apply grout as shown at right.

Call in a professional if the tiles have been set in a thick mortar bed. This is typical in older installations but is still practiced by some pros today.

If you have even a small hole or gap in your bathtub-surround grout, fill it immediately, before moisture can seep behind the tiles and loosen them. If your grout is developing cracks or gaps, if it is stained beyond cleaning, or if you just want to change the color (see the tip on the opposite page), remove it and apply new grout. Use unsanded grout for joints that are ⅛ inch or narrower; use sanded grout for wider joints. For strength and durability, mix grout powder with latex additive, not with water. Once the grout has hardened, apply sealer to keep it clean-looking and scrubbable.

Inside corners, especially the joint between the tub and the wall, should be sealed with silicone or bathtub caulk rather than grout. Grout will crack, while caulk is more flexible.

AMERISPEC® TIP | GROUT REMOVAL TOOLS

Removing grout from an entire tub surround can be tedious and time-consuming work. Fortunately, inexpensive power tools make the job quicker and easier. One setup features a guide and bit that attach to a rotary tool (far right). You can also buy a grout-removal blade for a reciprocating saw. If you have a small amount of grout to remove, use a hand grout saw (left and middle).

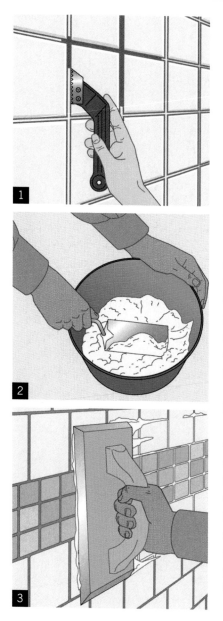

Regrouting

1 If grout is recessed, don't apply a thin layer on top, as it will likely flake off. Remove the grout all the way to the wall. To use a hand grout saw, use slow, deliberate strokes to avoid damaging tiles. Apply only moderate pressure, letting the saw do most of the work. When the going gets rough, replace the saw blade.

2 Pour some grout powder into a clean bucket. If the grout is fortified with polymer, mix it with water. Otherwise, use latex additive. Slowly add the liquid and mix with a margin trowel or a paint stirrer until the grout is the consistency of toothpaste and is free of lumps. Wait 10 minutes, then mix again. Add a little more liquid if it's needed.

3 Using a float, scoop some grout out of the bucket and smear it onto the wall. Working in sections about 4 feet square, push the grout into the joints. Hold the float nearly flat and sweep it diagonally across the surface so it does not dig in. At all points, press the grout in by moving the float in at least two directions.

1

2

3

Recaulking a bathtub

1 Remove all the old caulk first. Use a scraping tool that holds a straight razor blade. First scrape down the face of the tiles, then scrape along the bathtub rim. Some types of caulk can be softened with a heat gun. Finish by scrubbing the area with an abrasive pad.

2 You could simply apply caulk and smooth it with your finger, but here's a technique that will produce an extra-neat joint. Apply a piece of masking tape along both sides of the joint. Caulk the joint (see page 113), then smooth the caulk with your finger.

3 While the caulk is still wet, pry up one end of a piece of tape and pull it away, taking care not to smear caulk on the tub or wall. Do the same with the other piece of tape. Allow the caulk to dry for a full 24 hours before taking a shower or bath.

4 Tilt the float up and use it like a squeegee to wipe away most of the grout from the face of the tiles. Scrape diagonally so the edge of the float cannot dig into the grout lines. Once you have pressed and scraped one section, move on to the next. If the grout in the bucket starts to harden, throw it out and mix another batch.

5 Dampen a sponge and wipe the tiles gently. Rinse the sponge every few minutes with clean water. If you see a gap, push grout in with your finger. Pay close attention to the grout lines and aim to make them consistent in width and depth. Wipe the surface three or more times. Allow the grout to dry, then buff the tiles with a dry cloth.

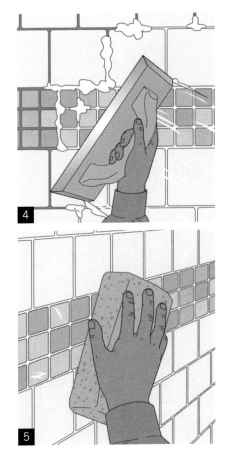

4

5

INSTALLING A TUB ACCESSORY

Some tub accessories, such as soap dishes, are attached to the surface of a tiled wall, while others are set into an opening in the tiles. Some installers prefer to attach a soap dish using a weak adhesive so the dish will pop out in one piece rather than break if it is pulled hard. If you are installing a new accessory, get one that will fit into the existing opening. Otherwise you will need to remove and cut a tile or two to make room for it. Clean the wall surface and allow it to dry. Spread construction adhesive, tile adhesive, or thinset mortar onto the back of the accessory. Push it into place and hold it there using pieces of masking tape or duct tape until the adhesive sets. The next day, caulk the joint between the accessory and the tiles.

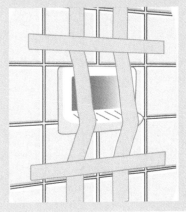

🔨 AMERISPEC® TIP **COLORING EXISTING GROUT**

At a tile or home center you can find products that permanently change the color of old grout. First clean the grout with a special solution. Apply the colorant with a small paintbrush or an applicator that comes with the product. Let it soak for the recommended amount of time, then wipe the tiles. It may take two or three coats to achieve the color you desire.

repairs to textured ceilings and walls

Many homes have ceilings and walls that are textured rather than smooth. Patching these surfaces is not as difficult as it may seem.

POPCORN CEILINGS Some ceilings are covered with an "acoustic" surface that resembles popcorn or cottage cheese. This finish saves time for installers, who spray it on rather than applying and sanding several coats of joint compound. It does have a slight sound-dampening effect, which vanishes once the surface is painted.

A small number of popcorn ceilings contain asbestos. You can send a sample to a testing agency (there are several on the Internet) for an inexpensive test. See page 13 for more information on asbestos.

If your popcorn ceiling is in good condition you can re-paint it. Be careful that the texture does not come loose while you paint. A textured paint roller works better than spraying. First apply a coat of alcohol-based primer (also known as white shellac), which will dry quickly and seal any stains. Then apply paint, taking care not to make any area overly wet.

If an area 4 feet square or smaller is damaged or has come loose, you can patch it using any of the techniques shown below. If the texture is coming loose in several areas, you probably need to remove it.

To remove a popcorn finish, clear out or cover everything in the room. Have a helper use a small pump sprayer filled with water to dampen a 4 by 4 foot ceiling area. Wait 5 minutes or so for the texture to soften, then use a 6-inch taping blade to scrape the texture off. (Ceiling paint is fairly porous. If the ceiling has been painted with semigloss, however, the water will likely not soak through to the texture.) Hold a bag under the scraper to catch debris. Proper wetting is the key, and it may take some experimenting to achieve. You want the texture to be dampened, but you don't want to wet the drywall, as that could seriously weaken it.

Once the texture is removed, you will probably find drywall that has received only one coat of tape and joint compound, so it is not smooth enough to paint. For a smooth finish, sand and apply a second and third coat. Or apply a wall texture (see opposite page). Paint with drywall primer followed by ceiling paint.

WALL TEXTURES If you have an old home with textured plaster walls, duplicating the texture is a job for pros. However, if your walls are made of textured drywall, patching is simply a matter of practice and finding the right technique. In most cases, using a hopper and perhaps a trowel will do the trick. If the wall has swirls, try duplicating them with a whisk broom. Many other textures are created with a trowel.

Patching a popcorn ceiling

DAB APPLICATOR To patch a very small area, buy a tube of popcorn ceiling patch equipped with a foam applicator. Gently scrape away any loose texture. Squeeze the tube as you press it against the ceiling. Use dabbing rather than sweeping motions to spread the texture.

SPRAY CAN You can buy an aerosol can of acoustic patch or spray devices that you load yourself. Scrape away a rectangular section of the ceiling. Protect the surrounding area with a cardboard box with its bottom removed (above) or by pinning up sheets of plastic. Spray until you achieve the desired texture.

ROLLED TEXTURE You can purchase acoustic ceiling patch in dry bags that you mix with water, or in premixed buckets. For a heavier texture, apply the patch first with a trowel, then go over it gently with a texture-paint roller. For a lighter texture, use the roller to apply texture paint.

Texturing walls

TEXTURE GUN A texture gun has a hopper on top, into which you load joint compound. It often is recommended that you first water down the compound. Adding a bit of sand increases the strength and produces a slightly grainy effect. With a texture gun you can achieve an orange peel texture, which is only slightly bumpy, or a spattered texture, which has more pronounced globs. Make sure you cover the floor and furniture before using the machine. Then fill the hopper and use the gun to spatter the walls until you have the desired amount of texture.

KNOCKDOWN TEXTURE A classic knockdown texture has a combination of flat and rounded areas. First spatter the wall using a hopper gun as shown at left. Before the compound starts to dry, gently run a large taping blade or flat trowel over the surface to flatten some but not all of the bumps. A pool trowel (shown above) helps you avoid streaks.

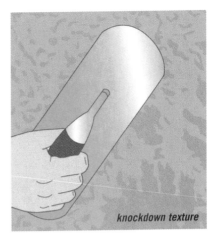

knockdown texture

hopper gun

AMERISPEC® TIP DEALING WITH STAINS AND MILDEW

If a stain cannot be cleaned away, cover it with alcohol-based stain-killing primer, then paint over it with latex paint. Treat mildew first by removing its cause, which is persistent moisture. Once the area is dry and you are certain it will stay dry, clean it with a commercial mildewcide or with a solution of 3 parts water to 1 part chlorine bleach.

CEILING TILES

Prefabricated ceiling tiles are attached either to an existing ceiling or to furring strips. Staples or nails (either with or without adhesive) or adhesive alone secures the tiles.

If ceiling tiles develop stains, paint with stain-killing primer, then with latex paint. Be aware that when you paint over ceiling tiles you lessen their ability to dampen sound.

If a tile is dented or chipped, follow the steps at right for removing and replacing it. You will need to remove one tongue and the back sides of two grooves in order to slip the new tile in.

Replacing a ceiling tile

1 Use a sharp utility knife to cut through all four joints around the damaged tile. Use a flat pry bar to remove the tile, then remove one of the tongue pieces left in an adjoining tile.

2 Using a straightedge and the utility knife, cut off one tongue and the back sides of both grooves on the replacement tile. Take care not to damage the visible portion of the tile. Test that the tile will fit.

3 Apply adhesive to the ceiling or to a furring strip. Slip the remaining tongue into an adjacent tile's groove, press the other side of the tile into place, and temporarily brace the tile until the adhesive dries.

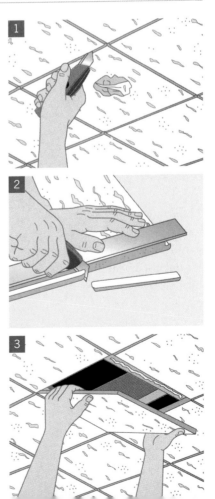

repairs to wood paneling

REPAIRING SOLID-BOARD PANELING

Solid-board paneling is made of ⅜- to ¾-inch-thick hardwood or softwood boards, or plywood strips ranging from 3 to 12 inches wide. Most are milled to overlap or interlock. Paneling is attached to studs, furring strips, or drywall.

If you can't repair damaged paneling to your satisfaction, you may want to replace one or more boards (see instructions below). Be sure to carefully match any new paneling and its finish with adjacent surfaces.

MINOR SCRATCHES AND GOUGES
One of the most common ways to conceal shallow scratches and gouges is to fill them with a putty stick, then wipe away any excess putty with a clean cloth. Choose a color that matches the finish of your paneling. You can also conceal minor scratches on paneling with furniture polish or wood color-match sticks.

DENTS AND DEEP GOUGES You may be able to restore dented wood fibers by removing all the finish from the dent site, then placing a damp cloth and a hot iron over the dent until the wood fibers rise to the level of the surrounding surface. Let the wood dry thoroughly before sanding it smooth and refinishing the area to match.

To repair a deep gouge or a nail hole, fill it with a matching wood putty, using a flexible putty knife to apply the putty. Let it dry, then sand the patch smooth with fine-grade sandpaper wrapped around a sanding block. Finish it to match the surrounding area.

Replacing a damaged tongue-and-groove board

1 Remove the baseboard (see step 1, opposite page). Adjust the blade depth of a circular saw to the damaged board's thickness. Saw up the board's center and then split the ends with a chisel.

2 Wedge a flat pry bar or wide chisel between the sawn edges. Pry the sections away from the wall one at a time. (You may find "blind" nails driven into the tongues.)

3 Place the damaged board over the new board and mark the correct length with a pencil and combination square. Use a power saw to cut the replacement board to length.

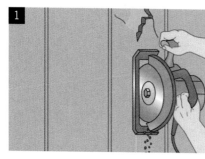

4 Remove the back of the new board's groove with a wood chisel (beveled side down) and a mallet, holding the board in a vise and using wood blocks to protect the board.

5 Align the replacement board with the adjacent one, starting at the ceiling. Fit the tongue of the new board into the groove of the adjacent board and slip it into place.

6 Tap the board into place with a padded block. Drive finishing nails at the top and bottom, sinking their heads with a nail set. Fill the holes and finish the wood, then replace the baseboard.

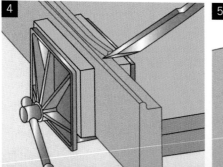
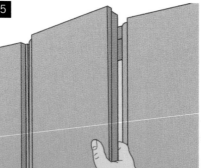
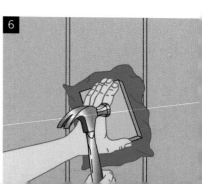

REPAIRING WOOD-VENEER SHEET PANELING

Sheet paneling may have a veneer of wood, simulated wood, or even fabric or vinyl. Of these, wood veneer responds best to repair, though even your most careful efforts may show.

Panels usually measure 4 by 8 feet and are fastened to either wall studs or furring strips with adhesive and/or color-matched nails. If you can't conceal the damage to your satisfaction or if the paneling has holes, you may want to replace a panel, as shown at right.

MINOR SCRATCHES AND NICKS

The simplest way to conceal a flaw is to draw over it with a colored putty stick. Wipe away any excess putty with a clean cloth. Putty sticks come in a variety of colors to match finished wood paneling. You can also hide scratches and nicks with shoe polish or floor wax.

For a more thorough repair, lightly rub the damaged area with fine steel wool or fine-grade sandpaper, applying less pressure toward the edges. Wipe away residue. Apply wood stain with a cotton swab.

After the stain is dry, lightly buff the area again with a fine abrasive and wipe away the sanding residue. Spray a light coat of varnish on the area and let it dry, then lightly buff it with a fine abrasive and wipe. If the original panels were waxed, wax the entire panel and buff it to a sheen with a clean cloth.

DEEP GOUGES AND CRACKS

Use a putty knife to fill deep gouges and cracks with wood putty. Sand smooth when dry. Use a small brush to stain or paint the putty so it matches the finish of the panel, or use colored putty that matches the finish.

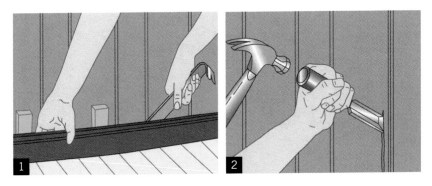

Replacing a damaged wood-veneer panel

1 Insert a pry bar between the baseboard and paneling, placing wood wedges in the gap. Pry off the baseboard and remove the remaining nails with pliers or a hammer.

2 Split the panel near one edge (not on a stud), using a hammer and chisel. The split should be large enough for you to insert a pry bar to peel the panel off the studs.

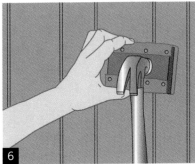

3 Pull the panel off the studs with a pry bar, being careful not to damage adjacent panels. Wedge a pry bar between the panel and studs to break any adhesive bond.

4 After pulling off the old paneling and scraping off any adhesive (or removing nails), apply a bead of adhesive along the length of the studs to hold the new panel.

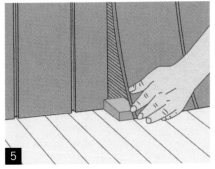

5 Position the new panel. Drive four finishing nails near the top of the panel to secure it. Then pull out the base, holding it with a wood block until the adhesive gets tacky.

6 Remove the block and press the panel into place. With a padded block, hammer along edges and over studs. Remove the finishing nails if they are not needed. Replace the baseboard.

floors and stairs

Before you make repairs or improvements to wood, vinyl, carpet, or tile floors, make sure you understand the substructure.

A FLOOR'S SUBSTRUCTURE The joists that support the floor are typically 2 by 8 or wider, and they are usually spaced 16 or 24 inches apart. The

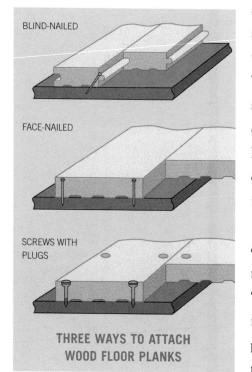

BLIND-NAILED

FACE-NAILED

SCREWS WITH PLUGS

THREE WAYS TO ATTACH WOOD FLOOR PLANKS

subfloor is nailed to the joists and sometimes also glued with construction adhesive. The subfloor is typically constructed of one or two sheets of plywood. In some prewar homes, diagonally laid 1-by-4 or 1-by-6 planks were used instead.

If your house is built on a concrete slab, the floor may be laid over 2-by-4 "sleepers" spaced every 16 inches or so, or on a base of plywood that is attached to the concrete with concrete

fasteners. In some older homes, tongue-and-groove hardwood flooring rests on 1-by-3 sleepers nailed on top of the planks and spaced about 12 inches apart.

If your home has a crawl space or basement, you may be able to check out the subfloor from underneath. If you can tell that it is plywood, look for a grade stamp that designates the thickness. Or look for a hole in the floor (perhaps for a pipe) and measure there.

FINISH MATERIALS Most wood flooring has a tongue on one side and a groove on the other so that the boards fit together snugly. Tongue-and-groove flooring is usually fastened with nails driven at an angle through the tongue, making the nail heads invisible. Less common plank flooring, which has no tongues or grooves, is fastened with nails or screws driven through the face of the boards. The fastener heads are sunk below the surface and covered with putty or wood plugs.

The thickness and stiffness of the subfloor determine the types of finish materials that can be put on top. If your house is built on a concrete slab, the slab can support almost any type of flooring. But with a plywood or plank subfloor, it's important to check out the type and thickness of the material to determine its limitations. A floor that is slightly

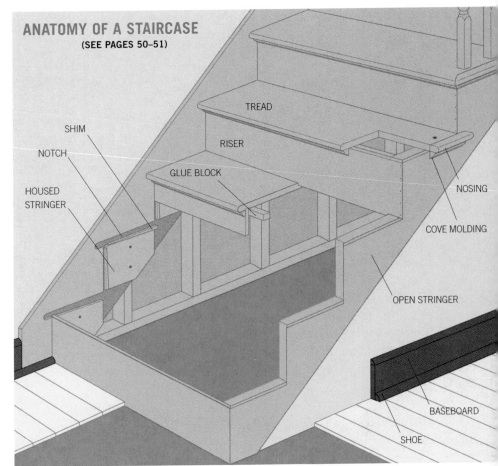

ANATOMY OF A STAIRCASE
(SEE PAGES 50–51)

SHIM
NOTCH
HOUSED STRINGER
GLUE BLOCK
TREAD
RISER
NOSING
COVE MOLDING
OPEN STRINGER
BASEBOARD
SHOE

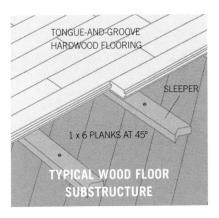

TONGUE-AND-GROOVE HARDWOOD FLOORING
SLEEPER
1 x 6 PLANKS AT 45°

TYPICAL WOOD FLOOR SUBSTRUCTURE

flexible or springy is not suitable for ceramic or stone tile, as the grout or tiles will likely crack. Wood flooring, laminate flooring, or carpet can be installed on a subfloor that is slightly springy and less than smooth. Vinyl tiles and sheet flooring can be installed on a springy floor, but the surface must be very smooth.

FLOOR PROBLEMS A few minor dips in a floor caused by the house settling are common. But if a floor sags more than 1½ inches or feels mushy when an adult jumps on it, the house could have a serious structural problem.

Look for evidence of rot. Discolored areas on the joists or subfloor usually indicate a plumbing leak. If you are faced with any of these problems, call a contractor.

You can repair most minor surface damage yourself. If your wood flooring squeaks or has separated, split, or warped boards, you can often reattach them and make the floor straight. Often, but not always, a moderately scratched or stained wood floor can be sanded and refinished. This chapter will also show you how to repair floor tile, vinyl, and carpeting.

fixing squeaky or warped wood flooring

Squeaks on a wood floor occur when pieces of wood rub together. Squeaks usually originate in the finished flooring, but they can also occur in the subfloor or even the joists.

DIAGNOSING THE PROBLEM Have an adult walk on the squeaky area while you lie on the floor and watch closely. If you see boards moving against others, the solution is to reattach them to the subfloor. If a section moves up and down, the damage is likely beneath the floor-ing. You may need to attach the subfloor to the joists or shore up the joists, as shown on the next page.

If the joists are visible from the basement or the crawl space, watch from below while someone walks across the floor above. You might spot some slight movement between the joists and the subfloor or per-haps loose bridging between joists.

CORRECTING SQUEAKS Simple but usually not permanent remedies include squirting powdered or liquid graphite between floorboards or dusting cracks with talcum powder. Use a paintbrush to work the pow-der into the gaps between boards, then sweep.

If floorboards are rubbing, face-nailing is usually the best solution. Experiment with various shades of wood putty to find the best color-match so the holes will not be too visible. If you can work from below, drive screws up through the sub-floor and into the flooring.

If the problem is below the floor-ing, drive shims into a gap between a joist and the subfloor, or add a cleat. If the joists themselves sag when the floor is walked on, add sister boards. If that does not do the trick, or if you see cracked joists or any that sag more than ½ inch, call a professional carpenter.

Three ways to silence squeaks from above

RE-SEAT To reseat loose boards before reattaching them, tap them sharply with a hammer and carpeted 2 by 4. As you tap, move in the direction shown in the inset below.

NAIL Drill angled pilot holes through the flooring, into the sub-floor, and, if possible, into a joist. Drive finish nails or flooring nails, countersink their heads, and fill.

DRIVE POINTS Coat old-style triangular glazier's points with liquid graphite, then use a putty knife and a hammer to drive them between boards.

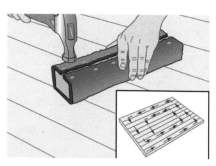
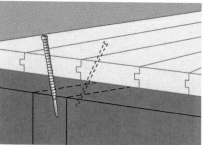
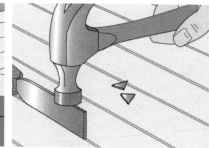

Three ways to silence squeaks from below

SHIM If you see a gap between the subfloor and a joist, drive shims every 3 inches or so into the gap using medium pressure only. Do not cause the floor to rise.

FASTEN WITH SCREWS Drill pilot holes, taking care not to poke through the flooring. Drive wood screws (¼ inch shorter than the total floor thickness) with washers.

ADD A CLEAT Under a large loose area, mount a cleat against a joist. Prop the cleat snugly against the subfloor and attach it to the joist with screws.

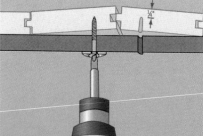
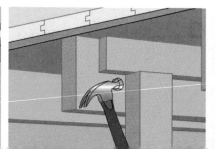

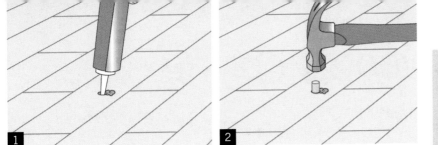

1	**2**

Filling with adhesive

1 If there is a gap under the flooring and face-nailing doesn't solve the problem, try gluing. Drill a ⅜-inch hole through the board and squirt flooring adhesive into the hole until it starts to ooze out.

2 Wipe away the excess adhesive. Cut a short length of ⅜-inch dowel, the same color as the flooring, and tap it into the hole. Wipe away the squeezed-out adhesive, allow it to dry, then sand it smooth and dab it with finish.

LOOSE DUCTS OR PIPES

Sometimes ductwork or water supply pipes can cause squeaks. The solution may be to tighten straps, install new straps, or wedge insulation between the metal and wood surfaces.

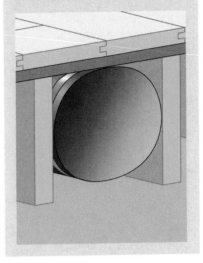

WARPED OR BUCKLED BOARDS

If flooring boards buckle upward or are warped so they do not present a smooth surface, the problem may be moisture. Take steps to ensure the area will remain dry. Place a damp towel over the area and weight the boards down by placing concrete blocks or other heavy objects on top. After a few days, the flooring will probably settle down at least partially. To fasten the floor down, drill pilot holes every few inches along the length of each warped or buckled board, then drive in finish-head screws. Fill the holes with wood putty and then finish.

> **⚘ AMERISPEC® TIP   SQUEAKS UNDER CARPETING**
>
> If a carpeted floor squeaks, the solution is to drive nails or screws through the carpeting and the plywood subfloor and into joists below. Depending on the type of carpeting, you can usually drive finishing nails or finish-head screws right through the carpeting and their heads will not be visible. Otherwise, you may need to pull the carpeting up first.

 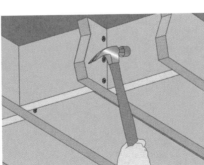 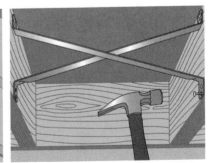

Firming sagging or bouncy joists

ADD A SISTER To strengthen a joist, install a "sister" joist alongside it. Cut the sister out of 2-by lumber, making it as long as possible. Wedge it against the bottom of the subfloor and drive pairs of 3-inch screws every 8 inches or so.

USE BLOCKING To strengthen an entire floor, cut 2-by blocking, the same width as the joists, to fit snugly between joists. Tap the blocking into place between the joists so the pieces are offset from each other, then attach with screws.

BRIDGING Steel bridging is not quite as strong as blocking, but is easier to install and will cut down on squeaks. Purchase bridging made to fit the spaces between your joists, usually 14½ inches. Wedge each piece tightly, then attach with nails or screws.

replacing wood flooring

I f some boards are severely scratched or stained, you may need to replace them. The instructions on these pages are for tongue-and-groove solid hardwood flooring. If you have laminate or engineered wood flooring, follow the same procedures. If you have plank flooring, you can usually simply pry loose a board without damaging its neighbor.

Too often, a repair to damaged tongue-and-groove flooring results in a rectangular patch that stands out like a sore thumb because its joints are not staggered. Make a rectangular patch (as shown on the next page) only if it will be covered with a rug or carpeting. A better approach is to remove boards or portions of boards so their ends are staggered in a way that blends with the surrounding floor. Because the pieces interlock, removing and patching tongue-and-groove flooring in this way is a time-consuming task that requires some skill.

PREPARING FOR THE REPAIR Buy replacement boards that match the existing flooring in size and color. On a solid hardwood floor, strip the finish from a piece of the removed flooring to determine what sort of wood to buy. Sanding, staining, and finishing may require more work and time than the actual repair. You can try to finish the new boards before installing them, but it is difficult to achieve an exact match. It may be necessary to sand and refinish the entire floor (see pages 42–43).

If you need to replace more than one board, plan the patch so that you end up with staggered joints. You may choose to remove full-length boards. If a damaged board is very long, however, you may choose to replace only a portion of it. If you are removing a full board, skip steps 1 and 5 (opposite page).

For a professional appearance, all the cuts—both to the existing boards on the floor and to the replacement boards—should be neat and at a perfect right angle. A power miter saw makes this easy, but you can achieve good results with a circular saw if you use a square as a cutting guide.

REMOVING A SINGLE BOARD

Using a circular saw, make two plunge cuts into the middle of the damaged board, cutting from one end of the board to the other. (Be careful not to cut into the adjacent boards.) Chisel down far enough to release each end. Pry out the central cutout section using the chisel. Now you can carefully pry out the grooved side and the tongue side.

Replacing a rectangular section

1 Use a framing square to mark the area to be cut. Mark first with a pencil, then with a knife, to prevent splintering. Adjust the blade depth of a circular saw to the boards' thickness. Start cuts in the center and work toward the ends.

2 Finish the cuts with a chisel, then pry the interior boards up. Cut away the exposed tongue on one side of the rectangle. Remove or sink any exposed nails. Cut a piece of roofing felt or construction paper to fit, then staple it into place.

3 Cut boards to fit snugly and blind-nail each into place. Remove the last board's tongue, use a woodblock to tap it down, drill pilot holes, and drive face nails. Countersink the nails, fill the holes with wood putty, and finish.

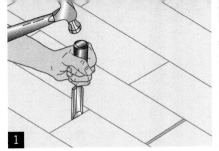

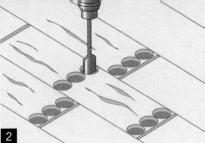

Weaving in staggered boards

1 Use a square and a knife to mark each cut line; this will prevent splintering when you cut the board. Hold a chisel with the bevel facing the area to be removed, then pound with a hammer until you cut about halfway through the board.

2 Bore a series of ½-inch holes across the width of the board just inside the cut lines. Take care that the holes do not cross the cut lines. Also bore a series of holes every 8 inches or so along the length of each board.

3 Use a 1-inch or wider wood chisel and hammer to split the defective areas. Pound with moderate pressure to avoid damaging adjacent boards. If the boards do not split, you may need to drill more holes.

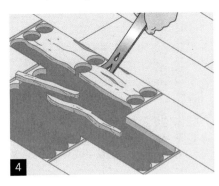

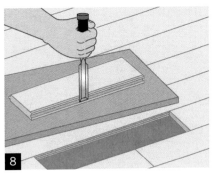

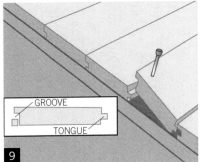

4 Using a flat pry bar and perhaps a small woodblock for leverage, pull out the split portions of the boards. Take care that you do not split a board past the cut lines.

5 Use a wide, sharp chisel to trim the ragged edges from each cut board. If a cut is not clean or at a precise right angle, make a new cut just behind it. In some cases, you can use a circular saw to start the cut.

6 Staple roofing felt to the floor to minimize squeaks. Slip the first new board's groove over an existing one's tongue. Tap the board in place with a mallet and a scrap of flooring, then blind-nail.

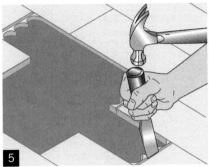

7 To blind-nail, drill an angled pilot hole just above the tongue and drive a finish or flooring nail. Continue positioning boards. You will probably need to cut off portions of tongues, using a chisel or a table saw.

8 Whenever possible, install boards with tongues and grooves intact, as this will allow you to blind-nail them. Where necessary, use a chisel to cut off a tongue or the area below a groove.

9 Wherever a tongue or the bottom edge of a groove has been removed, you must face-nail the board. Drill a pilot hole and drive a finish nail or a flooring nail so its head is at least ¼ inch below the surface. Fill the hole and finish.

sanding, finishing, and spot removal

Some wood floors are stained and then finished, but many have only a hard finish, which alone can change the appearance of the wood. Often this finish is an oil-based polyurethane, which tends to yellow after a year or two. In many parts of the country, oil-based poly is banned due to air-quality concerns. On some older homes, varnish was used. These factors can make color matching a challenge, so you may choose to sand and refinish the entire floor (see pages 42–43).

CLEANING AND RENEWING A WOOD FLOOR

Sometimes a dingy-looking floor can be restored to an attractive glow with a thorough cleaning, followed by an application of a finish such as polyurethane or floor wax. Whichever products you use, test them on an inconspicuous area before tackling the entire floor. If a section of the floor is bare of finish, treat it differently than the areas that have a finish; it is very easy to accidentally stain bare wood. Vacuum the floor thoroughly before attempting any type of cleaning.

If you have a wax buildup, wash the floor with a solution of dishwashing detergent and water, or use a professional wax stripper. Work in 4-foot-square sections, cleaning and wiping up before you move on to the next section.

For minor scratches or an ugly finish, clean the floor using a product that is made specifically for hardwood floors. Some products simply clean, while others add a finish as they clean.

If the wood has a spot, sand the surface to remove any finish and get to the bare wood. Wearing gloves and protective clothing, mix a batch of wood bleach (oxalic acid) according to the manufacturer's directions. Pour the bleach over the spot or discoloration, and let it sit for an hour or so. Rinse with a solution of 4 tablespoons of borax to 1 quart of water and let the wood dry. Bleach again if needed. (If bleaching does not remove it, you may have to sand the floor, as shown on pages 42–43.) Sand the area smooth, then apply a stain or finish.

⚑ AMERISPEC® TIP MATCHING STAINS

Spot-staining can be very tricky, as even slight differences in color will be apparent. Experiment on scrap pieces of flooring before applying stain to the floor. Sand the scraps as you will the floor, apply stain, wait a day, then apply the polyurethane or other finish. (The finish often changes the color of a stain significantly.) Once you are sure of a good color match, you can start on the floor.

Finishing a repair

1 With wood putty, fill the gaps between the old and new boards, as well as any other gaps. Use putty that receives a stain, or a colored putty that matches the stain you will apply. Press firmly to push the putty deep into the floor.

2 Sand the patch so it is smooth and level with the surrounding floor. A belt sander works faster than a vibrating sander, but work carefully to avoid pitting the floor. Start with 40-grit paper, then sand with 60-grit, then 80- or 100-grit.

3 If you will use a stain, apply it with a paintbrush, wait a minute or so, then wipe away the excess. Wait a day, then apply a hard finish such as polyurethane. Let it dry, sand lightly, and apply another coat of polyurethane.

repairing laminate and parquet flooring

Many of the repair techniques on pages 38–39 apply to other types of tongue-and-groove flooring. Where you need to remove a tongue or the bottom edge of a groove, you must facenail.

Most wood parquet tiles are sold stained and sealed, so you do not have to sand and refinish them.

However, it is a good idea to apply acrylic sealer or polyurethane for added protection and to seal the joints between tiles.

LAMINATE FLOORING Laminate flooring is composed of pressed board or plywood with a hard resin coating. It is very resistant, but not immune, to scratches. Dents can be filled, but it is usually not possible to successfully fill a scratch. The planks are 4 feet long. Depending on the damage, you may choose to replace an entire plank, or make a cut and replace only a portion.

ENGINEERED FLOORING Sometimes referred to as "laminated," this material is composed of plywood or pressed wood with a top layer of hardwood. Repairs are similar to those for a hardwood floor. Some types can be sanded and refinished once (see pages 42–43), but others have a veneer that is too thin.

Repairing a section of laminate flooring

1 Use a circular saw to cut out a portion from the middle that is about 1 inch from all edges. Complete the cuts with a sharp chisel. Pry this piece out. Next, make four short, angled cuts running from the cutout area to each of the corners. Complete the cuts using a chisel. Pry out the scraps.

2 Cut a new piece of laminate flooring to fit snugly into the cutout area. Use a circular saw or a table saw to cut off the edge below the groove. Test that this patch will fit. Apply glue to all the tongues and to the floor at each end. Slip the patch into place and weight it down for a day before walking on it.

PATCHING A HOLE IN LAMINATE FLOORING
Small areas of damage can be filled with laminate patching putty. Use a utility knife and a chisel to cut the hole (at least ¼ inch deep) and square up its edges. Squeeze putty into the hole. Using a putty knife, force putty down and scrape the surface. Wait an hour, then wipe the area with a damp cloth.

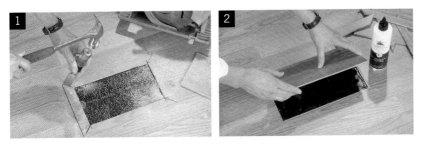

Replacing a section of parquet flooring

1 Set a circular saw to cut just through the tile. Make cuts in each direction across the tile. Take care not to cut an adjacent one.

2 Use a hammer and a wide chisel or a flooring scraper to pry the tile out piece by piece. Scrape the floor free of adhesive, which can be tenacious.

3 Use a circular saw to cut away the bottom edge of the replacement tile's two grooves, as well as one of its tongues. Trowel parquet tile adhesive onto the floor and set the tile.

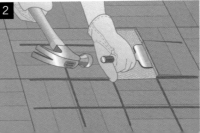

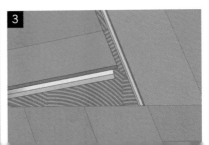

sanding and refinishing a hardwood floor

A damaged or dingy hardwood floor can often be rejuvenated with sanding and refinishing. A medium-sized room can be sanded and stained in a day. Allow several more days to apply coats of protective finish. You will need to work carefully, especially when using a drum sander with heavy-grit paper, to avoid gouging the floor.

SHOULD YOU SAND Make sure your floor is a good candidate for a thorough sanding, which typically removes up to ⅛ inch of wood. If the floor has only surface damage, consider an alternative to drum sanding (see tip, page 43).

Solid, ¼-inch-thick flooring can usually be sanded up to three times. In an older home, the floor may have already been sanded once or twice. To check, examine the top of the flooring in several places (check a damaged section or at the end of a board). If there is less than ⅛ inch of wood above the tongue, there is not enough to sand.

High-quality engineered flooring can be sanded only once. Consider using a random-vibrating sander instead of a drum sander.

Water or pet-urine stains on a portion of the floor that is unfinished (lacking a glossy coat) are usually too deep to sand away; you will likely need to replace the flooring. Burn marks may also run too deep.

If a hardwood floor was covered with underlayment and another flooring material, removing the underlayment will reveal a grid of nail or staple holes. These holes may remain somewhat visible after the floor is sanded and finished.

THE RIGHT EQUIPMENT Rent a drum sander designed for finishing floors. A machine that runs on 220 volts works quickly, but you will need to be extra careful or you could pit the floor. You will also need a 220-volt receptacle with a hole configuration that matches the sander's plug. A sander that runs on a standard 120-volt current is slower and safer. Buy drum sanding belts in three grits: typically 40, 60, and either 80 or 100. You will also need an edge sander to get near the wall and a pull-type paint scraper for tight spots and corners. To clean up and prevent dust from settling in cracks, use a shop vacuum. To apply the stain and finish, use an applicator made from lamb's wool and a paint brush. A pole sander equipped with 100-grit sandpaper speeds the job of sanding the finish between coats.

1 Make any necessary repairs to the floor (see pages 36–39). Remove the base shoe and, if necessary, the baseboard. Sanding creates dust that seeps through small openings, so open a window and point a fan outside to expel the dust and make the air breathable. Seal doors with masking tape and plastic.

2 At the rental store, ask for detailed instructions on the use of the drum sander. To load a drum sander with a sanding belt, unplug the machine and tip it up so you can get at the underside. Loosen one or two mounting nuts, then slip the sanding belt onto the rollers and tighten the nuts.

3 Tip the belt up and turn the sander on. Slowly lower the belt onto the floor, allowing the sander to pull forward. Do not allow the sander to remain in one place for even a second or it will dig into the floor. Overlap your passes by several inches. When the sander no longer sands effectively, change the belt.

4 Vacuum the floor thoroughly after each sanding. Examine the floor for exposed fastener heads. Countersink them to prevent damage to the sanding belt. Resist the temptation to skip one of the sandings. If you omit the medium- or fine-grit sanding, the floor will probably show visible sanding marks. Sand the surface a second time using the medium-grit paper.

5 Use an edge sander to reach most of the areas not covered by the drum sander. Wear a face mask and ear protectors, as this tool creates a lot of dust and is very noisy. Equip the sander with 60-grit disks for the first sanding. It will take a few minutes to get the knack of keeping the machine flat and steady as you work. It can run away from you if you are not careful.

6 Where the edger cannot reach, use a paint scraper with a sharp blade. Apply strong downward pressure as you pull the scraper. Whenever possible, scrape with the wood's grain. When you must go against the grain, bear down with less force to avoid splintering the wood. Change the blade (or rotate it if you have a four-sided type) as soon as the going gets tough.

7 After the second sanding, vacuum thoroughly. Fill any holes with wood putty. Choose putty that is stainable and close to the desired finish color of the floor. If you are not going to apply stain, try to match the color of the raw wood. When the putty is dry, sand the floor one more time using 80- or 100-grit paper. At corners where you used the scraper, smooth the floor with a hand sander.

8 The floor must be dust-free. Vacuum thoroughly, wait a bit, and vacuum again. Run your hand over the surface. If you pick up dust, vacuum again. If you choose to apply stain, mix it thoroughly. Apply the stain with an applicator to an area about 10 feet square. Wipe away any excess with a rag. Work quickly and systematically so you never apply stain to an abutting area where stain has already dried.

9 After the stain has dried, apply two or three coats of polyurethane finish. Apply the finish carefully, using smooth strokes to avoid creating bubbles. An applicator made from lamb's wool is the best tool for this job. Allow the finish to dry, then sand lightly using 220-grit paper. A pole sander makes the job easier. Vacuum thoroughly and apply one or two additional coats of finish.

✈ AMERISPEC® TIP | **ALTERNATIVES TO DRUM SANDING**

If the damage to your floor is not severe and you do not need to remove a water or pet-urine stain, consider this pair of options. To remove a floor's finish and perhaps some shallow scratches, rent a janitorial-type flooring buffer. Buy some flooring screens and a pad to hold them. Start with a heavy screen, such as 60-grit, and finish with a lighter 80- or 100-grit screen. You may find it takes 15 minutes or so to get the hang of operating the buffer. Replace a screen once it stops removing material from the surface of the floor.

A random-vibrating sander removes shallow scratches as well as the finish. It is safer to use than a drum sander because there is no danger of gouging the floor. Begin with 60-grit paper, then use 80-grit, and finally 100-grit.

replacing baseboard and shoe molding

Installed where the floor and walls meet, baseboards (also called base moldings) and shoe moldings hide uneven floor and wall joints and protect walls from damage caused by foot traffic, furniture, and cleaning tools. Often the boards become so dented or marred that they need to be replaced for appearance's sake.

The directions below show how to remove and replace lengths of baseboard and shoe molding that have square ends. For lengths that run into corners, you'll have to cut mitered or coped ends, as shown on the opposite page.

BUYING MATERIALS When you shop for replacement sections, take old pieces with you to ensure a good match. Many wood baseboards and

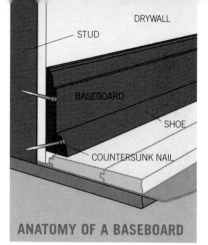

ANATOMY OF A BASEBOARD

shoe moldings come in standard shapes (called profiles), but some have profiles that are no longer made. If that is the case with your baseboards, either use standard moldings (perhaps combining two

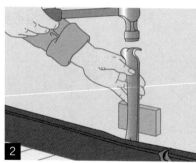

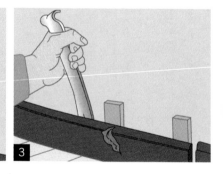

Replacing damaged baseboards

1 Insert the thin end of a broad-bladed pry bar between the shoe molding and baseboard. Loosen the molding by prying outward. Pull the molding free and remove the nails.

2 Place the thin end of the pry bar between the baseboard and wall and pry outward to make a gap. Use a woodblock to protect the wall.

3 Insert wooden wedges into the gap as you pry. When the baseboard is loose, pull it free. Remove any remaining nails from the baseboard and wall with pliers or a hammer.

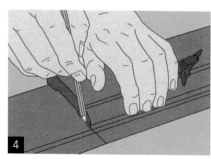

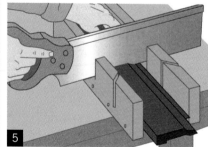

4 Measure the replacement baseboard and shoe molding against the damaged pieces and mark cutting lines with a pencil. (For corners, see opposite page.)

5 Use a miter box and backsaw to cut the replacement baseboards and shoe moldings. Saw the pieces on the waste side of the cutting lines.

6 Position the baseboard and drive nails at each stud location. Position the shoe molding and nail it into the floor or the base plate. Sink the nails, fill, and finish.

or more) to approximately mimic your moldings, or have a millwork shop make new pieces that match.

REPLACING BASEBOARDS AND MOLDINGS

If the molding is painted, cut a line between the molding and the wall with a utility knife so paint won't chip when you pull away the molding. To protect the wall, use a wood block behind the pry bar as you work, and pry only at studs.

Wherever possible, hold a new board in place to mark it for cutting. Where necessary, use a tape measure. A power miter saw makes it easy to achieve precise cuts, but you can also get good results using a miter box and backsaw. Practice on scrap pieces until you are confident you can make straight cuts.

CUTTING AND FITTING CORNERS

When replacing two pieces that meet at an outside corner, miter the ends of both pieces and install them as shown (above right). If the baseboards you're replacing meet at an inside corner, cope the end of one replacement to fit over the other (right). Cut and fit the ends of both base shoe pieces in the same way.

NAILING INTO FRAMING MEMBERS

Removing old baseboards will likely make it clear where the studs are. Lightly mark the wall for stud locations just above the top of the new molding. Make sure the nails will sink at least an inch into a stud or base plate. In most cases, 6-penny (6d) nails are long enough. However, if the baseboard is thick or if you have thick plaster walls, you may need longer nails. To prevent wood from cracking, drill pilot holes for all nails that are 3 inches or closer to the end of a piece of molding.

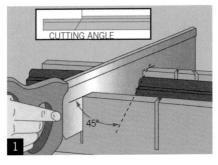

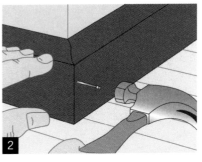

Installing an outside corner

1 Measure for the new pieces and draw cut lines. Use a miter box and a backsaw to cut each piece of the replacement baseboard at a 45° angle.

2 After nailing one new piece into place, butt the end of the second section against it, drill pilot holes, and drive nails through the joint.

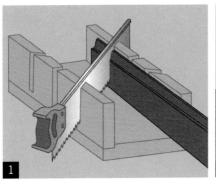

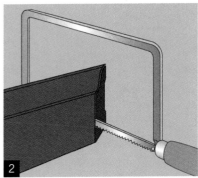

Installing an inside corner

1 Cut one piece straight and install it in the corner. Cut the other piece (which will be coped) at a 45° bevel.

2 Use a coping saw to cut along the molding's profile, following the curvature. Hold the saw at a right angle to the board as you cut.

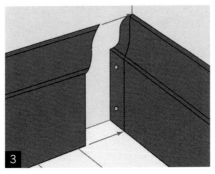

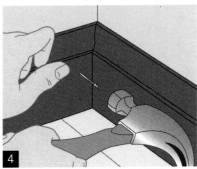

3 Hold the coped piece in place and check the fit. You may need to modify the cut using a knife or a rasp. Once the fit is tight, cut the other end of the board.

4 Drive nails through the baseboard and into the studs and sole plate. Sink the nails, fill the holes, and finish.

repairs to resilient flooring

Vinyl tiles and vinyl sheet flooring are the most common resilient materials. Others include cork, linoleum, and rubber tile. No-wax vinyl has a shiny top surface that cannot be mended if scratched or torn. Commercial tile, with flecks of color that run all the way through its thickness, can sometimes be mended if scratched. Try sanding it and then applying floor wax or acrylic sealer.

Resilient flooring will telegraph even minor imperfections in the underlayment that it rests on. If you see bumps or ridges and valleys, you probably need to replace or smooth the underlayment.

If you cannot find an exact match for a damaged resilient tile or section of sheet flooring, remove a tile or cut out a section from under the refrigerator or some other inconspicuous place.

There are two types of vinyl floor adhesive. With one type,

typically used for sheet flooring, you set the material in place while the adhesive is wet, then wait a day or so for the adhesive to dry.

The other type, commonly used for tiles, is allowed to dry to a tacky finish before the flooring is applied.

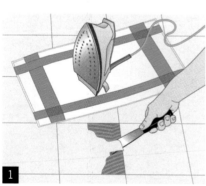

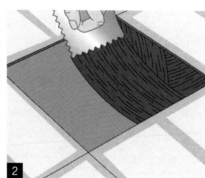

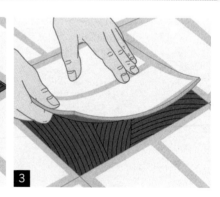

Replacing a damaged tile

1 If you cannot simply pry a tile up with a putty knife, soften the adhesive by placing a cloth on the tile, then pressing with a hot clothes iron. Scrape the floor smooth once the tile comes up.

2 Spread a thin, even layer of vinyl floor adhesive on the subfloor using a small-notched trowel of the size recommended by the adhesive manufacturer. Avoid getting adhesive on adjacent tiles.

3 Butt two adjacent edges of the new tile against two adjacent tiles, matching the pattern, if any. Press the tile into place and remove any adhesive smudges with mineral spirits.

FLOORS AND STAIRS

Three repairs for surface damage

CURLED TILE Soften the adhesive with an iron and cloth as shown on the opposite page, step 1. Gently lift the corner and scrape the adhesive off the floor with a putty knife. Spread a thin coat of adhesive, let it become tacky, and press the tile corner back into place.

BUBBLE Following a line in the pattern if possible, slit the bubble edge to edge using a utility knife. With a putty knife, force a small amount of all-purpose flooring adhesive inside. Press flat and weight the area overnight.

SMALL HOLE OR GOUGE This works best with commercial tile. Make a filler by mixing powdered leftover flooring and a few drops of clear nail polish. Mask the surrounding area and apply the filler. When it dries, buff it with fine steel wool.

✦ AMERISPEC® TIP | SEAL THE SEAMS

If you have sheet flooring with a seam where two pieces join, apply seam sealer every year or so to keep the two pieces from coming apart. Sealer is available at home centers and hardware stores.

Patching sheet flooring

1 Choose a section to replace that follows a line in the pattern so the seam will be less visible. Cut a piece of leftover flooring that matches the floor pattern and is larger than the section by at least 2 inches on each side.

2 Attach the piece to the floor with masking tape, carefully matching the pattern. Using a straight-edge and a very sharp utility knife, cut through both the patch and the flooring.

3 Pull up the patch and set it aside. Use a putty knife or a chisel to pry up the damaged flooring and scrape away the adhesive. Take care not to mar, pry up, or cut the adjacent flooring.

4 Test that the patch will fit snugly; you may need to trim it with a rasp or wood plane. Spread adhesive on the back of the patch with a notched trowel. Press the patch into place, clean away excess adhesive, and weight the area overnight.

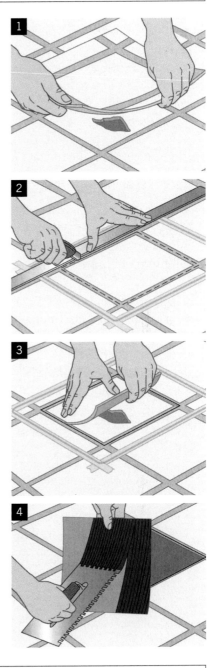

✦ AMERISPEC® TIP | POPPED NAIL

If a nail head leaves an impression in a vinyl floor, first use a nail set and hammer to pound it back in. The set will leave a small hole, which you can fill with seam sealer. If the nail pops up again, slice through the vinyl and pry out the nail with a flat pry bar. Reglue the vinyl and apply seam sealer.

ceramic and stone floor tile

This page shows how to replace one or two damaged floor tiles. If more than a few floor tiles have cracked, it is likely that either the tiles are not strong enough or the subsurface is not firm enough. You may need to tear up all the tiles and start again. If whole tiles are popping out, the adhesive is not strong enough. Remove the tiles, scrape away the old adhesive, and set the tiles in a bed of thinset mortar.

If the grout is cracking or chipping but the tiles are fine, the grout was likely not mixed with latex additive, so it is brittle. Remove the grout with a power tool (see page 28). Apply new grout that is polymer or latex reinforced.

Grout that is dingy but sound can usually be restored with grout cleaner. You can also purchase grout coloring agents that will transform the color of your grout. Once the grout is the color you desire, be sure to apply sealer regularly.

⚡ AMERISPEC® TIP | **REMOVING STAINS FROM FLOOR TILE**

A general-purpose tile cleaner will handle most stains. To remove food or drink stains or ink, first scrub with hydrogen peroxide, then laundry bleach. For oil-based stains such as paint or tar, first try mineral spirits, then paint remover. To remove rust, scrub with rust remover, then wash with an ammonia-based household cleaner. Clean whitish mineral deposits with a lime-deposit cleaner.

Replacing a ceramic floor tile

1 To avoid cracking adjacent tiles, first remove the grout around the damaged tile. You can try a grout saw (see page 28) but will likely need to tap the grout with a hammer and a small cold chisel.

2 With a hammer and cold chisel, strike the center of the tile until it cracks. Pry out the tile shards. If the tile does not crack readily, use a drill with a masonry bit to bore holes across the tile, then chip.

3 Use a putty knife or a wide cold chisel to pry and then scrape out all the mortar and grout from the area. Vacuum up the dust, then clean with a damp cloth. It may help to use a grout saw to clean the edges.

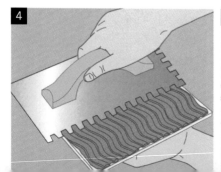
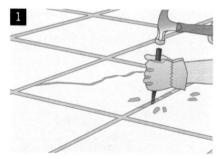
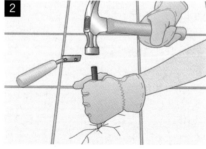

4 Test that the tile and mortar will sit at the right height. Mix a small batch of latex- or polymer-reinforced thinset mortar. Using a square-notched trowel, apply the mortar to the back of the tile.

5 Press the tile into place. Check that it is level with the surrounding tiles, then wipe away any mortar that oozes out along the sides. Make sure all the grout lines are the same width. Allow to dry overnight.

6 Mix a small batch of reinforced sanded floor grout and apply with a grout float. First press the grout into the joints, holding the float nearly flat. Then tilt it up and scrape. Clean with a damp sponge.

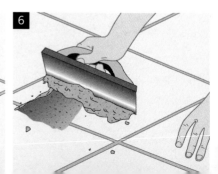

carpeting

arpeting is most often attached to the floor via tackless strips, which are pieces of wood that run around the perimeter of the room with barbs poling upward to grab the underside of the carpet. Carpet installers use special tools to stretch the carpet taut before tapping it to the tackless strips. You can usually pull up your carpeting (for example, to hide a telephone wire) fairly easily if you grab it with a pair of pliers near the wall and pull up.

In some cases, especially in a tricky area like a stairway, carpeting is attached with carpet tacks, small nails driven through the carpeting. Heat-activated carpet tape is usually used to join two pieces of carpeting, such as at a doorway.

Most modern carpeting has a stain-resistant finish that repels stains. To remove stains, first try products made for carpet spot removal. If you have pet stains, apply a protein digester enzyme treatment, typically sold in pet supply stores, then blot with a damp cloth. To remove pet odors, sprinkle baking soda, wait half an hour or even overnight, then vacuum.

To deep-clean a carpet, rent a rotary shampoo machine or a steam cleaner. Take care not to overwet the carpet, as that can cause discoloration or even shrinkage.

A few simple repairs are shown below. If a carpet is torn or ragged, or if it is wrinkled because it is not pulled taut, call in a professional for repairs or install new carpeting.

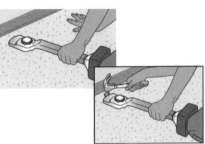

Three carpet repairs

INDENTATION If a furniture leg has caused a depression, try placing an ice cube on it; as it melts, the fibers will rise. Or hold a steaming iron just above the surface, then rub with a coin to raise the fibers.

LOOSE CARPETING NEAR A WALL If carpeting is loose and perhaps curled up at the edge of a room, it has likely come free from the tackless strip below. Using a rented knee kicker, pull the carpet taut, then tap it down with a hammer.

GAP AT A SEAM If carpeting has come loose at a seam, rent a carpet iron and purchase some heat-activated tape. Remove the old tape, set the new tape in place, and heat with the iron while you press the pieces together.

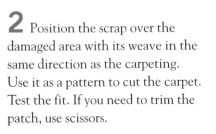

Piecing in at a damaged area

1 Place a scrap of replacement carpeting upside down on a piece of plywood and use a straightedge and utility knife to cut a patch that is a few inches larger than the damaged area in each direction.

2 Position the scrap over the damaged area with its weave in the same direction as the carpeting. Use it as a pattern to cut the carpet. Test the fit. If you need to trim the patch, use scissors.

3 Apply double-sided carpet tape around the hole so it will grab both the carpeting and the patch. Apply a small amount of construction adhesive along the sides, then set the patch into place.

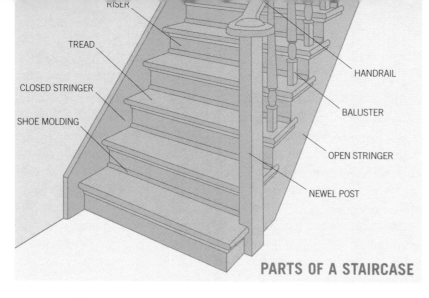

RISER

TREAD

CLOSED STRINGER

SHOE MOLDING

HANDRAIL

BALUSTER

OPEN STRINGER

NEWEL POST

PARTS OF A STAIRCASE

stair repairs

For a cutout illustration of a stairway's construction, see page 35. Squeaks are usually caused by a loose tread rubbing against a riser or stringer. Treads come loose when joints open as a result of shrinkage or when supporting blocks or nails work loose.

If the noise comes from where you step, concentrate your repair efforts there. If the noise comes from one side, or if it comes from the rear of the tread when you step at the front, first secure the place where you step. Then move to the apparent source of the noise.

If the stairs are accessible from underneath, work on them from below so your repairs won't show. Wear eye protection and provide yourself with plenty of light. Have a helper walk on the stairs while you pinpoint the problem areas.

BANISTERS

Banisters, also called balustrades, consist of one or two handrails, balusters, and one or more supporting newel posts. Wear and tear can weaken the joints, resulting in loose handrails, balusters, or posts.

Methods for tightening loose parts involve inserting shims or securing with screws. If you're using screws, drill pilot holes for them to prevent the wood from splitting.

If a newel post is loose and the measures shown do not solve the problem, call in a carpenter. The stairway may need to be disassembled and the newel support rebuilt.

Six ways to fix squeaky stairs

FROM ABOVE Drive and sink nails into angled pilot holes drilled through the tread into the riser (A), then fill holes with wood putty. Tap glue-coated shims between the tread and riser (B). Use a backsaw to trim the shims, then cover with molding. If you drive screws, you may choose to counterbore (C) and fill the holes with wood plugs.

FROM BELOW Tap glue-coated wedges between the tread and the riser, using a hammer and a small block of wood (A). Install metal brackets under the tread and riser (B). Glue and screw woodblocks under the tread and against the riser (C). Make sure screws are not too long, so their ends are at least ¼ inch beneath the tread or riser surface.

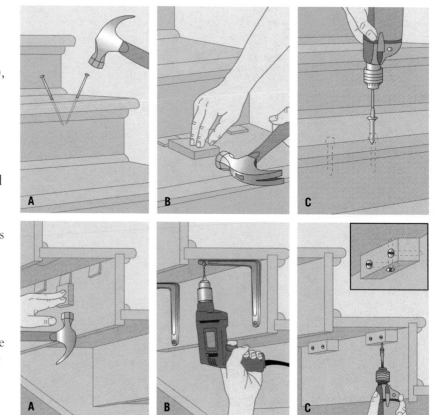

 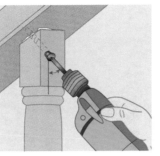

Two ways to tighten a loose handrail

SHIMS Tap a glue-coated shim between the handrail and baluster (above left). Tap gently so you don't pry up the handrail. Trim the shim with a utility knife.

SCREWS Drill an angled and countersunk pilot hole through the baluster and into the handrail. Drive in a glue-covered screw (above right). Fill the hole.

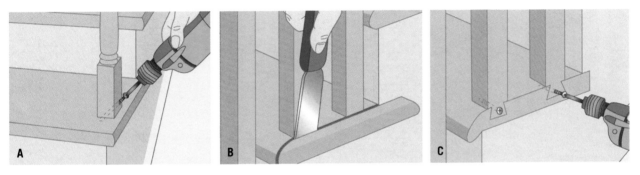

How to tighten loose balusters

BALUSTERS NAILED TO TREADS Drill an angled pilot hole through the baluster and into the tread, then countersink the hole. Drive a wood screw tightly (A). Fill the hole with wood putty, sand smooth, and finish.

NOTCH-AND-TENON BALUSTERS Pry off the molding with a putty knife or chisel (B). Drill a pilot hole through the tenon into the tread. Apply polyurethane glue or epoxy around the notch and tenon, then drive a screw (C). Replace the molding.

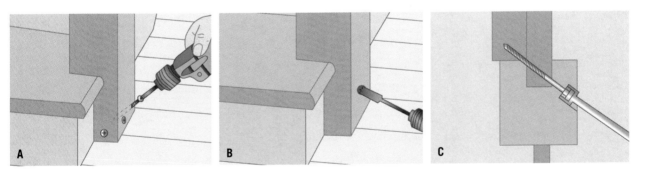

Two ways to tighten a loose newel post

GLUE AND SCREWS Drill angled pilot holes through the base of the post and into the floor; countersink the holes. Apply polyurethane glue between the post and floor and then drive wood screws (A). Fill the holes with wood putty, then sand and finish.

LAG SCREWS AND PLUGS Use a ¼-inch spade bit to drill a ¾-inch-deep hole into the newel post (B). With a ⁷⁄₃₂-inch bit, extend the hole into the stringer. Use a ⁵⁄₁₆-inch bit to enlarge the hole through the newel only and drive in a ⁵⁄₁₆-by-4-inch lag screw (C). Glue in a dowel plug, sand, and finish.

windows, doors, and cabinets

Windows and doors open to admit light, air, and people, and they must also close tightly to seal out the elements. This is a demanding assignment, so it's not surprising that windows and doors often need repairs. Moving parts that rub against each other can become worn, parts that are exposed to rain and snow can deteriorate, and hardware can wear out. This chapter will help you solve the most common window and door ailments.

MAINTAINING WINDOWS AND DOORS It is common for windows and exterior doors to leak air—and add to your energy costs. Even if you have a single-glazed window, most energy loss is probably through unsealed gaps rather than through the glass. Watch closely as you close a door or window to see if it is leaking anywhere. On a windy day, hold a piece of plastic food wrap up to a closed window or door to reveal any air movement. Seal small gaps with caulk; for larger gaps, use spray foam, preferably the non-expanding type. Installing new weather stripping may dramatically increase the energy efficiency of a door or window.

Keep exterior wood surfaces well sealed with paint (see pages 116–117 for complete instructions on prepping and painting exteriors). Peeling or cracks will let in moisture and damage wood siding. Take care when you paint a window or door, as buildup can cause moving parts to stick or create uneven seals. You might need to scrape or sand away existing paint before applying a new coat.

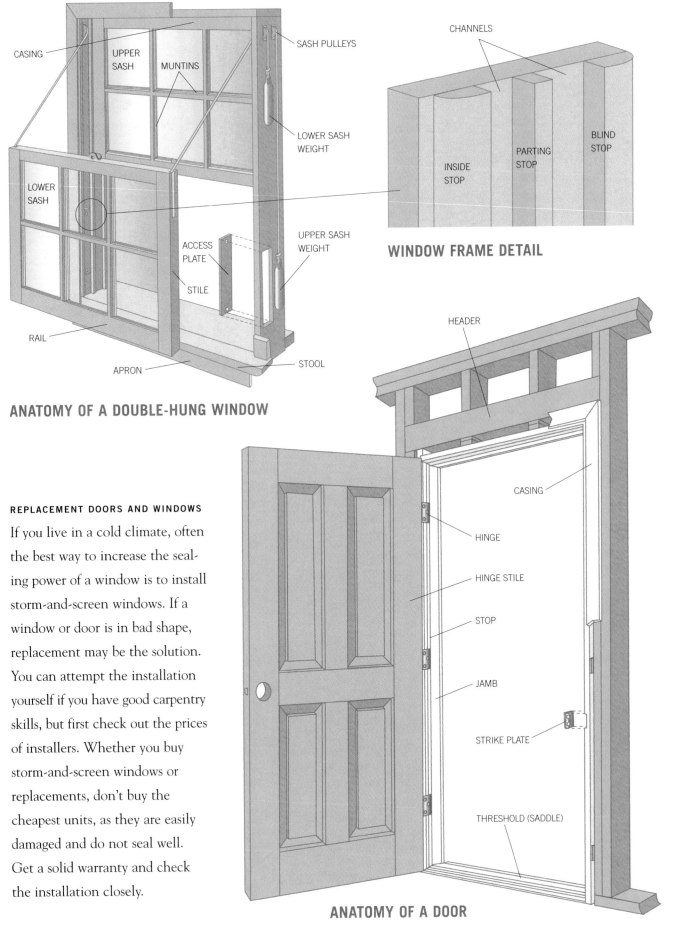

CASING

UPPER SASH

MUNTINS

SASH PULLEYS

LOWER SASH WEIGHT

LOWER SASH

ACCESS PLATE

STILE

UPPER SASH WEIGHT

RAIL

APRON

STOOL

ANATOMY OF A DOUBLE-HUNG WINDOW

CHANNELS

INSIDE STOP

PARTING STOP

BLIND STOP

WINDOW FRAME DETAIL

HEADER

CASING

HINGE

HINGE STILE

STOP

JAMB

STRIKE PLATE

THRESHOLD (SADDLE)

ANATOMY OF A DOOR

REPLACEMENT DOORS AND WINDOWS

If you live in a cold climate, often the best way to increase the sealing power of a window is to install storm-and-screen windows. If a window or door is in bad shape, replacement may be the solution. You can attempt the installation yourself if you have good carpentry skills, but first check out the prices of installers. Whether you buy storm-and-screen windows or replacements, don't buy the cheapest units, as they are easily damaged and do not seal well. Get a solid warranty and check the installation closely.

replacing broken glass

Replacing broken glass in a single-pane wooden window, especially a small one, is not difficult. When handling broken or new glass, wear heavy gloves, a long-sleeved shirt, and safety goggles. Before removing broken glass, tape newspaper to the inside of the sash to catch splinters. Pad glass shards with layers of newspaper before transporting the debris to the garbage.

To bed the new glass, you can use conventional glazing compound (also called window putty), which is like a thick paste and is applied with a putty knife, or a newer caulk-like compound that is applied with a caulking gun. The latter looks easier to apply but is often trickier.

Because panes larger than 2 by 3 feet are awkward and dangerous to handle, consider using a professional installer.

You can cut glass yourself, but it's easier and safer to have a hardware store or glass store cut it for you. Order it ⅛ inch smaller in height and width than the opening.

Replacing broken glass

1 Wearing safety glasses, tape the cracked pane with a crosshatch of duct tape to prevent glass shards from falling out as you work. When you're finished, you can tape newspaper to the inside of the window to help catch broken glass.

2 Use a 5-in-1 tool to remove the old window putty. If necessary, warm the putty with a heat gun, but be careful not to scorch the frame (keep a fire extinguisher nearby).

3 Remove broken glass and pry out metal glazier's points. Scrub the rabbeted area of the window frame with a wire brush. Dust it off, then use a small brush to apply a thin coat of linseed oil to the rabbet, where the glass and compound will go.

4 Glazing compound should be at room temperature or warmer. Roll it into a very thin rope with your hands and press it into place with your thumb. Use a scraping tool to press the putty firmly into place so it will seal the glass at all points.

5 Install the pane and secure it by pressing glazier's points into place. Use two points on each side for small panes and one point every 4 to 6 inches for larger ones. Be careful not to push against the glass, as the pressure could crack it.

6 Roll compound into a rope about ⅜ inch thick. Use your thumb to press it firmly into place. Dip a putty knife in linseed oil and use it to smooth the putty. Make sure the putty is not visible from the inside. If it is, flatten the bevel.

RESTORING OLD GLAZING COMPOUND
If glazing compound does not touch the glass, it is not sealing out air and moisture. If compound is cracked, peeling, or missing in spots, use a putty knife or glazing knife to scrape away any that is at all loose. Apply compound to the resulting gaps following steps 3–6 on page 54. If the putty is stuck fast to the wood but there are gaps between the putty and the glass, seal the gaps with exterior caulk.

CUTTING AND CARRYING

TWO GOOD TOOLS A glazier's knife has a solid scraper for cleaning out old putty and driving points, and a V-shaped blade for smoothing new compound. The groove allows excess compound to ooze out. A 5-in-1 tool also scrapes and drives points, plus it quickly opens paint cans and cleans rollers.

5-in-1 tool

glazier's knife

DUCT-TAPE GLASS HANDLE To easily and safely transport small panes of glass, use a strip of duct tape, about 8 inches long, to make a handle. After removing the handle, clean the glass with mineral spirits.

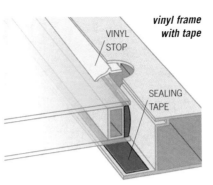

vinyl frame with tape

VINYL STOP

SEALING TAPE

Other ways to seal windows

VINYL STOP AND TAPE Many vinyl windows are held in place with a vinyl stop and sealed with a setting tape, which has a rubber surface. To reseal a window, pry out the stop and purchase replacement sealing tape. Apply the tape, set the glass on it, and press the stop back into place.

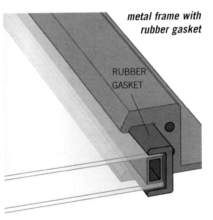

metal frame with rubber gasket

RUBBER GASKET

RUBBER GASKET Many metal frames have a rubber gasket that runs around the perimeter of the glass and fits snugly into the frame. To take out the glass, remove the screws and disassemble the metal frame. Buy a replacement gasket and either wrap it around the glass or press it into the frame, then reassemble.

WOOD STOP AND CAULK On some wood frames the glass is held in place with small strips of nailed molding rather than glazing compound. To remove the glass, pry out the molding strip and scrape away the old caulk. Apply a thin coat of silicone caulk, press the window into place, apply another layer of caulk, and reattach the trim. Take care not to hit the glass with a nail.

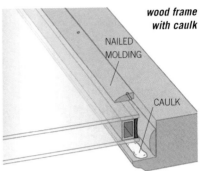

wood frame with caulk

NAILED MOLDING

CAULK

SPRING CLIPS On some metal frames, the glass is held in place by spring clips. To get at them, you may need to first pry out a thin strip of metal. Use long-nose pliers or a screwdriver to remove the clips, then replace the glass and reinstall the clips. You may choose to apply caulk to seal the window tightly.

spring clips

repairing double-hung windows

(see page 53)

A double-hung window (see page 53) has two sashes that move up and down. In many homes, the upper sash has been painted or nailed shut, which is fine as long as you can clean the window from the outside. Prewar windows typically use a pulley-and-weight system.

As a wood sash ages, it may no longer fit its frame or the balance system may break down. A simple sash or stop repair can often restore a window to good working order. If a sash is temporarily stuck because of high humidity, a change of weather may correct the problem. If a sash moves reluctantly, clean its channels. Windows that have been painted shut require a little more effort, but can also be opened.

If a window will not stay open, the balance system needs repair. See the next page for pulley-and-weight system repair and page 58 for other repairs. Replace all the cords at the same time, preferably with long-lasting chains or nylon ropes.

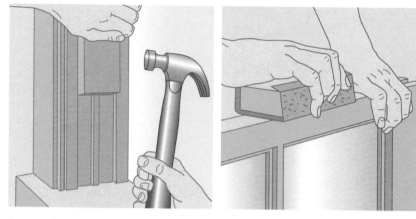

Loosening a tight sash

If the stop is binding against the sash, tap it with a hammer and woodblock to move it slightly to the side. If this doesn't work, reposition the stop.

If the sash is too wide, remove it (see opposite page) and sand each side. Check it for fit. Take care not to oversand or the sash could be too loose.

> **AmeriSpec® TIP** **DON'T PAINT IT SHUT**
>
> A few hours after you have painted a window, score the movable parts with a utility knife, then operate the window a couple of times to keep it from becoming stuck. A sash saw (right), also called a paint zipper, makes quick and clean work of cutting through paint that is holding a sash in place.

Freeing a stuck sash

1 Score the painted edges of the sash with a sash saw (see above) or a utility knife. Work a wide putty knife between the sash and window frame. Tap the knife with a hammer.

2 From the outside, wedge a flat pry bar between the sill and sash. Work alternately at each corner so the sash moves up evenly. Protect the sill with a woodblock.

3 Chisel any built-up paint off the edges of the sash, stops, and parting strip. Sand the edges smooth and apply paraffin or a window lubricator.

Repositioning the stops

1 Score the paint between the jambs and the stops, then pry off the stops, leaving the nails in them. (Remove the screws if the stops are screwed in.)

2 Chisel or scrape any built-up paint from the edges of the sash, stops, and parting strip. Sand the edges smooth and apply paraffin or window lubricant.

3 Nail the stops back onto the jambs using a thin cardboard shim as a spacing guide. Either refasten the old nails in the old holes or drill pilot holes and drive new nails.

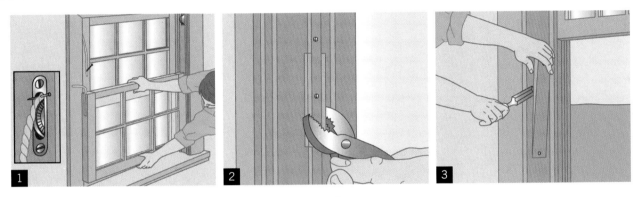

Removing wood sashes and replacing cords or chains

1 Remove the inside stops, then raise and angle the lower sash out. Untie and slip each cord or chain out of the groove. Use a nail to keep them from slipping through the pulleys.

2 Use pliers to pull out each parting strip, and use wood strips to protect the wood. Angle the upper sash out of the frame and disconnect the cords or chains as shown in Step 1.

3 Remove the screws holding each access plate and pry the plate off. In some cases, you may need to remove some of the weather stripping to get at the plates.

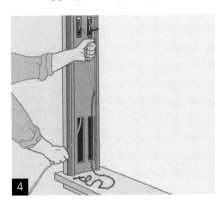

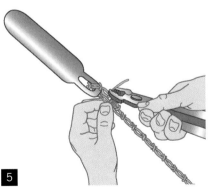

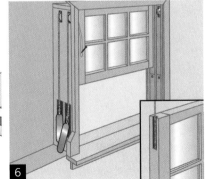

4 Tape an end of each new chain or cord to an end of each old one. Slip a nail through each cord or chain's other end. Untie the weights, then pull the old lines out of the openings.

5 Loop each line through the hole in each weight. Secure chains with wire or double-knot a new cord. Clear the access openings of any debris and replace the weights.

6 Adjust chains so the weights will be 2 inches above the stool when the sash is up. Secure the chains to the sash channels with short screws. Replace the access plates.

BALANCE SYSTEMS

Over the years, manufacturers have designed a number of balance systems. Here we show some of the most common ones. If yours is different, look for a manufacturer's name and search on the Web for replacement parts. If a certain window was commonly installed in your neighborhood, a local hardware store may carry parts.

TENSION-SPRING OR CORD SYSTEM

In a tension-spring balance system, sometimes called a clockspring system, each sash is operated by two balance units with spring-loaded drums inside. The units fit into the side jambs near the top. A flexible metal tape hooks onto a bracket screwed into a groove routed in the sash. A cord balance system (not shown here) works similarly, but the balance units contain nylon cords rather than tape.

Some units have an adjustment screw, which you can tighten if the spring does not hold the sash in place. If the spring or tape breaks, replace the unit. To find replacement parts, go to a window specialty store or type "sash pulleys" into an Internet search engine.

To remove the unit, take out the stop and pull the sash partway out. Unhook the tape from the sash and let it wind back on the drum. Unscrew and remove the drum from the jamb. Insert the new unit into the jamb pocket and screw it on. Pull down the tape (A), hook it to the sash, and reinstall the sash.

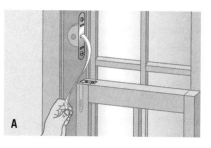

SPIRAL-LIFT SYSTEM Here, a spring-loaded spiral rod encased in a tube rests in a channel in the sash. The top of the tube is screwed to the side jamb, and the rod is attached to a mounting bracket on the bottom of the sash. If the sash does not stay put when raised, adjust the tension. If the balance breaks, replace it.

To adjust the tension, move the jamb liner to reveal the spiral balance. Release the side catches and pull the top of the sash out slightly. Unhook the balance from the jamb. If the window doesn't stay open,

increase the tension by turning the balance clockwise (B). Turn the balance counterclockwise if the window is hard to open.

To remove the unit, unfasten the tube from the jamb (C) and remove the mounting bracket from the sash (D). To install a new unit, attach the new tube to the jamb, tighten the spring, and fasten the new mounting bracket to the sash. Reattach the jamb liner and reinstall the sash.

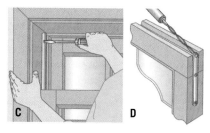

Window locks

SASH LOCK To replace a standard sash lock, first attach the piece that goes on the upper sash. Position the other part on the lower sash, making sure it will tightly close the sashes together, and attach with screws.

sash lock

SECURITY LOCKS A spring bolt screwed to the sill will secure almost any type of window. A locking pin pokes through a hole drilled through both the bottom and top sashes. Depending on where you drill the holes, the pin can secure the sash when the window is closed or partially open. The pin hangs from a short chain when not in use. You can also buy a keyed lock, which secures both sashes.

spring bolt

locking pin

keyed lock

WINDOW CHANNEL UNIT

Here, sashes slide through channels which contain springs to hold the sashes up. In some cases, the channels are part of the window frame, so you must replace the entire window. If a channel is detachable, remove any mounting nails or screws, as well as stops. Slide the sashes toward the middle and tilt the sashes and channels out. Buy replacement channels and slide the sashes in.

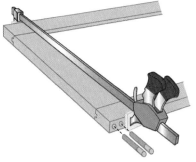

Mending a wooden sash

If a sash frame is coming apart, clamp the frame tightly together. Drill two long holes through one stile and well into the next, using a ¼-inch bit. Squirt in some wood glue and tap in ¼-inch dowels. Wait a day, trim the dowels, and paint.

1 If only a portion of a sash frame is rotted, chisel away all loose matter and drill a series of short holes in the damaged area. Pour wood hardener into the holes and the surrounding area.

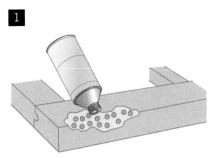

2 Wrap a scrap of wood tightly with plastic sheeting, as shown, and screw it against the damaged area. Mix and apply two-part wood filler or auto body filler. Scrape, sand smooth, and paint.

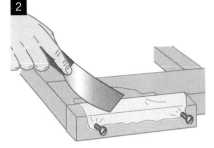

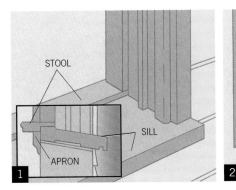

STOOL

SILL

APRON

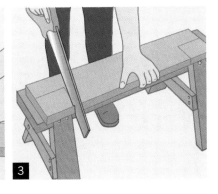

Replacing a sill

1 If a sill cannot be repaired as shown above, pry off interior casings and inside stops (see page 53) and pry off the apron. Remove any nails from the stool and take it out in one piece.

2 Measure the length of the sill between the jambs. Saw the sill into three pieces. Remove the center piece, then the end pieces. Cut off any nails with a reciprocating saw or hacksaw blade.

3 Using the old sill's end pieces as templates, mark the new sill to the correct length, allowing for any grooves in the jambs. Cut the new sill with a saw and bevel the ends for an easier fit.

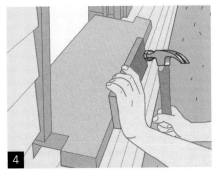

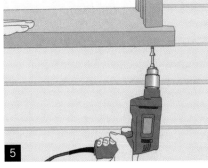

4 Tap the new sill into place using a woodblock to protect the edge. Don't force the sill. If it sticks, remove and recut it as needed.

5 Add shims under the sill for a snug fit, if needed. To secure the sill, screw it to the side jambs from underneath.

6 Fill the screw head holes and apply a coat of primer. Caulk the sill's edges and paint. Inside, replace the stool, apron, sash, stops, and casings.

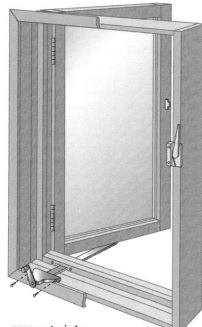

casement window

casement windows

A casement window, whether made of wood, vinyl, or metal, has a sash hinged at the side and is operated with a crank-and-gear mechanism. Clean and lubricate the mechanism regularly. If a part wears out, find the manufacturer's name and purchase an exact replacement.

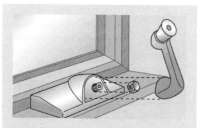

REPLACING A HANDLE

If a handle spins and does not open the window, try tightening the setscrew that secures the handle to the operator shaft. If that doesn't work, remove the handle. Install an adapter and a new handle that fits tightly.

RESTORING SMOOTH OPERATION If the window is difficult to operate or does not close completely, clean all moving parts and check that debris is not hindering the opening and closing of the sash.

If that doesn't do the trick, remove the cover from the operator; you may also need to remove the operator from the window. Inspect the gears. If the teeth are worn, replace the unit with a duplicate that cranks in the same direction as the old one. If the teeth are sharp but clogged with dirt, remove debris and grease with a soft wire brush or clean the assembly with a solvent such as mineral spirits. Lubricate gears with graphite powder, silicone, or gear grease. Turn the crank to spread the lubricant. Use silicone spray on nylon gears. If the gears still malfunction, replace the assembly.

CORRECTING A BINDING SASH If a sash sags or sticks, adjust the hinges as on a door (see pages 66–67). If the sash is paint-bound, use a knife or sash saw (see page 56) to free it. If a wood sash has swollen, sand or plane the part that's rubbing, then seal and refinish it. If the stop has swollen, remove it, sand as needed, and reposition it.

You can compensate for a mild warp in a wooden sash by adjusting the stops (page 57) or adding weather stripping (pages 64–65).

CLEANING AND LUBRICATING

Open the window and use a wire brush to clean the track. Remove any rust or mineral deposits. Treat the inside of the track with spray lubricant. As you close the window, watch to identify any spots that need further brushing or sanding.

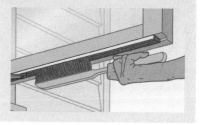

Servicing an operator

1 Open the window halfway, remove the screws, and pull the operator partway out. Slide the extension arm until it reaches the slot. Pull the assembly out.

2 Remove the cover and inspect the gears. If they look good, try lubricating. Otherwise, replace the unit with a duplicate.

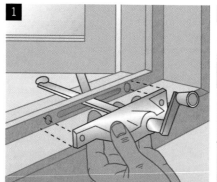

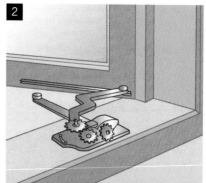

sliding windows

Sliding window sashes move along metal, wood, or vinyl tracks fitted into the window frame at the top and bottom. To ease their movement, large sashes often have plastic rollers attached to the top and bottom, or to the bottom only.

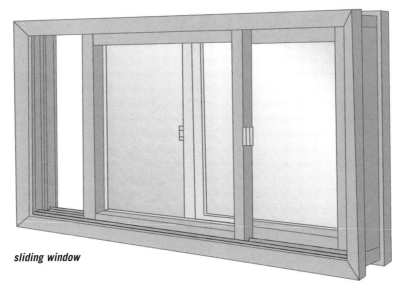

sliding window

RESTORING SMOOTH OPERATION

Often one sash is fixed and the other slides. You can usually remove the sliding sash by simply lifting it up and tilting its bottom out. If a sash is stuck or does not move freely, sand away any paint or finish that is rubbing against the frame. Use a wire brush to clean all the dirt from the track. For stubborn particles, use the blade of an old screwdriver to pry dirt loose. Lubricate the track with paraffin or window lubricant.

If rollers are sticking, treat them with graphite powder or spray lubricant until they move freely. If they're broken, you'll need to remove the sash and take it to a hardware store or glass shop to have the rollers replaced.

REPAIRING A CATCH Sliding windows are secured with a variety of catches, depending on the manufacturer and the material. If the window's catch doesn't work properly, you may need to remove the sash from the frame to fix it.

You may be able to reshape a bent catch. Note how much it will have to be reshaped, then remove the catch and clamp it in a vise. Use pliers or a hammer to bend the catch to the proper angle. Replace it and check the latch operation. It should click as the window closes, and it should need to be fully depressed for the window to open.

⚡ AMERISPEC® TIP   SLIDING-WINDOW LOCK

This quick-release track grip provides protection against intruders and can be positioned anywhere along a sliding door's track. Snap it into place to secure the window.

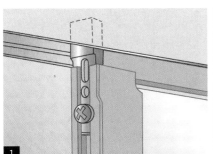

Straightening a bent track

1 To remove a sash, first unscrew and remove any security devices at the top. To remove a fixed sash, you'll probably need to take off corner brackets at the top and bottom.

2 Carefully lift the sash up to clear the track, then tilt the bottom out of the frame. You may need to align the rollers with notches in the frame in order to tilt it out.

3 Place a woodblock in the track. Using a hammer, tap the block against the bent metal until the side of the track is straight. Replace the sash and test the glide.

storm-and-screen windows

Most storm-and-screen windows can be left in place all year. However, it is a good idea to remove storm windows during hot weather, as they transmit a good deal of solar heat. Frames may be wood or metal, and the screening may be metal (usually aluminum) or fiberglass. If a room tends to get hot, consider installing dark sun-shading screening.

With regular maintenance, your storms and screens should last decades. Clean screening periodically by spraying it with a garden hose. If openings are clogged after the water has dried, dab with a bristle brush. Keep wood frames well protected with paint, but check that the frame will fit after you apply another coat. You may need to sand the edges before painting.

SMALL REPAIRS To mend a very small hole or tear in metal screening, use tweezers to twist the strands into shape, and then apply super-

glue. To repair a tear in fiberglass screening, sew it shut with a large sewing needle and clear fishing line, then seal the edges of the patch with superglue.

If screening has come loose from a metal frame, pull the screening taut and use a spline roller or putty knife to resecure the screening. If screening comes loose in a wood frame, partially pry up the screen mold, pull the screening taut, and reattach the mold with nails.

REPLACING STORM WINDOW GLASS
Replace glass in a storm window as you would in permanent windows (see pages 54–55). If the frame is metal, you may need to buy replacement gaskets or other parts that fit your window model.

FRAME REPAIRS A wood frame can be patched with mending plates, screws (next page), or dowels (see page 59). Working on a flat surface, disassemble the frame only as much

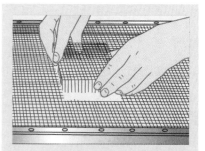

PATCH A SCREEN

For a large tear, cut a patch 3 inches wider and longer than the tear. Unravel each side, bend the end wires, and push them through. Bend the wires over on the other side and use superglue to secure the patch.

as necessary and then clean any paint or debris that inhibits a tight fit. Drill pilot holes before driving any screws or nails.

Metal frames have plastic parts and rubber gaskets that vary by manufacturer. Take your frame to a hardware store for replacement parts. If you can find the manufacturer's name, you may be able to buy parts over the Internet.

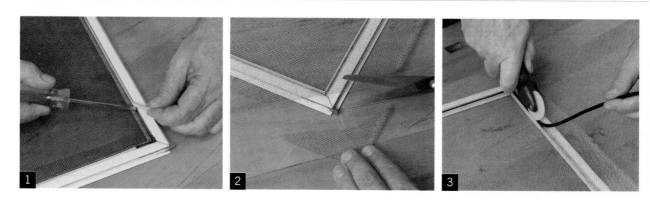

Replacing screening in a metal frame

1 Use a screwdriver to pry up the spline that runs around the perimeter of the frame. Pull out the spline and remove the old or damaged screen fabric.

2 Lay the new screen fabric over the frame. Using sharp utility scissors, trim it so that it is several inches larger than the frame in each direction. Then snip off the corners as shown.

3 Use a screen-spline roller to force the screen into the spline channel, stretching the screen fabric taut. Cut off the excess with a utility knife.

WINDOWS, DOORS, AND CABINETS

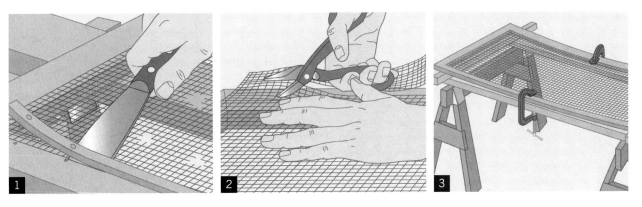

Replacing screening in a wood frame

1 Using a chisel or putty knife, carefully pry off the screen mold. Work from the ends toward the center. Remove the old screening.

2 Using tin snips, cut a new piece of screening 2 inches larger than the opening on all sides. Staple the screening to one end of the frame so the staples will be under the molding.

3 To end up with a taut screen, you need to bow the frame during installation. Place it on boards over sawhorses and put 1-by pieces under the ends. Clamp the middle. Staple the other end of the screening and remove the clamps.

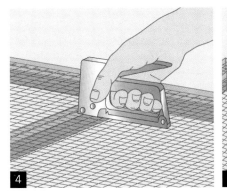

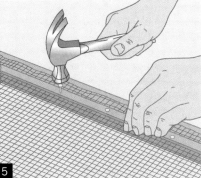

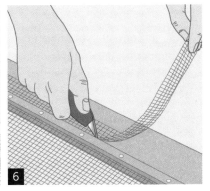

4 Working from the center toward the ends, staple each side of the screening, pulling it tight. Staple the middle rail last.

5 Nail on the molding. Pound the nails flush, or countersink them and fill the holes. Refinish any new molding to match the frame.

6 Use a utility knife to cut away excess screening around the molding. Cut gently so you don't slice a groove in the frame.

Repairing a wood frame with mending plates, corrugated fasteners, or screws

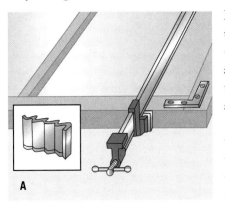

A

Hold one corner of the frame together tightly with a long clamp (A), and then drive screws to attach an angled mending plate at the corner. You can also hammer in a corrugated metal fastener (inset).

Or, glue the frame at the corner, then countersink a long wood screw through the corner joint (B). Cover the screw head with wood putty, then sand and paint it.

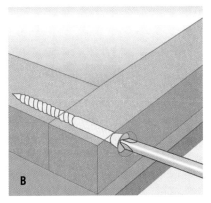

B

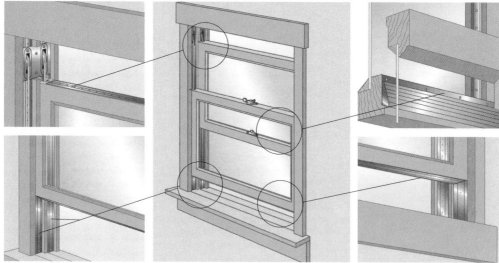

METAL STRIP ON TOP OF UPPER SASH

METAL STRIP BETWEEN TWO SASHES

SPRING BRONZE NAIL-ON STRIPS

METAL STRIP ON BOTTOM OF LOWER SASH

weather-stripping windows

Most newer windows are weather-stripped at the factory. You can also apply weather stripping yourself.

CAULKING AND SEALING Make sure the nonmoving areas are well sealed. If you can access cavities inside the wall around the window, see that they are filled with fiber-glass insulation or spray foam. (The cavities on either side that hold the ropes and weights for an older double-hung window cannot be insulated, because the weights need to move.) Apply caulk, both outside and inside, to any cracks.

AVAILABLE PRODUCTS Self-stick tapes are a good choice for metal or vinyl windows when nailing isn't an option, especially where parts of windows press together rather than slide against one another. Choose EPDM rubber or high-density foam. Vinyl V-strips are easy to install but wear out quickly.

Use nail-on strips for wood windows because they attach firmly. Gaps less than ¼ inch are best sealed with spring bronze. This material is especially suited to filling the gaps between a window sash and its

jambs. A tubular vinyl gasket works well where the gaps are large or uneven in width. The flange is often reinforced with metal to prevent the soft vinyl from tearing. Felt strips are not durable.

WEATHER-STRIPPING STRATEGIES The trick is to provide tight seals while allowing the window to open and close smoothly. Work methodically as you apply weather stripping, constantly checking for

Attaching spring bronze

1 Measure the side channels for both sashes and cut spring bronze strips with tin snips. You may need to cut separate pieces on each side of the pulleys. With the nailing flange against the sash stop, slide the strips up between the sash and the jamb. Attach the strips with brads.

2 Measure and cut horizontal strips that extend the full width of the window. Attach one piece to the bottom of the lower sash so the nailing flange is flush with the inside edge of the window. Hammer gently so the window doesn't crack. Attach the other horizontals in the same way.

⚞ AMERISPEC® TIP | **INCREASING THE TENSION**

If a bronze strip does not seal because the gap is too wide, use a putty knife to gently pry it farther open. Do this a little at a time, until it seals without binding.

both seal and smooth operation.

Before you start, make sure the window lock pulls the sashes tightly together. If it does not, adjust its position. Check for problem areas, as you may need to apply weather stripping to only some areas and not others.

To seal a double-hung window, insert spring bronze between the sashes and the jambs, then attach them to the top of the upper sash, the bottom of the lower sash, and the bottom face of the upper sash.

OTHER PERMANENT WEATHER-STRIPPING PRODUCTS

PLASTIC SELF-ADHESIVE V-STRIPS
Take particular care to clean the surfaces so the adhesive will stick well. Cut the pieces to length with scissors. Position them as you would for spring bronze, then peel off the backing and press them into place.

SELF-STICK FOAM This is easy to apply. Choose a foam of the right thickness so it will seal but still allow the window to close. To ensure a good bond, make sure the surface is smooth and clean.

Remove any loose paint, clean the surfaces with a mild detergent, and allow them to dry. Measure strips and cut them to length with scissors. Peel off the backing and press the foam into place.

TUBULAR VINYL Unlike spring bronze and plastic V-strips, tubular gaskets are applied to the outside of the window and are thus visible. (Painting them is not recommended, as it will inhibit their flexibility.) Measure the strips and cut them to length with scissors (or tin snips if the strips are reinforced with metal). Close the window, then

Temporary solutions

ROPE CAULK Just before the weather turns cold, press removable rope caulk into the joints between the sashes and the jamb, between the sashes and the sill, and at the top of the bottom sash where it meets the top sash. Remove it in spring.

HEAT-SHRINK PLASTIC

1 This effectively seals an entire window in minutes. Clean the window casing and sill and apply strips of double-faced tape all around. Peel away the protective paper. Press the plastic sheet onto the tape.

2 Use a hair dryer to heat the plastic at all points until it shrinks tight and all wrinkles are removed. Use a utility knife to trim excess plastic around the perimeter.

SEALING THE PULLEYS
To prevent air leaks around sash cord pulleys, cover the pulleys with self-adhesive pulley covers. Clean the pulley surface thoroughly, then peel off the backing from the cover and position it over the pulley. Pull the sash cord out to snap it into the pulley and then press the cover into place.

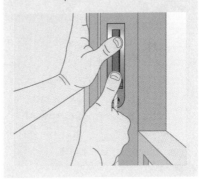

butt the tube section snugly against the part to be sealed while keeping tension on the strip as you drive in the brads.

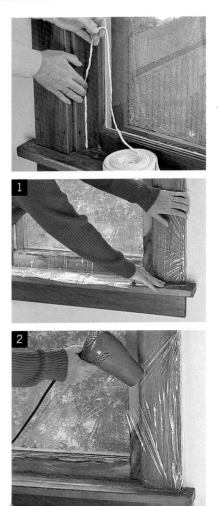

door repairs

All hinged doors (see page 53) have the same basic framework, sometimes hidden under a solid veneer.

A paneled door has a visible frame of stiles and rails that supports two or more panels. A flush door is faced with hardboard, wood veneer, metal sheathing, or a fiberglass composite. A flush door for exterior use should have a solid core of several layers of hardwood, foam-insulation fill, or particleboard. An interior hollow-core flush door has narrow interior stiles and a network of corrugated cardboard strips. The wood surface is ¼-inch-thick plywood or hardboard.

A door frame consists of jambs, casing, and stops. At the floor there is usually a threshold, and sometimes there is a sill. The jambs form the sides and head of the frame, while the casing acts as trim and as support for the jambs. The stops are wood strips that the door fits against when closed. On exterior doors, a sill fits between the jambs, forming the frame bottom. The threshold is fastened to the sill or to the floor.

REPAIRING A DOOR

Age and continual use can cause even a well-fitted door to loosen, bind, or warp. Often the latch no longer works properly. The most common repairs are covered in the following six pages. A door that's badly warped should be replaced.

LOOSE DOORS If an exterior door is leaking air, weather stripping is usually the solution (see page 77). If a loose door is causing latch problems, you may be able to adjust the latch. If a door rattles or is difficult

to close, you may need to move the stop. If there is a gap at the top or bottom, a door can be extended as long as it will be painted.

BINDING DOORS Binding or sticking can have a number of causes, from a buildup of dirt and paint to a door that sags. Adjusting the fit of the door usually solves the problem.

LATCH PROBLEMS When a latch fails to work, the trouble may be with the fit of the door or with the lockset (see pages 74–75).

REMOVING A DOOR

If you're working on just one hinge at a time or on the top of a door, you need only open the door partially and wedge shims underneath the latch side to hold the door steady. But for other work, such as sanding or planing the side or bottom, you must remove the door and lay it on a workbench.

To remove the hinge pins, close the door securely. Using a hammer and a flat pry bar or screwdriver, gently tap on the bottom of the lowest pin or on the underside of its head to drive it up and out of the hinge barrel. Remove the middle pin, if there is one, then take out the top pin. Lift the door off its hinges.

When you reinstall the door, replace the top pin first, then the middle and bottom ones. Drive the pins home only after the hinges are correctly aligned.

BINDING DOORS

Binding can result from house settlement (when the door frame moves), from a buildup of paint or dirt, or from a misaligned or sagging door. The cure is usually to adjust poorly set or loose hinges, or to plane the door edges.

Open the door, grab the knob, and watch the hinges as you lift. If a hinge leaf is loose, try tightening the hinge screws. If they spin and don't tighten, follow the steps on the next page to tighten the holes. After tightening the hinges, check to see if the door is binding even slightly. Fix the cause of the bind or the screws will come loose again.

If the hinges are OK, identify the spots that bind by inserting a thin strip of cardboard or paper between the door and jambs. Look for a buildup of dirt or paint on the door edges or jambs. Chisel or plane off any globs of paint, then sand.

If the door binds badly or isn't square in its frame, you can diagnose the problem fairly easily (see opposite page) and determine which repairs are needed. The hinges may have to be shimmed or set in deeper mortises (see page 68).

If you must remove excess wood from the door edges, sand with coarse followed by finer paper. Keep the sanding as even as possible. Plane only if necessary. When sanding or planing the stiles, concentrate on the hinge side, since the lock side is usually beveled to allow for a tight fit.

⚲ AMERISPEC® TIP | **IF THE HINGE PIN IS STUCK**

If a hinge is rusted or painted tight, try squirting it with penetrating oil. If it still doesn't come loose, it may be easier to remove the screws from one of the hinge's leaves. That will allow you to remove the door, with the hinge attached to either the jamb or the door.

Diagnosing and adjusting a binding door

If the door binds as in (A), reset the upper hinge (repair the screw holes and tighten the screws, or deepen the mortise) and/or shim out the lower hinge. If the door binds as in (B), do the opposite: reset the lower hinge and/or shim out the upper one.

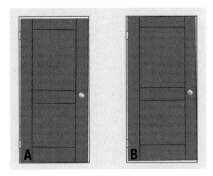

If the door binds on the hinge side (C), shim out the hinges, or remove the door and sand or plane the hinge side. If it binds on the lock side (D), sand or plane that side and perhaps deepen the hinge mortises.

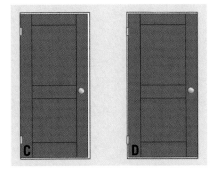

If the door binds along the top (E), wedge it open and sand or plane the wood along the top. If it binds along the bottom (F), remove the door and sand or plane the wood along the bottom.

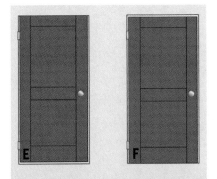

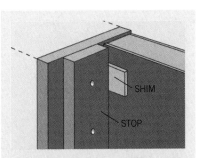

Strengthening a loose hinge

1 If any hinge screw holes are stripped, remove the screws and the hinge leaf from the jamb. Coat small wooden dowels or matchsticks with glue and pack them in the holes. Wipe off the excess glue and trim the plug flush.

2 After allowing the glue to dry, hold the hinge leaf in position and drill new pilot holes for screws. Then drive in the screws. For extra strength, you can substitute longer screws for the original ones.

> **✈ AMERISPEC® TIP   QUIETING SQUEAKY HINGES**
>
> Silence a noisy hinge by coating it with silicone spray or light penetrating oil. If the squeak persists, remove the pin and thoroughly clean the pin, barrel, and hinge leaves with steel wool. Coat them lightly with silicone spray or light penetrating oil and replace the pin.

CURES FOR A WARPED DOOR

The best insurance against warping is to seal the door on all surfaces to prevent moisture from swelling the the wood. A badly warped door should be replaced.

If there's a slight bow on the hinge side, installing a third hinge between the top and bottom ones may pull the door into alignment.

If the bow is on the lock side and the door latches only when slammed, reposition the stop as for a window (see page 57). If necessary, adjust the strike plate (see page 69).

If the top or bottom of the door does not meet the stop on the lock side, try repositioning the stop or the strike plate. You may also have to place half shims, as shown at right, under each hinge leaf either on the side of the leaf that's closest to the pin or on the opposite side, depending on the warp. Usually, the other hinge is shimmed in the opposite way.

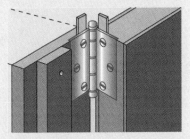

ADJUSTING A WARPED DOOR
Reposition the stop (see page 57), spacing with a thin cardboard or wood shim, then nail the stop into place.

To adjust the angle of a door, loosen the hinge screws and slip a small shim of cardboard or thin wood under each hinge leaf, then retighten the screws.

techniques for working on doors

plane

sureform tool

Techniques for repairing a door include planing edges, cutting or deepening hinge mortises, and making shims for hinges. Support a door so it holds still while you're working on it. One simple way is to set one edge on a pad and wedge the other into a corner of the room.

A carpenter's plane is the best tool for shaving wood. A sureform tool is less expensive and is easier to use, but it leaves a rough surface that you must sand smooth. If only a small amount of wood must be removed, sandpaper wrapped around a sanding block is the best choice. Another alternative is to use a belt sander, but work carefully to avoid creating unevenness.

Use a plane that's long enough to ensure flat cuts. The blade should be wider than the thickness of the door so the cuts will be even. Though a jack plane (14 to

Planing a door

1 On both faces of the door, use a pencil to scribe a line in the area to be planed. Plane everywhere you cannot slide a dime between the door and the jamb.

2 Stabilize the door and adjust the plane to cut paper-thin slices. Place the plane flat on the surface, and push it with moderate pressure. If it digs in and gets stuck, try planing in the other direction. At the door's top and bottom, you will plane across the grain. Plane from the corner towards the middle to avoid splitting the ends of the stiles.

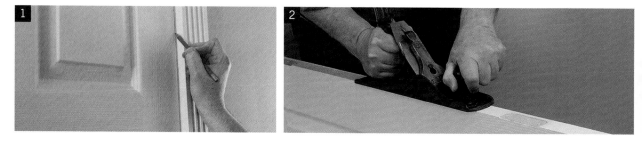

Cutting a hinge mortise

1 Using a hinge leaf as a template, mark the placement and depth lines for a new hinge or a depth line for a deeper mortise. Carefully score this line with a hammer and chisel.

2 Make shallow, parallel cuts to the desired depth using a hammer and chisel held almost vertically as shown. Then lower the chisel to a 30-degree angle, bevel side down, and gently chip out the wood to the desired depth.

3 Make the final smoothing cuts from the side, holding the chisel bevel side up, almost flat. Position the hinge leaf and check that it's flush with the surface of the door or jamb. Drill pilot holes and drive hinge screws.

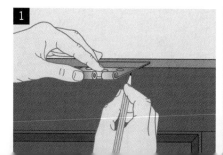

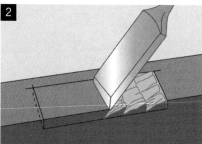

15 inches long) is preferable, a 9- to 10-inch-long smoothing plane will do the job.

To avoid gouging the wood, plane with the grain. Testing on a scrap of wood, adjust the blade to make paper-thin cuts so you don't remove too much wood.

If you're working on a binding door, plane the top or bottom rail if the door is binding there, or the hinge stile if the door binds on the hinge side. It's best to avoid planing a binding lock stile, since it involves maintaining the beveled edge along that side and, in some cases, repositioning the lockset. Instead, plane the hinge stile whenever possible to correct the problem.

You'll need to remove the hinge leaves before planing. Use a utility knife to cut through any paint around the leaves, then unscrew and remove the hinges. After you plane, deepen the hinge mortises as shown on the previous page. If you must plane near the top or bottom of the lock stile, be sure to re-form the bevel afterward.

CUTTING HINGE MORTISES Hinge mortises are recesses into which hinge leaves are fitted so they sit flush with the door and jamb surfaces. You'll need to cut them if you're adding a middle hinge to

USING A PLANE
Use two hands when operating a jack plane, gripping the rear handle with one hand, the front knob or one edge with the other. At the beginning of the cut, apply slightly more pressure on the plane's toe. Even out the pressure as you continue the stroke, and then near the end gradually switch pressure to the heel.

straighten a warped door or if you're hanging a new door. If you're adjusting the position of the door in a jamb or you've planed the hinge stile, you'll have to deepen the mortises. To do so, mark the new depth on the edge of the door or jamb and then go to Step 3 on the previous page.

MAKING SHIMS To move a door closer to the lock side of the jamb,

ADJUSTING BALKY LATCHES
If a door latch doesn't catch or won't operate smoothly, the latch bolt on the door may not be lined up properly with the strike plate on the doorjamb. Repairs range from minor latch adjustments to repositioning of the door.

If the latch does not operate smoothly, lubricate it with graphite. If it does not catch, close the door slowly to watch how the latch bolt meets the strike plate. The bolt may be positioned above, below, or to one side of the strike plate. (Scars on the plate may give you a precise clue as to the degree and direction of misalignment.) The problem also could be that the door has shrunk and the latch no longer reaches the strike plate.

Once you've determined what adjustment is needed, use one of the three remedies illustrated at right. If the door has warped only slightly, adjust its angle. To do this, you can either insert shims on the side of each hinge leaf that's closest to the pin, angling the door inward, or reposition the stop closer to or farther from the door so the latch can engage the strike plate (see page 67).

If the lock is the problem, turn to pages 74–75 for information on lock repairs.

you can insert a shim under the hinge leaves. Use dense, hard-surfaced cardboard such as that used for file folders.

Using a hinge leaf as a pattern, cut a shim and make the screw holes (a paper hole punch works well for this). The shim should be minutely smaller in each dimension than the hinge. Don't glue the shim in place, as you may want to remove it later.

Three ways to adjust a strike plate
For less than a ⅛-inch misalignment of latch bolt and strike plate, remove the plate and file its inside edge to enlarge the opening.

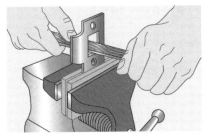

For a larger misalignment, remove the strike plate and extend the mortise higher or lower. Replace the plate, fill the gap at the top or bottom with wood putty, and refinish.

If the latch doesn't reach the strike plate, shim out the plate or add another strike plate on top of the first. If it still won't reach, shim out the door's hinges. Replace the door with a wider one if necessary.

CUTTING OR EXTENDING A DOOR

If you install new flooring or carpeting on top of old, you may need to cut a door's bottom so it does not scrape. Allowing a door to scrape will eventually damage both the flooring and the door. If a doorway goes out of square because the house settles, you may need to trim the top, bottom, or latch side of a door. (Before trimming a door's latch side, make sure the latch will still work after the door has been cut.) If you need to remove ¼ inch or less, you are likely better off using a plane or a power plane rather than a circular saw.

EXTEND A DOOR

You can extend a solid door, though the difference in grain will be visible unless you paint it. Cut an extension piece to size, test the fit, and apply wood glue. Clamp the extension, drill pilot holes, and drive screws that penetrate at least 2 inches into the door. After the glue dries, sand the area smooth.

🐕 **AMERISPEC® TIP** | **PATCHING A HOLLOW-CORE DOOR**

Hollow-core doors can be easily dented or cracked, even with a bare fist. You can patch a small hole or medium dent using two-part wood filler. If you sand carefully, the patch will not be visible after you paint it. If the door has a larger hole, you're better off buying a replacement.

A circular saw will cause splinters in a board's face when cutting crosswise to the grain, so use a utility knife and a straightedge to slice a line just above where you will cut, to prevent splintering. When cutting a hollow-core door, you will need to replace the bottom rail, as shown below.

REPLACING A DOOR

Hanging a replacement door in an existing frame takes a lot of patience, especially if the frame is not perfectly rectangular (and it usually isn't). If the existing jamb and casing are in bad shape anyway, consider tearing them all out and installing a prehung door (see page 71).

Before purchasing a replacement, remove the old door and measure the opening from top to bottom on both sides. Then measure across the opening at two or more points, checking the upper corners with a framing square. Be sure the replacement door you purchase will fit your opening (keep in mind that a hollow-core door has only a ½-inch trim margin). Double-check all measurements before cutting.

Here are some tips to help make this difficult job go a bit more smoothly:

■ Sand or plane any excess wood up to ¹/₁₆ inch on the door's top and bottom, and up to ¼ inch on the sides. If you need to remove more, cut with a circular saw, then sand.

■ Leave a ¹/₁₆-inch clearance around the door on the top and sides. Bottom clearance should be at least ½ inch (more if you need to clear carpet or a rug).

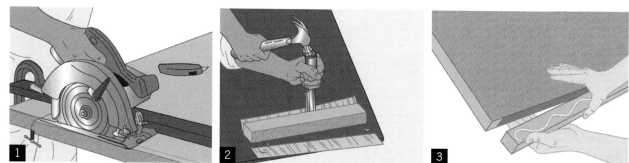

Cutting a door

1 Using a straightedge, draw the cut line, then use a utility knife to score a line ¹/₁₆ inch above the cut line. Clamp a straight board to use as a cutting guide, then cut the door with a circular saw. Sand the cut edges smooth.

2 If the door has a hollow core, you may need to fill the bottom with wood. Use a chisel to remove the veneer and glue from the cut-off piece. This will leave you with a wood piece that fits snugly inside the opening at the bottom of the door.

3 Test that the piece fits (you may need to trim it slightly). Apply wood glue to both sides, slip it into place, and either clamp it or place weights on it to hold the parts tight. After the glue sets, sand the edges.

■ Bevel the lock side of the door ⅛ inch so the door will clear the jamb as it opens and closes. If the door is already beveled, install it so the beveled edge is on the lock side.

■ When installing a hinge on the door, leave at least a ⅜-inch margin between the edge of the door and that of the hinge leaf.

■ If you're hanging a new door in an existing frame, use the existing hinges if possible. If you're hanging new hinges, place the top one about 7 inches below the top of the door, and the bottom one 11 inches above the bottom of the door. Center a third hinge between the others.

PREHUNG DOORS

A prehung door may cost more than a simple slab, but will save plenty of work and hassle. It will also probably fit together better than a slab door you install yourself, no matter how carefully you work. It comes with the door perfectly cut inside the jamb and installed on its hinges. Usually the casing is also supplied. The holes for the latch and the strike are already bored and mortised. You can buy prehungs that are hollow-core, solid-core, or panel types, for interior or exterior applications.

Some prehungs come with one-piece jambs that are 4⅝ inches wide. This is fine for most interior walls, which are 4½ inches thick. If you have thicker walls (as is often the case with plaster walls), buy a prehung with a split jamb so it can fit walls of various thicknesses.

Be sure to get the correct swing. A door with a right-hand swing has its hinges on the right and the handle or knob on the left when you push it open. A left-swing door has hinges on the left when you push it open.

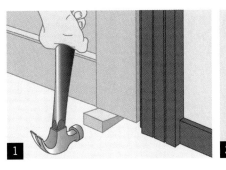

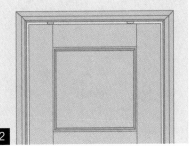

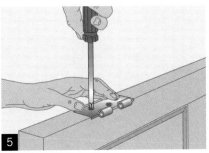

Hanging a replacement door

1 Rough-cut the new door so it fits fairly tightly. Place the door in the opening and then shim at the top for a ¹⁄₁₆-inch clearance. Shim the bottom to hold the door in place. Mark and cut the bottom, leaving a minimum ½ inch clearance.

2 Wedge the door snugly against the lock side, maintaining the ¹⁄₁₆-inch top clearance. Mark a trim line for a ⅛-inch clearance on the hinge side and then trim. Bevel the lock side if it's not already beveled.

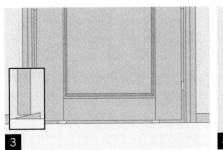

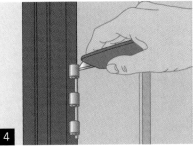

3 Hold the door in position with shims and wedges and double-check the clearances—¹⁄₁₆ inch on the top and sides, a minimum of ½ inch on the bottom. Lightly sand where it is needed.

4 Remove the hinge-side shims and push the door tightly against the hinge jamb. Mark the hinge locations on the door with a utility knife, using the hinge leaves on the jamb as guides.

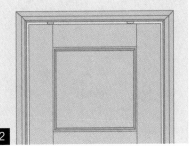

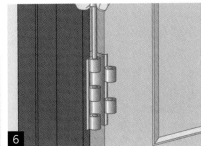

5 Outline the hinges using the marks made on the door. Cut mortises with a hammer and chisel (see page 68). Position the hinge leaves in the mortises, drill pilot holes, and drive the screws.

6 Slip the hinge leaves together and tap in the pins. Check that the door swings freely and install a new lockset (see pages 74–75). Coat all wood surfaces with a sealer or primer to prevent swelling and warping.

sliding doors

There are three basic types of sliding doors. A sliding patio door has heavy doors that are usually mostly glass. It typically rests and glides on rollers at the bottom, while the top track acts as a guide only. Top-hung sliding closet doors typically hang on rollers that run in an overhead track, and a short track at the floor keeps the doors from wandering. A pocket door works much like a sliding closet door, but the hardware must be hefty enough to handle a heavier set of doors and the door disappears into a cavity in the wall.

PATIO DOORS

Regularly vacuum out the bottom track and brush away debris from the top track. Apply lubricant only as recommended by the manufacturer; too much can actually act as a magnet for debris. If a track gets bent, you can often tap it back into shape.

If the track is clean but the door does not slide easily, try adjusting the height. If that does not work, remove the door and inspect the rollers; clean out any debris. If the rollers appear worn and do not spin easily, replace them.

A patio screen door is often subject to abuse. Repair screening as shown on page 62. Replace rollers when they are worn. If the main door is bent or out of square, it should be replaced.

Fixes for a patio sliding door

ADJUST DOOR ROLLERS Each of the two rollers can be adjusted up or down. Pry off the cap that covers the adjusting screw, then turn the screw. Adjust the door so it glides smoothly, its side is parallel to the side track, and the latch operates.

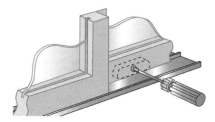

ADJUST A SCREEN DOOR A screen door's rollers can also be adjusted. The screws are usually directly above the wheels. Adjust them so the screen door glides smoothly and stays securely in the track.

STRAIGHTEN A TRACK Use a hammer and woodblock to straighten a bent metal track. If the track cannot be straightened, you can usually replace it without difficulty, as it is separate from the rest of the frame.

REMOVE A DOOR The door is heavy, so work with a helper. Lower the rollers, move the door to the middle of the frame, lift it straight up, and tilt the bottom outward.

SERVICE OR REPLACE ROLLERS Remove the screws and pry out the roller unit. If cleaning does not restore smooth operation, replace the assembly with a duplicate made by the same manufacturer.

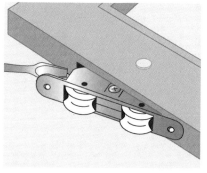

REPLACE SCREEN WHEELS Remove a screen door by lifting it and tilting the bottom out. Remove the adjusting screw and pull out the roller assembly. Replace it with one made for your door.

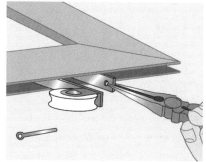

⚡ AMERISPEC® TIP | GARAGE DOOR SAFETY

An older garage door with an automatic opener may pose a risk to young children. Many lack electric-eye or pressure-sensitive sensors that reverse the door when they detect an obstacle, or have sensors that do not work properly. To be sure your garage door is safe, consult the owner's manual and inspect it yourself, or call in a specialist.

SLIDING CLOSET DOORS

If a top-hung sliding door pops out of its track, check for dirt in the track, a section that's worn or bent, or a guide that's out of alignment. Unscrew and remove the bottom guide on the floor. Reinstall the door and the bottom guide.

If a door is tilted so its side is not parallel to the door frame, adjust one or both of the top rollers. There should be a ⅜-inch clearance between the bottom of the door and the floor or rug. If a door is tilted outward or inward, the bottom guide needs to be moved so the door can hang freely.

Some sliding closet doors are made of inexpensive particleboard, which is subject to warping. If you cannot compensate for a warped door by adjusting the top roller or moving the bottom guide, then replace the door.

Three fixes for a top-hung sliding door

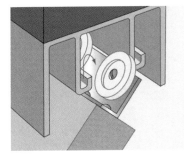

REMOVING AND REINSERTING A DOOR Lift the door straight up and angle it to lift the rollers out of the track. Some top-hung doors have slots on the track that you must align with the rollers before you can lift the door out or reinsert it.

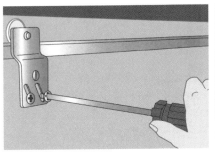

ADJUSTING DOOR HEIGHT To adjust a top roller, loosen one or two screws, move the door up or down, and retighten the screws. If adjusting the door causes it to scrape at the bottom guide, you may need to cut or plane the door.

ADJUSTING THE BOTTOM GUIDE If the guide is loose, the doors will bind. Align the guide so the doors slide freely, then drive longer screws to ensure the guide will stay put. If the door slips out of the guide, install a shim under the guide.

POCKET DOORS

If you have an old pocket door that has been out of service (and perhaps sealed inside the wall) for decades, it may be possible to revive it. In most cases, the upper track is in good shape but the rollers no longer run smoothly. Remove the rollers and look for a manufacturer name. Even if you can't find the maker, you can likely find compatible rollers at a specialty hardware store or by typing "pocket door hardware" into an Internet search engine.

You can typically install rollers by screwing them to the top of the door. If the screws do not grab in the old holes, move the roller over a couple of inches, drill new pilot holes, and drive the screws.

You can probably adjust the rollers up or down by turning a screw or a nut. If you have a pair of pocket doors, set their sides perfectly parallel to each other.

At the bottom of the door, there is usually a channel that fits over a guide attached to the floor at the jamb. Less commonly, a metal guide at the bottom of the door runs through a metal channel that is set into the floor.

If the track is damaged or if you can't find rollers to fit in it, you can install a new track. You will probably first need to cut two access holes in the wall to the side of the opening so you can drive screws to attach the track.

If you have the hardware but not the door, buy a new door to fit. Install rollers at the top and cut a groove in the bottom of the door to run over the guide.

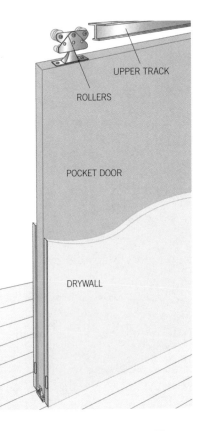

UPPER TRACK

ROLLERS

POCKET DOOR

DRYWALL

door locksets

Many exterior doors have a handle lockset (also called a cylindrical lockset) of the type shown below. This variety has a round body that fits into a hole drilled through the door. Some exterior doors, especially front doors, have a mortise lockset, with a squared body that slides into a deep notch in the door's edge. A mortise lock may have a combined latch and deadbolt mechanism. In addition to the handle lockset, it is a good idea to install a deadbolt lock on exterior doors, as shown on page 76. Most interior doors have round knobs, with or without locks. In pre-war homes you may find mortise latch assemblies, as shown at right.

When doorknobs or latches cease to work properly, first check that the door itself is not binding (see pages 66–67). See that the latch or bolt is aligned with the strike plate on the jamb and make adjustments as needed (see page 69). Also try disassembling and cleaning the mechanism. Often, however, replacement is the easiest and fastest solution. And new hardware is a quick way to dress up a door.

If you need to drill holes to install a new lockset, be sure you have the right size hole saw and spade bit on hand (usually a 2⅛-inch for the lock hole and a 1-inch for the latch hole). A sharp chisel is also a must.

Servicing a mortise latch assembly

1 If scraping paint off the cover does not restore smooth operation, remove both handles. (You may need to loosen setscrews or unscrew a knob.) Remove two screws and pull out the latch case.

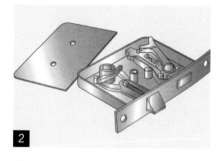

2 Lay the case on a flat surface and carefully remove the cover. Examine the inner workings closely. If the parts are in good order, clean out any debris and spray the unit with lubricant. If that doesn't work or if parts are broken, replace the case.

⚑ AMERISPEC® TIP   **SOLUTIONS FOR A BROKEN KEY**

If a key has broken off in the lock, first try using a thin but stiff wire to pry the fragment out. If that doesn't work, disassemble the mechanism and use the wire to push from the other side. Or take the mechanism to a locksmith.

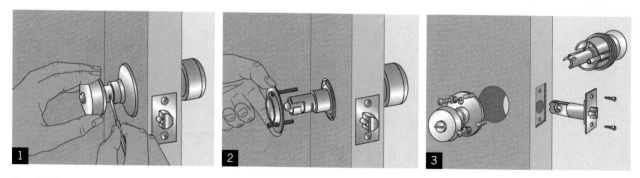

Replacing a handle lockset

1 To take out the interior knob, remove screws from the inside face. If there are none, look for a small slot in the shank. Push the tip of a small screwdriver or nail into the slot and then remove the interior knob and trim.

2 Unscrew and remove the mounting plate. Pull on the exterior handle to slip out the cylinder. Unscrew and take out the faceplate and latch assembly. Remove the strike plate from the doorjamb.

3 Insert and screw on the new latch assembly and faceplate. Holding the exterior knob and cylinder, slide the cylinder in through the latch assembly. Attach the mounting plate, handle trim, and knob. Install the new strike plate.

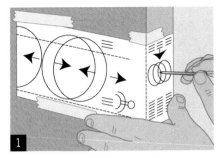

Installing a new handle lockset

1 A template and instructions should be included with your new lockset. Place the knob 36 to 37 inches above the floor. Tape the template to the door, then use a nail or the tip of a drill bit to mark the centers of the lock and latch holes.

2 Using a hole saw, bore the lock hole. As soon as the guide bit exits the opposite side of the door, stop and continue from the other side. Use a spade bit to bore the latch hole, as shown. Take care to drill straight, level holes.

3 Insert the latch assembly. Holding it square, trace the outline of the faceplate with a sharp pencil. Then use a utility knife or chisel to score the outline. Alternatively, trace around the faceplate with a utility knife, as shown.

4 With a knife or chisel and hammer, cut into the wood about ¼ inch on all sides. Working from the center of the mortise, tap the chisel to the bottom and then to the top. Insert the latch. If necessary, shave off a bit more wood.

5 Install the lockset as shown on the opposite page, then test for smooth operation. Close the door until the latch just hits the jamb. With a pencil, mark the spot where the center of the latch contacts the jamb.

6 Using the pencil mark as your guide, hold the strike plate against the jamb and trace its outline with a pencil. Score the outline and then chisel a shallow mortise. After checking the alignment, attach the strike plate to the jamb with screws.

FIXING COMMON LOCKSET AND HANDLE PROBLEMS

TIGHTENING THE HANDLES If the handles on an old mortise latch set are rattling, loosen the setscrew. You may be able to simply twist the

handle to tighten it. If not, remove the knob and look for setscrew holes along the spindle shaft. You may be able to tighten the knobs by inserting the setscrews for both knobs into new holes.

IF A LOCKSET DOES NOT OPERATE SMOOTHLY If a handle lockset or a deadbolt does not slide smoothly when the door is open, remove the handles or the cover and watch closely while

you operate the mechanism with a screwdriver. If you see a part rubbing against wood, remove the lockset and use a drill or chisel to widen the opening as needed. If the mechanism is balky even when it is out of the door, buy a replacement. If the latch operates smoothly with the door open but has trouble engaging with the strike plate, adjust the strike plate so it aligns with the latch or bolt, both vertically and horizontally.

DEADBOLTS

Security experts say that a high-quality deadbolt offers one of the most important measures of protection against intruders. Here we show how to install a high-security deadbolt, which drives a bolt 1 inch or deeper into a metal strike box mounted with long screws that extend into the framing, not just the jamb. This makes it nearly impossible to jimmy a door open.

Install a single-key deadbolt with a thumbscrew on the inside, unless the door has a glass pane that intruders could break to reach the thumbscrew. In that case, you may want to install a double-key deadbolt. To ensure that people can quickly exit during a fire or other emergency, keep a key nearby.

Installing a high-security deadbolt

1 Unless you are replacing an old deadbolt, use the manufacturer's template as a guide (as for a handle lockset, see page 75) and drill holes in the door. Insert the bolt assembly and screw the faceplate to the edge of the door.

2 Following the manufacturer's instructions, insert the exterior cylinder's tailpiece through the slot in the bolt assembly. Make sure the lock hole is facing the right way. Secure a cylinder retaining plate, as shown, and then attach the interior cylinder, which may have a keyhole or a thumbscrew.

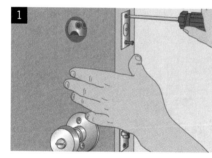

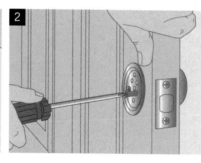

3 Dab the end of the bolt with lipstick or rub with a crayon, close the door, and turn the handle to mark the location of the strike hole. Use the strike plate to mark the doorjamb for a mortise. Drill holes deep into the jamb (and perhaps the framing as well) and chisel the opening so the strike box can fit (see next step). Cut a mortise for the strike plate.

4 Check that the bolt is aligned with the center of the hole. Following the manufacturer's instructions, insert the strike box, then the cover plate. Drive long screws through the jamb and into the framing behind. Depending on the model, the strike box may or may not be attached separately. (No strike box is needed if the door jamb is made of metal.)

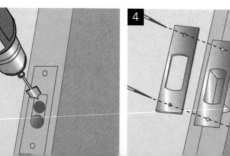

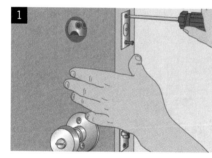

MORE SECURITY DEVICES

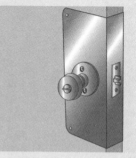

REINFORCER PLATE A metal plate like this makes it very difficult to pry a door open, and it makes a door-handle lock much more secure. To install one, remove the handles, slip the plate into place, drive screws, and reinstall the handles.

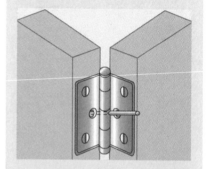

SECURITY HINGE PIN If your door has hinges exposed on the outside, an intruder can simply pop the hinge pins and remove the door. A hidden security pin like this makes it nearly impossible to remove the door on the hinge side.

PEEPHOLE A wide-angle viewer like this lets you see who's at the door. To install one, simply drill a hole, insert the pieces from each end, and screw them together. Some models come with installation kits.

weather-stripping a door

Doors are generally easier to seal than windows because they have fewer moving parts. Doors use some of the same products for weather-stripping as those used for windows (see pages 64–65). Spring bronze or plastic V-strips do a good job at the top and sides. The bottom, however, should be sealed with a weather-stripping threshold, a sweep, or a shoe. The illustrations at right show the most common ways to seal a door against drafts.

To add weather stripping so it doesn't cause binding, it's best if you first even out the gaps around the door (see pages 66–69). As you work, check that the weather stripping is not causing the door to bind or the latch to become difficult to operate. You may need to adjust the weather stripping so it is looser.

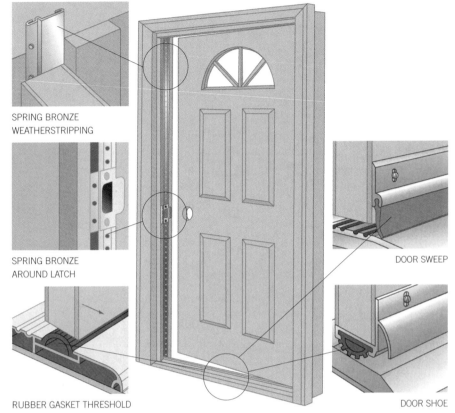

SPRING BRONZE WEATHERSTRIPPING

SPRING BRONZE AROUND LATCH

RUBBER GASKET THRESHOLD

DOOR SWEEP

DOOR SHOE

Sealing the sides and bottom

SPRING BRONZE First cut a short strip of spring bronze for the latch area, to fit behind the strike plate up against the door stop. Then measure and cut longer strips and attach them with brads to the sides and top of the doorjamb.

TUBE GASKETS WITH METAL BACKING To add an extra measure of protection, close the door and cut pieces of tubular plastic-and-metal weather stripping. Press gently against the door and drive screws or nails to attach the stripping.

DOOR SWEEP This is the simplest seal to apply to a door bottom, because you can leave the door on its hinges. Cut the sweep to match the width of the door. Close the door, position the sweep so it contacts the threshold, and drive screws.

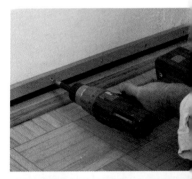

DOOR SHOE Door shoes make a better seal than sweeps. You will probably need to trim the door to allow for the thickness of the shoe. Remove the door and cut it. Cut the shoe to the width of the door, slip it on, and attach it with screws.

door thresholds and sills

The thresholds inside your house and the sills and thresholds in exterior doorways are exposed to continual foot traffic and the elements, and may eventually need to be replaced.

The sill forms the bottom of the frame of an exterior doorway and serves the same function as a windowsill, diverting water from the door and house. The sill fits snugly under the casing and against or under the jambs.

Fastened to the sill is a threshold, which helps seal the air space under a door. Thresholds are often used inside as well to make a neat transition between different flooring materials. Thresholds, also called saddles, are available in either hardwood or metal (usually aluminum). You can also get special thresholds that act as weather stripping (see page 77).

REMOVING A THRESHOLD OR SILL
Remove a damaged threshold or sill very carefully so you don't damage the door frame or any flashing under a sill. If necessary, you can cut them out, as shown for windowsills on page 59. Unscrew and remove a metal threshold.

INSTALLING A NEW THRESHOLD OR SILL If possible, use the old threshold as a template for cutting the new one. Check that the clearance between the bottom of an exterior door and the new threshold is about ⅛ inch. If it's less, mark the bottom of the door using the new threshold as a guide, then sand or trim the door to fit. If you are adding weather stripping at the door's bottom, follow the manufacturer's recommendations for clearances.

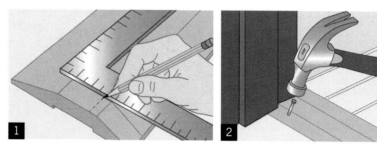

Installing a new treshold

1 Mark the new threshold to fit between the jambs. Cut, notching the ends to fit around the stops. Sand all cut edges. Caulk the underside and ends and center it under the door.

2 Drill pilot holes and nail the threshold to the sill with 6d casing nails. Countersink the nail heads and fill the holes with wood putty. Finish the threshold as desired.

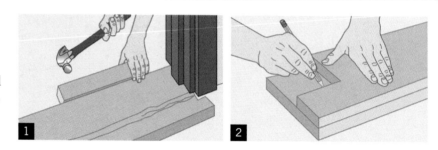

Replacing a sill

1 After removing any nails, drive out the old sill or saw it into three pieces and remove the center, then the ends. Take care not to damage any flashing underneath.

2 Using the old sill as a template, mark and cut the new sill to fit. If the old sill isn't in one piece, fit it together and make accurate measurements before cutting the new sill.

3 Gently tap the new sill into place, being careful not to force it. (A woodblock protects the sill from dents and splitting.) Sand or trim the sill for a snug fit.

4 Shim the sill if necessary. Drill pilot holes and drive nails or screws into the framing below. Sink the fastener heads and fill the holes with putty.

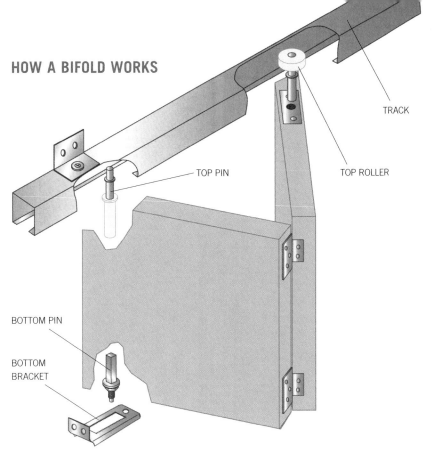

TRACK

TOP PIN

TOP ROLLER

BOTTOM PIN

BOTTOM BRACKET

gently snap shut. If they do not, you can easily adjust the door positions at the top or the bottom.

If a door scrapes the carpet even after it has been adjusted as high as it will go, cut the bottom following the techniques shown on page 70, then deepen the hole for the bottom pin. After the door is cut, you may need to shim the bottom bracket up.

To remove a bifold set, simply grab the side of the door where the pivot pins are, pull up, and tilt the bottom out. If the door will not come out, lower the door as far as it will go, and try again.

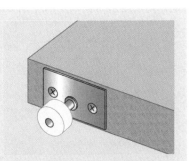

INSTALLING A REPAIR PIN

Bifolds sometimes crack around a top or bottom pin or roller. If this happens to yours, purchase a repair pin or roller, which has a bracket that spans the pin hole. To install it, drill pilot holes and drive screws.

repairing bifold doors

B ifold closet doors are usually lightweight, with light-duty hardware to match. Some are flush with hollow cores. Others are made of panels, perhaps with one or two louvered sections. Most repairs are simple. If one panel of a bifold door is damaged, buy a new set of two. It's not worth the small amount of money you'll save by trying to assemble an old panel onto a new one.

The doors should line up parallel to the side frame. If there are two sets of bifolds, they should meet in the middle just tightly enough to

Three bifold fixes/adjustments

ADJUST AT THE BOTTOM To move the bottom of the door to the left or right, grab the door near the bottom pivot pin, pull up until the pin disengages from the bracket, and move the pin over.

ADJUST AT THE TOP To move the top of the door to the left or right, open (fold) the door until the top bracket is accessible. Use a screwdriver to loosen the bracket's setscrew, slide the bracket over, and retighten the screw.

ADJUST THE HEIGHT To raise or lower the door, use an open-end wrench or a pair of pliers to grab the bottom pin's nut and twist it. If the door is heavy or the pin is difficult to reach, remove the door before making adjustments.

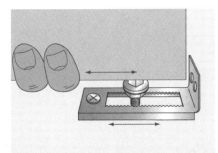

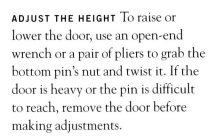

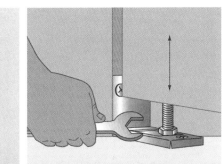

resurfacing cabinets

If your kitchen cabinets are ugly but in sound condition on the inside, and if you don't need to change their sizes or orientation, there are a number of sprucing-up strategies that can be accomplished quickly and inexpensively. The simplest is to apply a good coat or two of paint, as described on this page. If you install new hardware (see page 82) while you're at it, you could end up with an entirely new look. Applying veneer, drawer faces, and doors, as shown on the next page, will cost more but may not take much more time than applying two coats of paint.

PAINTING CABINETS

Whether you want to lighten dark and dingy cabinets or liven up your room with bold colors, paint can provide a relatively quick makeover. However, not all cabinets can be painted. Solid-wood or wood-veneer cabinets take paint well, as do metal ones. Cabinets covered with plastic laminate or thinner melamine plastic cannot be painted, as paint will not bond properly.

You can paint cabinetry with a bristle or foam brush, a roller, a pad, or a spray gun. Brushing paint on large surfaces will leave brush marks; a foam brush or a pad will leave less visible marks. Sprayers are expensive and require an enclosure to contain overspray. Rolling is fast and inexpensive, and it works exceptionally well on large surfaces. A short (4- or 6-inch) foam roller is a good choice because it lets you cover the frames with a single stroke and also quickly handle wider doors.

Painting cabinets

1 Remove all hardware—including screws, hinges, knobs, and pulls—and set aside whichever ones you will reuse. Remove the drawers. (Although you can try to paint your cabinetry with the doors and drawers in place, it is a lot easier to remove them.) Number the doors, drawers, and hardware to make them easy to replace when you are done painting.

2 Thoroughly clean all surfaces with trisodium phosphate or a TSP substitute. Rinse the surfaces completely with fresh water and allow them to dry. If you will install new hardware, fill all the mounting holes with putty and allow it to dry. Sand all surfaces with 150-grit open-coat sandpaper and then vacuum to remove any dust. Wipe with a slightly damp cloth.

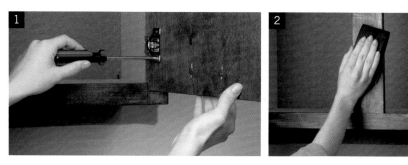

3 Mask all adjacent surfaces and use drop cloths to protect countertops and flooring. First paint the frames, then doors and drawers. You may choose to paint only the faces, as shown; the faces plus the edges of the frame pieces; or the insides of the cabinets as well. In the last two cases, you will need to use a brush. Also paint the insides of the doors.

4 While the doors dry, paint the drawer fronts, then the door fronts. If you need an additional coat, allow the first coat to dry overnight, then sand all surfaces with 220-grit wet/dry sandpaper. Vacuum thoroughly (or wipe with a tack cloth) and apply the next coat. Once the paint is dry, reinstall the drawers and doors.

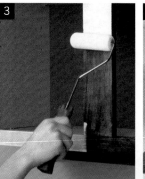

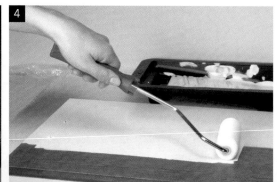

RESURFACING WITH NEW DOORS, DRAWER FACES, AND VENEER

Before you tackle this job yourself, consider hiring a cabinet resurfacing company to do it. It will cost more, but the company may have a wider range of colors and styles to choose from than you can find yourself.

You will need to buy new drawer fronts and doors, as well as matching self-adhesive veneer for the frames and ¼-inch plywood for any exposed cabinet sides. If a home center does not have what you want, check out a kitchen specialty store or see if a refacing contractor will sell materials without installation.

First cut plywood to fit over exposed cabinet surfaces and make sure it fits. Apply contact cement to the back of the plywood and the surface to be covered and allow it to dry to a tacky feel. Press the plywood into place very carefully, as you cannot move it once it's set.

Sand the frames and apply veneer. Then install the new drawer faces and doors.

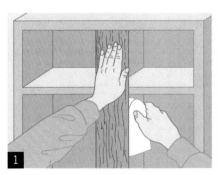
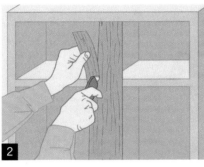
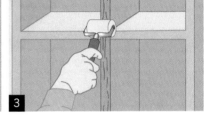

Applying veneer to the frames

1 Peel off a corner of the veneer backing, align the veneer on the face of the frame, and press it into place as you peel off the backing paper.

2 With a utility knife, use the sides of the frame as guides as you carefully cut away the veneer.

3 Use a hard rubber roller to press the veneer into place and activate the adhesive. Gently sand the edges smooth.

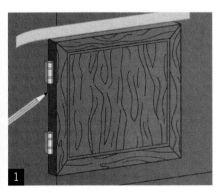

Installing new doors

1 Install the hinges (either old or new) on the frame, using the old screw holes if possible. Apply a piece of painter's tape to mark for the tops of all the doors. Position the door against the hinges and mark their positions on the door's edge.

2 Use a square to transfer the marks to the back of the door. Open the hinges and hold the door against the marks. Drill one pilot hole and drive one screw into each hinge. Test the fit, then drill holes and drive the other screws.

INSTALLING A DRAWER FACE

If the existing drawer has a face that can be removed, remove it. If not, cut away the face's overhanging edges. Position the new drawer face, clamp it, and drive screws from inside the drawer to secure it.

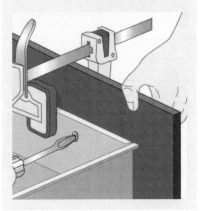

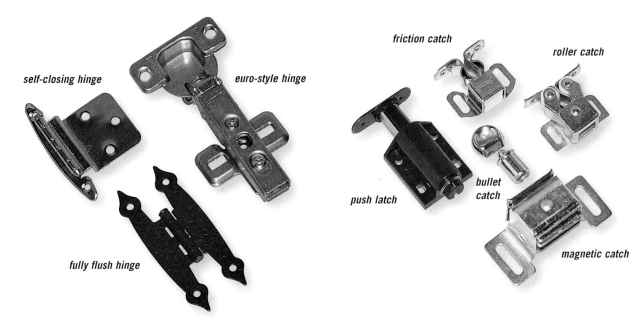

self-closing hinge

euro-style hinge

fully flush hinge

friction catch

roller catch

push latch

bullet catch

magnetic catch

REPLACING HINGES, CATCHES, AND PULLS

Changing your pulls can greatly improve the look of your cabinets, and replacing hinges and catches may make them operate more smoothly.

HINGES If your cabinet doors droop or shut poorly, first try tightening the screws. If a screw won't tighten, remove it, squirt some wood glue into the hole, force in some tooth-picks and break off the exposed ends, drill a new pilot hole, and drive the screw back in. If the hinges themselves are loose or damaged, replace them.

Take an old hinge with you when you buy replacements. If possible, get new hinges with holes in the same places or try to find hinges that will cover the old holes. Otherwise you will have to fill and sand some screw holes.

CATCHES AND LATCHES When catches wear out and lose their holding power, replace them. Magnetic catches don't have to be precisely aligned. Friction and roller catches have more holding power but must be installed with precision. Push latches have a high-tech feel, as they open a door when you push on it.

PULLS AND KNOBS A knob attaches with only one screw, so it can usually easily replace an existing knob. If you have existing pulls—which use two screws—or want to install new pulls, make sure the holes align. Otherwise you will need to fill, sand, and redrill holes.

Tips for installing knobs and pulls

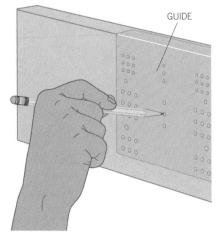

GUIDE

Install pulls carefully; a mistake in drilling can be hard to hide. To drill new holes, use a guide to ensure that all the pulls will be the same distance from the edge. Or make your own template using a piece of cardboard or plywood.

To install a door pull or knob, drill the exact hole size recommended by the manufacturer. Poke the screw through the hole. Drive the screw or screws into the pull.

REPLACING DRAWER GLIDES

Cabinet drawers are usually mounted on metal glides, or slides. Good glides allow drawers to be pulled out smoothly and silently. Cheaper models rattle and may let the drawer droop when extended. Solid metal glides with ball-bearing or nylon rollers are recommended. The best of the bunch have bumpers to cushion the impact of the drawer as it closes, so the drawer stays in place instead of bouncing open again.

full extension

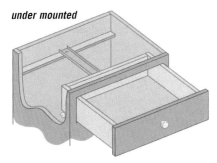

Glides can allow a drawer to open three-quarters of the way or fully. Full-extension glides are usually worth the extra cost because they make it easier to get items from the back of the drawer.

under mounted

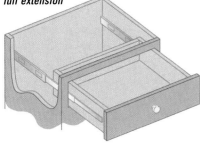

If you have under-mounted glides, you should replace them with bottom-mounted or full-extension glides. These are available at hardware stores and home centers and are easy to install if you follow the manufacturer's instructions.

bottom mounted

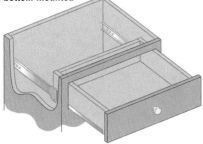

CLEANING AND REPAIRING COUNTERTOPS

Stains

Use a mild dishwashing solution for regular cleaning. For stubborn stains, follow these tips:

CERAMIC TILE The grout is usually the problem area. Clean it with a bleach solution (½ cup of liquid chlorine bleach to 1 quart of water). Once clean, it should be sealed.

GRANITE If your granite is not sealed, you may need to remove stains. Make a paste by mixing a cup of flour with 2 tablespoons of liquid dishwashing soap. Apply it to the stain, cover with plastic wrap, and let it sit overnight. Scrape away the mixture with a wooden utensil and rinse. If the stain is oil-based (containing grease, oil, or milk), use hydrogen peroxide instead of dishwashing soap. For coffee, tea, or fruit stains, mix hydrogen peroxide with a couple of drops of ammonia. Use straight hydrogen peroxide to remove ink or marker stains. Once the stains are removed, apply a granite sealer and reapply it every year or two.

FORMICA AND LAMINATE Avoid abrasive cleaners. For stains, apply a paste made of lemon juice and baking soda. Let the paste dry, then rub vigorously with a damp cloth. For ink, try rubbing alcohol.

SOLID SURFACES (Corian and others) Use scouring powder and a damp sponge to scrub away stains. Smooth away minor burns, scratches, and other blemishes with sandpaper. Start with 200- or 300-grit, followed by a very fine (800-grit) sanding. Apply countertop polish (see "Worn finish").

WOOD OR BUTCHER BLOCK Seal regularly with bar wax or apply a thin coat of mineral oil when the wood looks dull. Let the oil soak in for an hour and then wipe away any excess.

Repairing damage

For damaged counters, home centers carry products that can help you make the best of the situation. Read the fine print to be sure the product you purchase is recommended for the surface you need to repair.

SCRATCHES AND CRACKS Look for a colored filler specially formulated to fill in cracks and scratches. It is inexpensive and easy to use. Apply it to a clean surface following the manufacturer's instructions, then wipe off any excess.

CHIPS The tricky part is matching the countertop color. Look for a kit that contains a repair compound in a variety of colors, together with a mixing chart. Once you have the desired color, apply the compound to the damaged area and let it dry. It will harden as it dries. Then sand and apply a clear finish over the repair.

WORN FINISH If your laminate counter has lost its luster in heavy work areas, look for a counter polish product that contains silicone. Clean the surface and apply the polish. Let it dry and then buff the area. Apply every few months, following manufacturer's instructions, to keep your counter looking new and clean.

LOOSE COUNTER EDGES If you have a formica or laminate counter that is peeling along the top or edge, you can glue it back in place with contact cement. Follow the manufacturer's instructions carefully. The glue needs to dry partially so that it's tacky before the loose area is pushed into final position. Put a weight on the area or tape it to hold it in place. Let it dry for 24 hours and then sand away any overhanging edges.

basements and attics

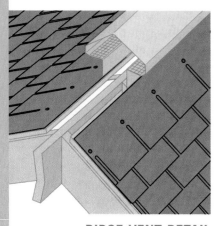

RIDGE VENT DETAIL

The basement and attic are important parts of a house's structure. Keeping them well ventilated and insulated, and keeping cracks sealed will go a long way toward making your home more comfortable and holding down energy costs.

BASEMENTS An old basement may have walls made of boulders held together with mortar. Most basements have walls of concrete block or poured concrete. Basement floors are almost always made of poured concrete. If you have an old basement with a dirt floor, consider hiring a contractor to pour a concrete floor. You may be able to lower the floor at the same time.

A basement should have at least one drain hole in the floor, and preferably more. Keep the hole covered with a drain plate, and keep the area around it clear so water can easily get there in case of a plumbing leak or a flood. Run a hose to test that the drain works. It should be joined to a pipe that leads to municipal storm and sewage lines, or to a dry well (a hole in the ground filled with gravel). Consult a plumber or your local building department if you are not sure. If the drain does not work, use a power auger to clear it. If that

---

⚡ AMERISPEC® TIP **WATCH YOUR STEP IN THE ATTIC**

If an attic floor has exposed joists and/or insulation, be very careful when walking around. One misstep between the joists and you could poke your foot through the ceiling below. If you need to work in the attic, or if you want usable storage space, place pieces of plywood up there and fasten them to the joists.

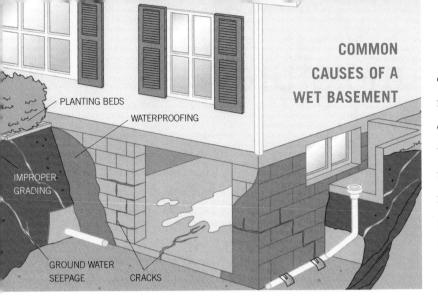

PLANTING BEDS

WATERPROOFING

IMPROPER GRADING

GROUND WATER SEEPAGE

CRACKS

doesn't work, contact a plumber for other solutions.

The most common basement problem is water seeping up through the floor or in through the walls. This chapter shows how to keep a basement dry. In many cases, several measures should be taken, including adding a sump pump, extending gutter downspouts, improving grading around the house, and dehumidifying the basement.

If you have a crawl space instead of a basement, there are usually fewer maintenance issues. Make sure that the space is well ventilated and that no puddles of water remain after a rain. Make sure rot is not developing where the house's wooden beams or joists meet masonry supports.

ATTICS It pays to spend half an hour periodically checking out your attic. Take a light up with you and inspect the attic floor

and ceiling. A minor roof leak may not appear inside the house until it becomes a serious problem. If you notice signs of leaking, see Chapter 8 for various roof repairs.

Because heat rises, insulating an attic is often the best way to make a home more energy efficient. At the same time, however, an attic must be well ventilated or moisture will collect and cause all sorts of problems. If it snows in your area, compare your roof with

others of a similar pitch in your neighborhood. If snow has melted on your roof and not on others, then you are probably losing too much heat through your roof and need more insulation and ventilation. In summer, place a thermometer in your attic near the top of the roof. If it registers more than 20 degrees warmer than the outside air, you probably need additional ventilation.

Usually, the best approach is to apply insulation with a vapor barrier to the conditioned space while making sure that air can flow freely up through eaves and out the ridge vents or the gable ends. This chapter will show you general insulation and ventilation strategies, as well as techniques for installing some of the most common insulation materials.

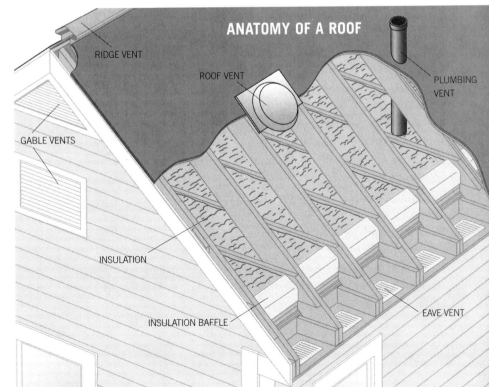

ANATOMY OF A ROOF

RIDGE VENT

ROOF VENT

PLUMBING VENT

GABLE VENTS

INSULATION

INSULATION BAFFLE

EAVE VENT

controlling moisture in a basement

Water problems in the basement range in seriousness from damp walls and floors to water gushing from cracks. The source may be humid air condensing on cool surfaces, or groundwater finding its way in. Before you can correct the problem, you'll need to determine the source of the entry water.

WHERE'S THE WATER COMING FROM?

If you can see water flowing out of a crack in a wall or floor, you know the source is groundwater. Otherwise, you'll have to perform the aluminum foil test (see opposite page) to see if water is coming from the ground outside or from moist air inside.

REDUCING CONDENSATION

When the basement air is humid, the moisture in the air may condense on cool surfaces, such as a concrete floor, plumbing supply pipes, and duct work.

The following suggestions will help to lower the air's humidity:
■ Check that the clothes dryer is efficiently venting moist air to the outside.
■ Install a dehumidifier in the basement (either have the collected water run into a drain, or plan to empty the tray daily).
■ Insulate cold-water pipes (see page 155).
■ Insulate basement walls (see page 92).
■ Improve ventilation by opening basement windows or installing an exhaust fan in the basement.

■ Cover any exposed dirt with 6 mil plastic sheeting.

CONTROLLING GROUNDWATER

When water collects next to a foundation wall or when the water table (the water level under your property) is higher than your basement floor, hydrostatic pressure can force water through joints, cracks, and porous areas in concrete walls and floors and through cracked or crumbling mortar joints in masonry walls. Poor construction practices are frequently the cause. These include easily clogged or nonexistent footing drains, poorly applied or nonexistent moisture-proofing on the foundation, through-the-wall cracks, and improper grading.

Minor problems can often be solved with some fairly simple steps. If they don't work, contact a foundation engineer or contractor for a more lasting solution.

EXTERIOR REMEDIES

Roof and surface water collecting next to the foundation can cause dampness in the basement. Use the following checklist and correct any problems you find.
■ Gutters and downspouts should be clear and should direct rainwater well away from the foundation. A splash block or downspout extension may be the solution (see opposite page).
■ Check that your grading directs rainwater away from the house. The ground should drop at least 1 inch per foot for the first 10 feet from the foundation walls.
■ Planting beds next to the foundation may allow water to collect or pool there. If they do, move or modify the plantings.
■ Wells around basement windows should be free of debris, have good drainage, and be properly sealed at the wall. See that the surrounding ground slopes away from the well.

INTERIOR REMEDIES

Minor moisture problems can sometimes be solved from the inside.
■ For a general moisture problem, brush or roll on waterproofing paint or trowel on crystalline waterproofing (CWM). Look for coatings at home improvement or masonry supply centers.
■ Patch cracks in walls and floors with hydraulic cement (see page 88), which expands and hardens quickly, even under wet conditions.
■ If you cannot seal a basement floor or wall crack yourself, hire a professional basement sealing company. They will likely use special equipment to inject epoxy into the crack.
■ Many basements have a sump pump, which pumps groundwater away from the house before it can well up in a basement floor or lower wall. See page 89 for maintaining and replacing a sump pump.

⚡ AMERISPEC® TIP   **WATCH THOSE CRACKS**

If you see horizontal cracks in a wall that's bowing inward, or long, vertical cracks wider than ¼ inch, or a crack that's getting wider (measure it periodically), you likely have a structural problem. Call a contractor who specializes in basement repair.

SEEPAGE OR CONDENSATION?

To test whether moisture is seeping through the wall or is simply the result of humid air, tape a 12-inch-square piece of aluminum foil tightly to a basement wall in an area that tends to get wet.

After three days, peel back the foil. If the room side is wet, you have damp basement air. Improve the ventilation or use a dehumidifier. If the wall side is wet, you've got seepage; follow the advice on the next four pages.

Diverting rainwater

A downspout extender easily attaches to the bottom of the downspout. Some types are flexible.

A roll-up extender stretches outward when it fills with water. It works well on smooth areas.

A splash block extends the flow of water away from the house and directs the water toward a wider area.

Efflorescence

1 A powdery white substance called efflorescence sometimes forms when bricks or other masonry materials stay moist for long periods.

2 Follow the steps above for diverting water away from the wall. Once you are sure it will stay dry, remove most of the efflorescence with a scraper and a wire brush.

3 Clean efflorescence with a masonry cleaner. Wear protective clothing when working with acid.

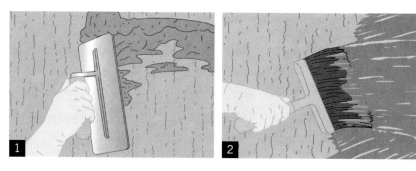

WATERPROOFING PAINT

Once you have directed most of the water away from the house, apply the first coat of masonry paint with a stiff brush, working it into the masonry. Apply the second coat using a paintbrush or roller.

Applying crystalline waterproofing (CWM)

1 Scrape away any loose matter and wire-brush the wall so the water-proofing can penetrate. Mix a small amount and then apply it with a trowel, pushing as you spread.

2 Immediately run a stiff brush over the material to create a fairly even texture. Cover the area with plastic or occasionally mist it to keep the coating moist for two days.

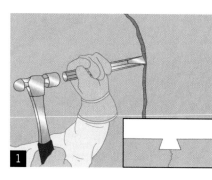

Patching a wall crack

1 Chisel out any crack wider than ⅛ inch, undercutting it (see inset) and beveling the edges. Clean out the crack. Directly outside, run a garden hose.

2 Once water starts to come through the crack, mix a small batch of hydraulic cement to the consistency of putty and roll it into a rope shape.

3 Press the cement into the hole and keep pushing until the leak stops. If it doesn't stop, pry out the patch, rechisel, and try again.

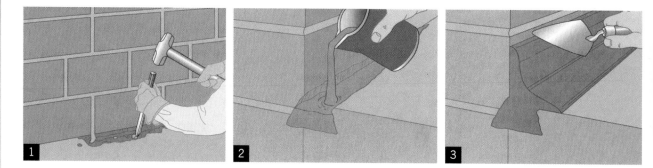

Patching a floor-to-foundation joint

1 Wearing goggles, chip out the joint with a hammer and cold chisel to make a groove 1 to 2 inches deep. Undercut the edges.

2 Clean out the groove. Pour a soupy mixture of hydraulic cement from a bent coffee can to within ½ inch of the top of the groove.

3 Fill the rest of the groove with a stiffer mixture of the cement, and use a trowel to cove it several inches up the wall and along the floor.

SUMP PUMP

A sump pump collects groundwater in a container, then pumps it out of the container and away from the house. In an older home the pump may simply sit in a pit in the basement floor. More commonly, it rests in a plastic liner.

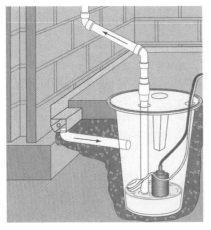

In many cases, a series of drainpipes, which may be made of clay or plastic, bring water into the sump liner via a single pipe that runs into the liner, as shown above. In other installations, there is no drainpipe. Instead, the pit liner is perforated with a number of holes and set in a bed of gravel so water under the basement floor can seep into it from all directions, as shown below.

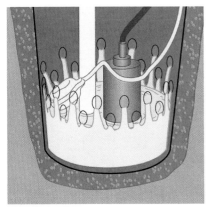

If you have no sump pump and often have standing water or a very moist basement floor, installing one may be more practical than digging a trench around the house and sealing the basement walls (see box

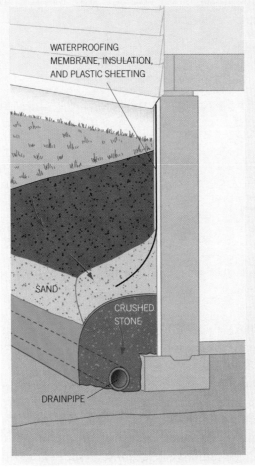

WATERPROOFING MEMBRANE, INSULATION, AND PLASTIC SHEETING

SAND

CRUSHED STONE

DRAINPIPE

THE PROFESSIONAL SOLUTION

If the steps here do not solve a serious basement water problem, call in a specialist. The solution is often to dig a trench next to the leaking wall, then apply waterproofing membrane, rigid insulation, and thick plastic sheeting to the outside of the wall. Flashing may be installed on top of the insulation. A drainpipe is typically installed near the bottom of the wall, sloped away from the house, and surrounded with crushed stone. Sand or other backfill is laid on top of that, and the plastic sheeting is embedded so it is angled away from the house. Finally, topsoil and sod or other plantings are added.

above). A professional can install a sump pump with a perforated liner in a basement that lacks underground drainpipes.

There are two basic types of sump pump. A submersible model sits in the bottom of the sump liner. A pedestal pump protrudes up out of the liner. A submersible is quieter but more expensive. Both types are controlled by a float-operated switch, so they come on when the water reaches a certain level.

Because electrical power is often interrupted during a storm—when you are likely to need the pump—it's a good idea to install an auxiliary pump powered by a rechargeable 12-volt battery (see right).

Test a pump by running water into the liner. The pump should kick on and run without undue noisiness. Clean the inlet screen

every year or so. Pumps typically last about 20 years, so don't be surprised if you need to replace one. Unplug the pump and disconnect it from one or two pipes, carefully noting how things are connected. Buy a replacement with the same connection points and replace any rubber connectors while you're at it. If the installation is not clear to you, hire a pro.

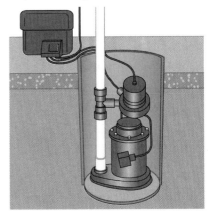

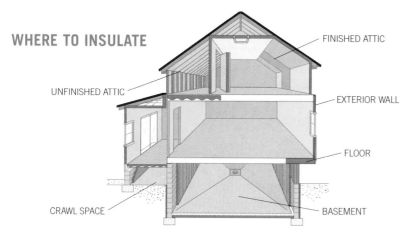

UNFINISHED ATTIC · FINISHED ATTIC · EXTERIOR WALL · FLOOR · CRAWL SPACE · BASEMENT

insulating and ventilating a home

For a home to remain comfortable and energy efficient, it must be well insulated and well ventilated. The primary focus of insulation is the attic, though the next five pages will also touch upon wall insulation.

INSULATION BASICS

Heat passes through ceilings, walls, and floors from the warm side to the cool side. Insulation slows this transfer. A well-insulated house requires less heating and cooling—and therefore lowers energy bills.

In an unfinished attic, you can easily measure insulation thickness. To check finished exterior walls for insulation, remove a receptacle cover plate near the baseboard (after shutting off power). Reach into the wall beside the box with a coat hanger bent into a hook and fish out some insulation.

The illustration above shows where to check for or add insulation. A climate map and companion chart on the opposite page show how much insulation you need, depending on where you live.

UNDERSTANDING VENTING

In hot weather, good ventilation keeps attics from overheating and radiating heat into living spaces below (A, top right). When an attic is not well ventilated, the heat flowing from the attic causes your air conditioner to work harder. Even when attic floors are well insulated, heat can seep down into the house. Installing a series of vents will allow warm air to flow up and out of the attic, to be replaced by cooler air brought in through the eaves or soffits. Ventilating an attic can easily lower its temperature from 150 to 115 degrees Fahrenheit.

In winter, ventilation clears the attic of warm, moist air that may seep up from living spaces (B, bottom). Allowed to remain in the cooler attic, this humid air would deposit its moisture as condensation on joists, rafters, and attic insulation, reducing its effectiveness.

Cold air directly below the roof also helps prevent ice dams, a buildup of ice along eaves that can cause roof leaks (see page 93).

THE VALUE OF FANS

Some parts of your house need to be well ventilated in both summer and winter. In hot weather, a whole-house fan mounted on the attic floor can pull cool outside air through the entire house and substantially reduce the amount you spend on air conditioning.

Ceiling fans that circulate air within a room also help cut cooling bills. They gently draw cool air up from the floor, where it tends to collect on hot days. Reversed in winter, a ceiling fan circulates warm air that accumulates near the ceiling.

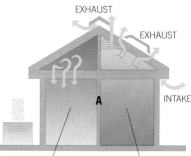

EXHAUST · EXHAUST · INTAKE · A

WITHOUT PROPER VENTILATION ATTIC HEAT BUILDS, PENETRATES LIVING AREAS

WITH PROPER VENTILATION HEATED AIR IS EXHAUSTED. COOLER OUTSIDE AIR IS TAK

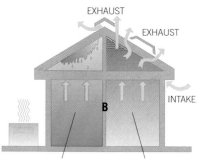

EXHAUST · EXHAUST · INTAKE · B

WITHOUT PROPER VENTILATION MOISTURE-LADEN AIR RISES INTO ATTIC AND CONDENSES

WITH PROPER VENTILAT MOISTURE-LADEN AIR I EXHAUSTED OUT OF AT

🔺 AMERISPEC® TIP | **DOES IT STILL INSULATE?**

If insulation has compacted because it has gotten wet, it will lose its fluffiness and therefore its insulating value. This can happen over a period of years in an attic that is periodically damp. It is probably best to replace the insulation. If yours does not look or feel fluffy, have it checked by a professional.

HOW MUCH INSULATION DO YOU NEED?

This map and chart, developed by the United States Department of Energy, show how much insulation your house needs, depending on its location and the fuel you use for heating. Amounts of insulation are given as R-values. The higher the R-value, the thicker the insulation.

1 2 3 4 5 6

Zone	Gas	Heat Pump	Fuel Oil	Electric Furnace	Attic	Wall	Floor	Crawl Space	Basement
1	X	X	X		R-49	R-18	R-25	R-19	R-11
1				X	R-49	R-28	R-25	R-19	R-19
2	X	X	X		R-49	R-18	R-25	R-19	R-11
2				X	R-49	R-22	R-25	R-19	R-19
3	X	X	X	X	R-49	R-18	R-25	R-19	R-11
4	X	X	X		R-38	R-13	R-13	R-19	R-11
4				X	R-49	R-18	R-25	R-19	R-11
5	X				R-38	R-13	R-11	R-13	R-11
5		X	X		R-38	R-13	R-13	R-19	R-11
5				X	R-49	R-18	R-25	R-19	R-11
6	X				R-22	R-11	R-11	R-11	R-11
6		X	X		R-38	R-13	R-11	R-13	R-11
6				X	R-49	R-18	R-25	R-19	R-11

Insulation Types	Description	Where to Use	Installation Method
Batts and Blankets	Flexible rolls (blankets) or precut strips (batts) of fiberglass. Batts are easiest to handle, but blankets can be cut for a perfect fit.	Unfinished walls, attic floors, and floors over unheated basements and crawl spaces. Good choice with standard stud and joist spacing in uncovered surfaces.	Batts and blankets are precut to fit between studs and joists and can be used both between and on top of attic floor joists.
Loose Fill	Loose fill fibers or granules of cellulose, fiberglass, rock wool, and other materials.	Good choice for finished walls, unfinished attics, and hard-to-reach locations.	Usually blown into wall and ceiling cavities with machines. The loose material easily fills nooks and crannies.
Rigid Foam	Made from extruded or expanded plastic foam that has been formed into panels. Expensive but offers higher R-values per thickness inch than other products.	Basement walls (interior and exterior), concrete floors, and some roof applications.	Usually glued in place and covered with a finish material, such as flooring or drywall.

VENT OPTIONS

House vents come in a wide variety of shapes, sizes, and types. Below are some of the most common ones. Intake vents should be placed as low as possible, often at the eaves. Place exhaust vents as close as possible to the peak of the roof.

EAVE VENTS (left) may be circular or rectangular. They are set into the eaves, one to each space between rafters, on two sides of the house. To be effective, eave vents must not be blocked by attic insulation.

A RIDGE VENT (see page 84) is a metal or plastic extrusion that covers a gap built or cut into the roof sheathing at the ridge. Louvers in the vent allow air to escape while preventing rain from entering. The vents run the full length of the roof.

ROOF VENTS (right) are typically small, square metal structures built to let air pass but keep rain out. Some are equipped with a thermostatically controlled fan to speed the removal of hot air from the attic. Turbine vents (left) have spe-

cially shaped vanes that turn in the slightest breeze to pull hot and humid air out of the attic.

GABLE VENTS (below) are common on older homes and can be either rectangular or triangular to fit into the angled space at the roof's peak. Because they're located at the ends of the attic, they're not as effective as roof-mounted vents. However, gable vents are the easiest to install.

INSULATING AN UNFINISHED ATTIC

This is likely the most important insulation project you can undertake. First measure your existing insulation and then use this table to determine the R-value of any insulation you already have.

FIBERGLASS (batts/blankets)	R-3.0/in.
FIBERGLASS (loose fill)	R-2.5/in.
CELLULOSE (loose fill)	R-3.4/in.
ROCK WOOL (loose fill)	R-2.8/in.

APPLYING ATTIC INSULATION

MEASURING THE INSULATION Slip a ruler between a joist and the insulation to measure the thickness. Average several measurements taken from different parts of the attic, then multiply the average by

the R-value per inch of insulation (see table, below left). To figure out how much insulation to add, subtract your finding from the R-value recommended on page 91. You may put new insulation over old, and you need not match types.

INSTALLING BATTS AND BLANKETS
If the attic floor is uninsulated, use insulation with a vapor-retardant face and place the facing next to the ceiling. In hot, humid climates, or if the attic is already insulated, use unfaced fiberglass. Start at the perimeter and work toward the attic access door. Place the insulation between joists, cutting it to length as shown on page 94. For higher R-values, lay additional insulation across the joists.

ADDING LOOSE-FILL INSULATION
Rent a loose-fill insulation blower from a home center, making sure you have enough hose to reach all corners of your attic. With a helper to load the blower with insulation as needed, start at the perimeter of the attic and work toward the attic access door. Fill every joist space completely and evenly with the insulation, leaving attic vents uncovered. You can shield vents with pieces of cardboard to avoid covering them. Level uneven spots with a rake.

⭐ AMERISPEC® TIP   CONTROLLING MOISTURE

Water vapor that condenses inside insulation ruins it. The solution is to install a vapor barrier. Some kinds of rigid foam insulation serve as their own vapor barrier. Polyethylene sheeting works well with most insulation. Fiberglass batts and blankets are available with a vapor-retardant facing on one side. Vapor barriers are most often placed on the interior side of the insulation, but in hot, humid climates, they go on the exterior side.

CONTROLLING ICE AND SNOW ON YOUR ROOF

An ice dam (below) forms at the eaves and can cause water from melting snow to back up under the shingles and leak into the house. Ice dams can result from alternate thawing and freezing of snow on the roof during a period of warm days and cold nights, or from heat loss through the roof of a poorly insulated and badly ventilated house. Either can cause the snow to melt and then, in cold weather, freeze again at the colder eave area. The result can be a great deal of damage to your roof.

KEEPING THE ROOF COLD The solution is usually to make sure the attic does not get too warm. Adequately insulate the attic and be sure that warm air from inside the house is not leaking into the attic. Check around all light fixtures that penetrate the attic floor, as well as ducts, plumbing stacks, and attic hatches. Fill any openings with stuffed insulation or caulk.

A good combination of eave, roof, and gable vents can help cool and dehumidify an attic. See pages 90 and 92 for venting strategies. Make sure that any eave vents are not blocked by insulation.

STRIP VENT   BREATHER VENT

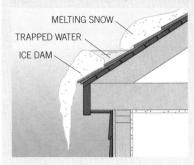
MELTING SNOW
TRAPPED WATER
ICE DAM

DE-ICING CABLES If you have a severe ice-dam problem, consider installing electrically heated cables along roof eaves and in gutters and downspouts. These cables, which are insulated for safety, are clipped to the shingles in a zigzag pattern or run along gutters and inside downspouts. They need to be plugged into an electrical receptacle. They create drainage channels for water that otherwise would back up behind an ice dam or freeze inside the gutters and downspouts.

INSULATING A FINISHED ATTIC

Uninsulated space in a finished attic is an oven in summer, a refrigerator in winter. So, in all likelihood, your attic living space already has some insulation. If not, or if what's there is insufficient, you can add more.

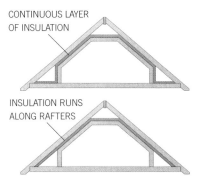
CONTINUOUS LAYER OF INSULATION

INSULATION RUNS ALONG RAFTERS

Insulating this space before the drywall is fastened to the ceiling and knee walls (short walls near the eaves) is no more difficult than insulating exposed studs, joists, or rafters elsewhere in the house. However, once wall and ceiling coverings are in place, the task becomes much more complicated and can require tearing down the ceiling and walls. Unless you are an adventurous and accomplished carpenter, call in a professional.

rafter vents

WHERE IT GOES Insulation is installed above the ceiling. Below the ceiling, the insulation can follow the knee walls to the attic floor, then across toward the eaves (see illustration at right). The insulation is installed with the vapor barrier toward the interior of the house.

MAINTAINING VENTILATION If your roof is equipped with soffit and ridge or roof vents, have an insulation contractor check for ventilation between the insulation and the roof. To ensure adequate ventilation, install vents between rafters.

Stapled to the roof decking, the vents allow a continuous airflow from the soffit to the ridge even after insulation batts have been placed over them.

The vents also keep moisture from the roof from soaking the insulation. With the rafter vents in place, the spaces between rafters can be filled. For maximum R-value, cover the batts with rigid foam insulation, then finish with drywall.

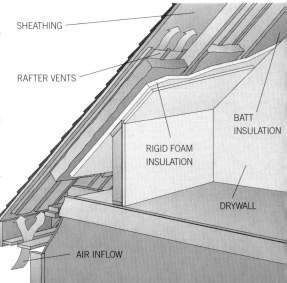
SHEATHING
RAFTER VENTS
RIGID FOAM INSULATION
BATT INSULATION
DRYWALL
AIR INFLOW

INSULATION FOR A STUD WALL

For walls with exposed studs, such as in a garage, fiberglass batts are usually the best insulation choice, although blankets will also work. Walls are usually framed with studs spaced 16 or 24 inches on center, and fiberglass batts are available to fit snugly into either of these spaces. If you use unfaced insulation, you'll need to staple a layer of vapor-retardant polyethylene plastic over the insulation to keep it dry. Batts and blankets with a vapor-retardant facing save this step.

CUTTING FIBERGLASS INSULATION
Place the fiberglass batt on a piece of plywood as a cutting board. Measure the height of the space between studs you wish to insulate and transfer it to the batt, laying a 2 by 4 or other straightedge across the batt to serve as a cutting guide (above). Compress the insulation with the cutting guide, then slice through the fiberglass with multiple strokes of a sharp utility knife.

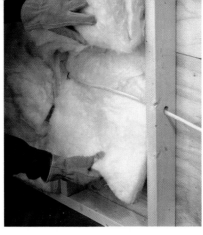

WORKING AROUND OBSTRUCTIONS
To fit insulation behind wires or pipes that pass through studs, peel the front half of the batt away from the back half (above). Slide one half behind the obstruction, then use the other half to cover it. Around electrical boxes for receptacles and light switches, split the batt unequally so that the thinner part fits behind the box. Cut out the front section with scissors or a utility knife for a snug fit around the box.

ATTACHING FACED BATTS Fiberglass batts and blankets with vapor-retardant facing on one side have flaps along the edges. Tuck the insulation between studs with the facing toward you as you work (below). Then staple the flaps to the studs.

BLOWING INSULATION INTO A WALL

If the exterior walls of your house need insulation, you can blow it into the spaces between studs without removing drywall or paneling. The best choice is often blown-in cellulose, which flows past obstructions in the wall and fills cavities around existing insulation better than other loose-fill products. Cellulose seals air leaks, making a separate vapor barrier unnecessary.

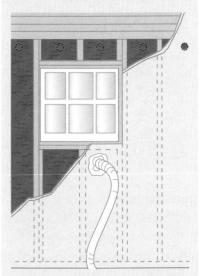

Many homeowners prefer to leave the job to a professional contractor, but some have achieved satisfactory results for themselves. The idea is to blow insulation into each space between studs, one at a time. Doing so requires that you cut a 2- to 3-inch hole in the wall between each pair of studs and as near the top of the stud space as possible. A hole saw makes short work of this part of the job. Save the drywall cutouts for repairing the holes later.

Feed the blower hose deep into each cavity while a helper operates the blower and controls the mix of air and cellulose. Plug the hole around the hose with a rag to prevent insulation from escaping. As the space fills, gradually withdraw the hose from the hole.

excluding critters

Exclusion means removing things in your yard or house that attract squirrels and other nonhuman intruders. It is the easiest, cheapest, and most humane way to deal with a squirrel problem.

SEAL THE GAPS It is often an on-going struggle to seal the gaps in a house that admits squirrels. They are persistent creatures that can gnaw through metal and wood. Often, after a gap has been filled, squirrels find a way back in, especially if the carpentry work is flawed. Common problem areas, listed below, should be checked regularly.

■ Areas covered with trim are usually the first places where cracks appear. Check high spots with binoculars. Look for dark rub marks from animal fur around or near a hole. Check at ground level too. Squirrels can enter a crawl space and work their way up through walls. Repair gaps or defects in house trim with pressure-treated wood or sheet metal and galvanized nails.

■ Rooftop ventilation fans can be problem areas. Many are made with aluminum screening, which is easy for a squirrel to chew through. Rescreen the fan with galvanized

steel wire in the form of hardware cloth, available at home centers.

■ Aluminum gutter spouting (for air conditioning or other utilities) that runs to upper floors can provide a rodent "ladder" to your home's attic. The bottoms and tops of the gutter spouting should be pinched off and then caulked.

■ Vents not built to code or other building anomalies may cause squirrel problems.

■ Tree branches can provide easy access to your home's rooftop. Trimming them so they are six feet away will help reduce squirrel traffic.

THINGS THAT DON'T WORK These measures seem not to bother squirrels much:

■ Moth balls
■ Sonic or magnetic devices
■ Ammonia, bleach, or bay leaves
■ Loud rock music

REMOVING SQUIRRELS Squirrels will leave on their own when the weather warms up, because they prefer the outdoors during warm months. This is the best time to seal gaps. If you can't wait that long, you may have to resort to trapping. It's best to do this before

winter sets in so the squirrel has time to set up a new nest. Bait a live squirrel trap with a peanut butter sandwich, then drive the captured creature at least five miles away to a new home. Contact your local wildlife agency for additional advice or information.

BAT CONTROL If you have a bat in your home, first determine whether it is an accidental intruder—possibly a lost youngster looking for a safe escape—or a roosting bat. The presence of dark droppings beneath the potential roosting area probably indicates bats that have taken up residence.

If it's an accidental intruder, use a shoebox and a piece of cardboard to capture the bat and release it outdoors. While the bat is perched on a wall, cover the animal with the shoebox, then slide the cardboard under the box to trap the bat. Release it outdoors.

Bats that roost in your home fly out almost daily (depending on weather) to find food. Bats can enter through openings as small as ½ inch in diameter. Common entry points include open windows or doors, broken or loose screens, missing shingles or tiles, places where flashing or boards have come loose, and places where pipe or wiring enters a building. Openings often appear where walls meet the eaves at the gable ends of an attic, where porches attach to the main part of a house, or where dormers meet the roof. Other points of entry are associated with siding.

To exclude bats, secure netting along the top and side of the opening. Leave the netting unattached along the bottom edge and allow it to extend 18 to 24 inches below the exit point. That way, a bat will be able to escape but not get back in.

fireplaces and chimneys

A welcoming hearth is an asset to most any room in the house. An older home may have a traditional built-in brick fireplace, but since the 1960s other types have emerged, including zero-clearance metal units. Wood-burning stoves have also grown in popularity.

Whichever type of fireplace you have, use it with care. Don't light a fire until you are certain your fireplace is safe. This chapter shows some ways you can inspect and repair a fireplace and chimney yourself, but be sure to call an expert for evaluation if you are not completely sure of your unit's safety.

A traditional fireplace has a warm ambience but may suck more heat out of a room than it generates. See pages 102–103 for some ways to make an old fireplace more energy efficient.

Dense plumes of smoke coming from the chimneys of traditional fireplaces or older woodstoves show why home fires have come under scrutiny in recent years. In certain areas, weather conditions called inversion layers trap pollutant-laden air close to the ground, generating thick, stifling, health-threatening smoke and gases. As a result, many regional air quality agencies now ask homeowners to limit or forgo fires.

These concerns have spawned a new generation of fireplaces and woodstoves—as well as inserts for existing fireplaces—that burn fuel so cleanly that most are exempt from limitations or prohibitions.

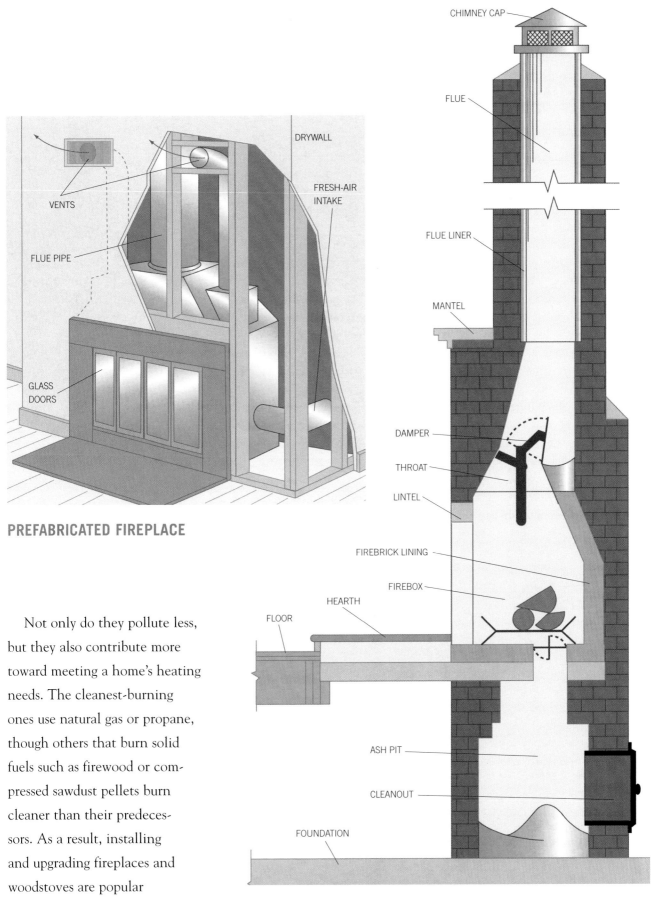

PREFABRICATED FIREPLACE

DRYWALL

FRESH-AIR INTAKE

VENTS

FLUE PIPE

GLASS DOORS

CHIMNEY CAP

FLUE

FLUE LINER

MANTEL

DAMPER

THROAT

LINTEL

FIREBRICK LINING

FIREBOX

HEARTH

FLOOR

ASH PIT

CLEANOUT

FOUNDATION

Not only do they pollute less, but they also contribute more toward meeting a home's heating needs. The cleanest-burning ones use natural gas or propane, though others that burn solid fuels such as firewood or compressed sawdust pellets burn cleaner than their predecessors. As a result, installing and upgrading fireplaces and woodstoves are popular home improvements.

WOODBURNING FIREPLACE

understanding and using a fireplace

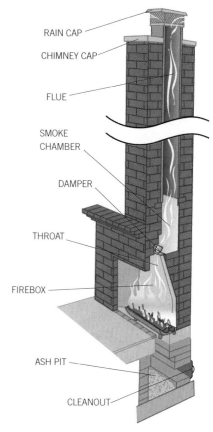

RAIN CAP
CHIMNEY CAP
FLUE
SMOKE CHAMBER
DAMPER
THROAT
FIREBOX
ASH PIT
CLEANOUT

A fireplace must be built correctly so it will draw smoke out of the house yet keep most of the heat inside. Have your fireplace cleaned and serviced once a year for safe use.

MASONRY FIREPLACES A masonry fireplace has a solid firebox leading upward to a damper, a smoke shelf, a smoke dome, and a chimney. The firebox and chimney can weigh more than 5,000 pounds, requiring them to rest on a reinforced concrete foundation. The firebox is built of brick or concrete block lined with special heat-resistant firebrick or tiles. It is shaped with a narrow "throat" that holds in some heat and directs smoke into a fire chamber just above. Natural convection sucks smoke up through the chimney. The damper is a small metal door that is opened to allow smoke to escape and closed when the fireplace is not in use. For economy, the ash pit may be omitted, but the flue and hearth are safety features every fireplace needs.

PREFABRICATED WOOD-BURNING FIREPLACES Factory-built prefabricated fireplaces (see the illustration on page 97) come in both radiant and heat-circulating designs. Unlike masonry fireplaces, they have metal fireboxes and outer metal shells that allow them to be placed near wood framing. These models, often called zero-clearance fireplaces, are relatively lightweight (600 to 800 pounds) compared with their masonry counterparts.

These units generally have fewer safety issues than masonry fireplaces. However, creosote can build up in the flue and possibly cause a dangerous fire (see pages 100–101).

In many cases, you can eliminate creosote by burning a special creosote-eliminating product and so avoid having the flue cleaned.

GAS LOG FIREPLACES Many gas log units do a good job of imitating the look of natural wood with far less

GETTING A GOOD LOOK

To see the inside of your firebox, your damper, and part of your chimney, position a large mirror at an angle, as shown, and hold a shop light just to the side of the mirror. To inspect the upper portion of the chimney, go up onto your roof (if it's safe) and use a strong flashlight, or dangle a shop light down into the chimney. Here are some things to look for:

■ An old fireplace may not have an inner flue, also called a lining. This is potentially dangerous because, without a lining, any gaps in the brick mortar can allow smoke and sparks to reach the house's structure and interior spaces. If your chimney has no inner flue, consult several contractors to see if it can be relined with metal or tile. A number of methods can be used.

■ If your mantel or the wall around the firebox is sooty, the firebox may not be burning correctly, or else the

fireplace has been used when the damper was closed.
■ Crumbling mortar joints, inside or outside, should be repointed (see page 114). If the bricks themselves are crumbling, call in a mason for an evaluation.
■ The damper should operate smoothly and close fully. Close the damper, light a piece of paper, and hold it inside the firebox as you blow it out. If smoke readily moves upward, the damper is not sealing well. Install a new damper or install a top damper operated with a pull chain. Also consider glass doors or an insert (see page 102).
■ The chimney top should be in sound condition and should be topped with a metal cap to keep animals out and arrest sparks (see page 103 for repairs).
■ Check the flue for creosote and have the chimney cleaned when needed (see pages 100–101).

mess and maintenance. There are two basic types.

A vented gas log unit produces a great deal of heat, but also requires a working chimney. If the chimney does not draw well, dangerous carbon monoxide may enter the living area. A vent-free unit has more efficient burners that produce less carbon monoxide and an oxygen depletion sensor, which turns off the fire if too much oxygen is depleted in the room. As a result, a vent-free fireplace can be installed most anywhere in a room, as long as it does not abut combustible surfaces. Vent-free fireplaces often do not look as realistic as vented units.

A vented gas log fireplace produces a great deal of water vapor. A vent-free unit produces less moisture but none of it gets vented to the outside, so it may produce excess moisture in the room.

WOOD-BURNING STOVES

Some older woodstoves are dangerous and inefficient, but newer versions generate a good deal of heat from only a few logs and produce little pollution. See that your stove is in compliance with local fire and emissions codes. Make sure that the chimney and the flue, as well as the fire-safe surfaces below and behind the stove, are installed with the clearances specified by the manufacturer.

The hearth under the stove and

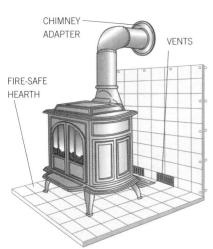

CHIMNEY ADAPTER

VENTS

FIRE-SAFE HEARTH

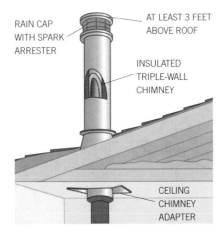

RAIN CAP WITH SPARK ARRESTER

AT LEAST 3 FEET ABOVE ROOF

INSULATED TRIPLE-WALL CHIMNEY

CEILING CHIMNEY ADAPTER

the wall behind it should be covered with fire-safe materials large enough to keep the floor and walls safe. In most cases, the hearth should extend at least 18 inches on all sides. It's a good idea—and it's sometimes required by code—to provide an air vent that supplies outside air on the floor or a nearby wall. Alternatively, an air duct can be connected directly to the stove via a small stovepipe at the bottom.

The chimney is usually made of double- or triple-wall construction, so it is warm rather than hot. This is especially important wherever the chimney touches the house. Make sure the chimney is attached securely.

When creosote builds up, clean the chimney with a brush (see pages 100–101) or burn a creosote-removing product.

A catalytic converter is a feature of many newer woodstoves. It reburns smoke to dramatically reduce pollution. Catalytic converters are often required by local codes.

PELLET STOVES

These burn small pellets made from wood byproducts. Some stoves have large glass doors and ceramic logs to create the illusion of a bigger fire. A microprocessor directs air and fuel intake. An electric auger feeds the pellets from a hopper into the fire chamber, where blown air creates a superheated firebox. The fire burns at such a high temperature that the smoke is literally burned up, so no chimney is needed. As with a clothes dryer, waste gases are vented outside through a duct.

The outside intake is operated by an electric motor. Another small electric fan blows the heated air from the fire chamber into the room. The electronic microprocessor controls the operation, allowing the pellet stove to be controlled by a thermostat.

Pellet stoves are easy to operate and can burn for up to 80 hours without having to be refueled. An additional advantage is that the pellets come in easy-to-store plastic sacks, eliminating the need for cutting, hauling, and stacking firewood. Before deciding on this option, however, check the price and availability of pellets in your area. Also make sure you can easily obtain parts and service.

🏠 AMERISPEC® TIP **SAFE USE OF A FIREPLACE OR STOVE**

■ Open the damper fully before lighting a fire. Keep the damper open until the fire is completely out and no longer smoking.

■ Burn only dry wood that has been aged for at least a few months. Wet or green wood can cause dangerous flare-ups and quick accumulation of creosote.

■ Don't use a fireplace to burn trash or pressure-treated lumber. These can produce toxic fumes. Never burn flammable liquids.

■ Install detectors for smoke and carbon monoxide in the room (see page 12) and keep a fire extinguisher on hand (see pages 10–11).

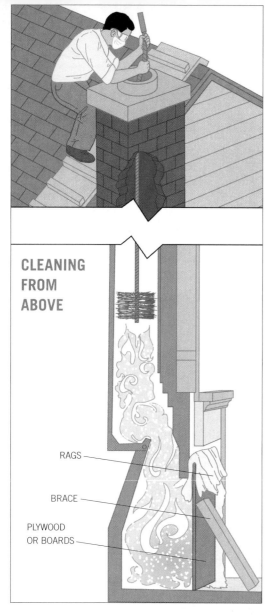

CLEANING
FROM
ABOVE

RAGS

BRACE

PLYWOOD
OR BOARDS

PLASTIC
SHEETING

CLEANING
FROM
BELOW

cleaning and maintaining a fireplace and chimney

R egularly cleaning and occasionally sealing a fireplace will go a long way toward keeping it in good working order. If a chimney is leaning or if bricks are missing, consult a professional. To repair chimney flashing that is leaking or corroding, see pages 122–123.

CHECKING FOR CREOSOTE Burning wood causes creosote—a black, sticky substance that is highly flammable—to build up inside a chimney. Creosote has three forms: first-degree creosote is gray and somewhat fluffy; second-degree creosote is dark gray and forms into crusty globs that look like blackened popcorn; third-degree creosote is very stiff and fairly smooth. Third-degree creosote catches fire easily and can set the other two types ablaze as well. A chimney fire can get extremely hot and burn for a long time, creating a very dangerous situation.

So at least once a year, or after burning a cord of wood or so, check for creosote buildup. Hire a pro to test for creosote, or test yourself. Open the damper and use a putty knife or screwdriver to scrape the ledge just above it. If creosote is more than ⅛ inch thick, it's time to clean the chimney.

CLEANING A CHIMNEY You can clean first- or second-degree creosote yourself. If you have third-degree creosote, hire a pro. In any case, you may want to hire a chimney sweep to tackle this messy job.

If you do it yourself, purchase or rent steel chimney brushes, handles, and extension rods. Make sure the brush is sized to fit your flue, and have enough extensions so you can reach all the way down to the firebox.

Wear long clothing, gloves, protective eyewear, and a dust mask. Seal the interior fireplace opening with boards and rags, or duct tape and plasting sheeting. Cover the room's carpeting and furniture with drop cloths.

Unless you have a top-mounted damper, you will probably want to work from the top down. See page 121 for tips on working safely with a ladder and on the roof. Attach a rope to the brush, in case you accidentally let go while working. You may need to attach weights to the brush. Push the brush down, then scrub the chimney walls by vigorously brushing up and down.

Once one section is clean, add an extension and continue cleaning until you reach the damper.

Working from the bottom up, open the damper and use plastic sheeting to seal the fireplace. Slit a hole in the sheeting, insert the brush up through the firebox, and seal the slit as tightly as possible. Work the handle up and down, adding extensions as needed until you reach the top of the chimney (see illustration, opposite page).

Once you have finished cleaning, wait for the dust to settle. Remove the plastic and vacuum the dust up with a shop vac.

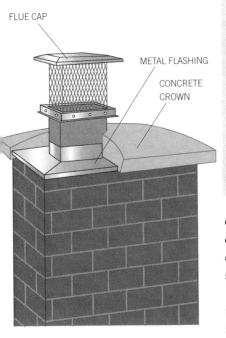

FLUE CAP

METAL FLASHING

CONCRETE CROWN

UPPER CHIMNEY MAINTENANCE
The part of the chimney that protrudes above the roof is particularly

CHIMNEY TOP FIXES

IMPROVING THE DRAW If your fireplace does not draw well, the chimney may not be tall enough. Ask a fireplace expert whether extending the chimney would help pull the smoke out. Other options include installing a wind-powered ventilator or an electric fan at the top of the chimney.

CAULKING A CHIMNEY CROWN If there is a gap in the joint between the crown and the flue, seal it tightly with masonry caulk or butyl caulk (upper left). Do the same for any minor cracks in the crown.

INSTALLING A FLUE CAP Rainwater can mix with creosote to produce an acid that damages masonry surfaces. An easy-to-install flue cap (left) will act as an umbrella, plus it will keep out small animals and arrest sparks. Measure your flue and buy a cap to fit; there are only a few standard sizes. Slip the cap over the flue, see that it is reasonably level, and tighten screws to hold it firm.

exposed to weather and is a notorious trouble spot. If the crown is damaged or if bricks are failing, see page 103 for repairs.

It's a good idea to seal the upper portion of a chimney using a masonry sealer designed to allow the bricks to breathe. Apply it with a paintbrush (right) or a pump sprayer.

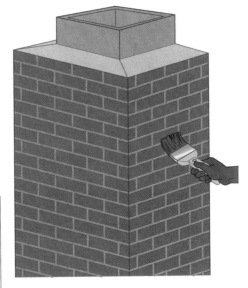

🕌 AMERISPEC® TIP | **IF YOU HAVE A CHIMNEY FIRE**

A chimney fire may start slowly, then suddenly burst into large flames. If you see excessive smoke coming from the top of a chimney or down through the damper, get your family out of the house and call the fire department. If possible, quickly douse the fire and close the damper (if you can safely reach it). If the fire department does not come right away, wet the roof and the chimney with a hose.

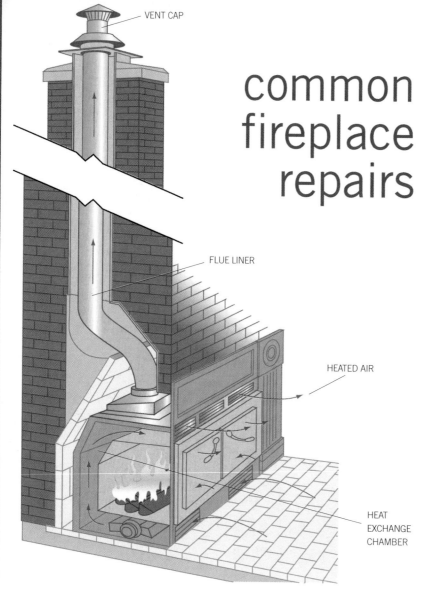

VENT CAP

FLUE LINER

HEATED AIR

HEAT
EXCHANGE
CHAMBER

common fireplace repairs

room when there is no fire. It is a good idea to install a vent that brings combustion air from the outside to the firebox.

LINER AND INSERT A wood-burning insert, as shown on this page, is usually more efficient than glass doors. It functions much like a wood-burning stove (see page 99) that is set into a fireplace opening. It has a heat-exchange chamber surrounding the firebox that pulls in cool air from the bottom and sends out warm air through the top. Its flue arrangement ensures that only hot air, and no smoke, will enter the room.

First, a properly sized liner is run into the existing flue (below). Because the metal is corrugated, it can be worked up into the flue from the room below. The main body of the insert then slips inside the firebox (right, opposite page). The flue is connected to the insert's top, and flanges seal the unit to the surrounding surface.

MAKING AN OLD FIREPLACE MORE EFFICIENT

Most masonry fireplaces don't supply much heat to a room. Because wood needs oxygen to burn, the fire draws air through cracks around doors and windows, displacing the warmer room air, which goes up the chimney along with flue gases. The two basic solutions shown on this page can be installed by a determined homeowner, but it's usually well worth the extra expense to hire a professional.

GLASS DOORS AND VENTS To improve heating efficiency, you can add tempered glass doors to the front of the fireplace. These limit the amount of warm air pulled into the fireplace and also the amount of cold air that can be pulled into the

★ AMERISPEC® TIP | NEW CHIMNEY CROWN

If your chimney crown is in bad shape, hire a mason to cast a new concrete crown. It should overhang the bricks on all four sides and have a groove running under the perimeter of the bottom edge to prevent rain water or snow melt from traveling to the bricks.

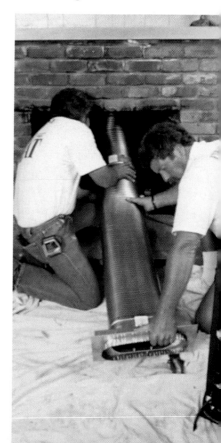

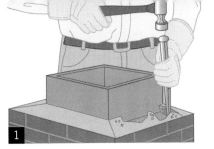
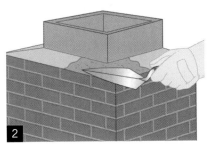

Repairing a chimney crown

1 If a crown has a portion crumbling but is basically sound, use a hammer and cold chisel to chip away the crumbling section. Take care not to damage the bricks or the flue.

2 Mix a batch of latex-reinforced patching concrete, and apply it with a wood or magnesium float. Smooth the surface at the same slope as the rest of the crown.

WHEN TO CALL IN A FIREPLACE PROFESSIONAL

The repairs shown on this page can be accomplished by a handy homeowner. If exterior mortar joints are generally failing, repointing is often the answer (see page 114). If a chimney is leaning noticeably, or if bricks are crumbling, call in a mason for evaluation and repairs.

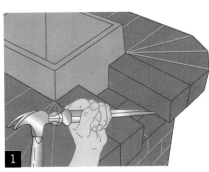
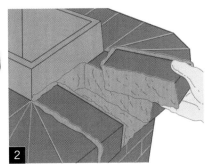

Replacing a brick cap

1 Remove any loose bricks using a hammer and cold chisel. If bricks are damaged, buy replacements, which you may need to have cut to size. Clean away any particles.

2 Mix a batch of latex-fortified mortar mix and wet the bricks. Apply mortar to the bricks and tap them into place. Use a brush to clean the joints.

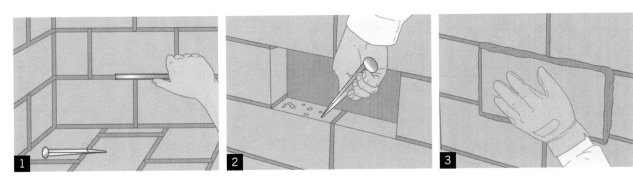

Repairing firebricks

1 If some mortar in the firebox is missing or loose but the bricks are firmly attached, mix a small batch of refractory mortar, apply it with a trowel, and smooth it with a striking tool.

2 If bricks are loose or damaged, remove them one or two at a time. Use a cold chisel, then a wire brush, to clean mortar from the edges of surrounding bricks. Buy replacement bricks if needed.

3 Apply refractory mortar to the surrounding bricks and to the replacement brick, then carefully slide it into place. If mortar falls off, creating a large gap, remove the brick and start again. Smooth the joints as in Step 1.

siding

Whether it's wood, vinyl, steel, aluminum, masonry, stucco, or composite materials, the exterior wall covering on your house is called siding. In addition to its decorative role, siding gives strength to exterior walls and protection for the inner walls. It also acts as a water shed system, protecting your house from the elements.

Siding may be plagued by a variety of ills, from obvious problems like peeling paint to less obvious insect infestation and dry rot. Many problems can be remedied if caught early on; regular inspection and maintenance are crucial (see pages 106–107). More modern cement-based composite sidings require little or no maintenance, so consider them if you are replacing siding.

ANATOMY OF A WALL Wood-frame walls are usually constructed from 2-by-6 or 2-by-4 studs. Insulation is placed between the studs, which are then covered with sheathing. An older home may have 1-by-6 plank sheathing, while postwar homes have sheathing made of plywood, oriented strand board (OSB), or a fibrous material.

The sheathing is covered with building paper. Older homes usually use roofing felt (tar paper) or rosin paper. Since the 1970s, spun-olefin building paper has grown in popularity. Some walls provide a vented air space between the building paper and the siding to help keep the wall dry. Then the siding is nailed onto the sheathing and/or studs.

For masonry walls, a veneer of brick or stone is applied. Each course, or tier, of bricks or stones is attached to the underlayment with short metal strips called ties. The bricks or stones are mortared in place. Some prewar homes have double-wythe walls, meaning there are two thicknesses of brick.

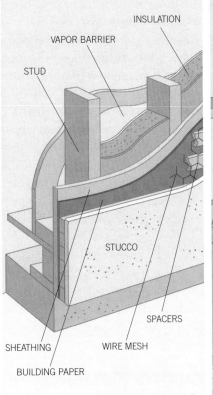

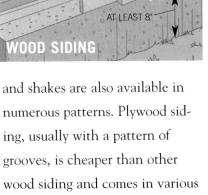

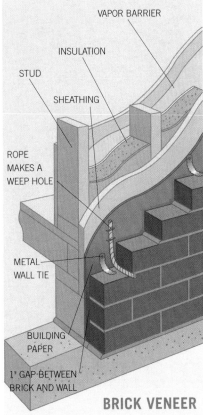

STUCCO SIDING

WOOD SIDING

BRICK VENEER

STUCCO For stucco siding, wire mesh is nailed directly to sheathing covered with building paper, or the mesh is nailed to spacer strips, as shown above. The stucco is then applied over the wire mesh in three layers. Stucco is a cement- based plaster. It can be bought already mixed and colored. The finish coat can be tooled in several textures.

WOOD SIDING Horizontal beveled siding, also called clapboard, is the most common wood siding. Other types may be installed vertically or horizontally. Shingles

and shakes are also available in numerous patterns. Plywood siding, usually with a pattern of grooves, is cheaper than other wood siding and comes in various patterns and surface textures.

MASONRY SIDING Brick walls may be laid in various patterns and bricks come in a wide range of sizes, colors, and textures. Stone veneer can also be laid in a variety of patterns. Mortar, a mixture of Portland cement, sand, lime, and water, holds the bricks or stones together. A gap between the bricks and the sheathing in

addition to a series of weep holes allow moisture to vent out. Masonry siding is practically impervious to weather.

MANUFACTURED SIDING Aluminum, steel, vinyl, and concrete-based composite siding panels are applied either horizontally or vertically. They usually come with trim pieces into which panels are fitted, and they are available in multiple colors and textures. Depending on maintenance and exposure to the elements, these types can last from 20 years to the life of the house.

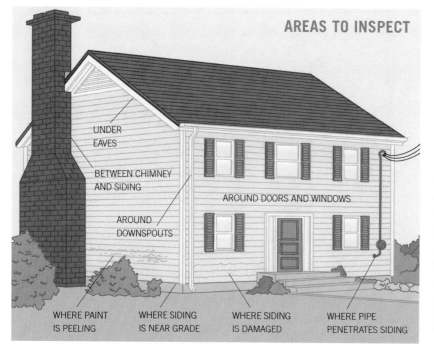

UNDER EAVES

BETWEEN CHIMNEY AND SIDING

AROUND DOORS AND WINDOWS

AROUND DOWNSPOUTS

WHERE PAINT IS PEELING

WHERE SIDING IS NEAR GRADE

WHERE SIDING IS DAMAGED

WHERE PIPE PENETRATES SIDING

inspecting and maintaining siding

With maintenance, your siding should last for many years. To keep your house looking its best, inspect your siding for damage in spring and fall, make any needed repairs promptly, and clean and repaint regularly.

INSPECTING YOUR SIDING

Look for obvious problems such as warped boards, missing or damaged shingles, holes in stucco, crumbling mortar, cracks, and defective paint (see photos on opposite page). Don't ignore less obvious interior problems such as dry rot and termite damage, as they can eventually destroy your house.

Begin with a visual inspection of vulnerable areas indicated in the drawing above. When you make your inspection, let the following list of problems and solutions guide you.

DETERIORATED CAULKING Note any caulking that has dried out and renew the seals (see page 113). Check the seals around windows and doors, around protrusions, and where a deck or masonry fireplace adjoins the house. Also caulk any cracks in board siding.

CRACKS Long vertical cracks in masonry walls may indicate settling. Place tape over a crack and leave it in place for several months. If the tape twists or splits, consult a professional to determine whether there is a serious structural problem. Otherwise, caulk and paint the cracks.

MOLD AND MILDEW Combined heat and humidity may result in mold or mildew on wood and painted surfaces. Take steps to keep the siding dry, and see the cleaning tips at right.

EFFLORESCENCE Brick or stone veneer may become covered with a white powder called efflorescence, formed when water-soluble salts are washed to the surface. This may indicate a leak that should be fixed. Once you have taken steps to keep the wall dry, clean it (see below).

ROT AND TERMITE DAMAGE Wet rot appears as dark or black areas that look much like burned wood. If you spot wet rot, find out why the area often stays wet, then solve the problem. Boards that feel mushy when you poke them with a screwdriver should be replaced. Dry rot is a fungus that causes wood to crumble.

Termites destroy wood by chewing out its interior. They can devour framing and siding so inconspicuously that they escape your notice. See page 110 for solutions.

CLEANING YOUR SIDING

To keep siding in good shape, hose it down and, if necessary, scrub it with a carwash brush that attaches to a hose. Spray vinyl panels and sponge them with a mild liquid detergent.

If brick veneer suffers from efflorescence, scrub the siding one small area at a time with a mild solution of muriatic acid (1 part acid to 10 parts water), and rinse the wall with clear water.

You can retard the growth of mold or mildew by washing the siding with a solution of ⅓ cup detergent and 1 quart household bleach in 3 gallons of water. Brush the walls, then rinse. After cleaning the siding, repair any caulking (see page 113) and paint or stain any areas that are chipped or peeling.

> **CAUTION** *When working with cleaning agents, wear goggles and gloves, and cover plants with a plastic tarp.*

SIDING

PAINT PROBLEMS

Exterior paint ills can result from a number of causes. Daily exposure to the elements takes a toll on painted surfaces. Other factors—including poor surface preparation, incompatible paints, or sloppy application—can hasten decay. Depending on the symptoms, surfaces may need to be stripped bare or may require no more than a light sanding or scraping.

inter-coat peeling

INTER-COAT PEELING Applying latex finish coats over surfaces previously painted with gloss alkyd often results in poor adhesion. To treat, sand off the latex paint, prime the surface with an alkyd or alcohol-based primer, and then apply latex finish coats. Some top-of-the-line acrylic paints can be applied over old alkyd paint without primer, but thorough sanding is required first to give the surface some bite.

CHALKING Chalking is the normal breakdown of a paint finish after long exposure to sunlight. To treat, wash off the loose, powdery material and repaint.

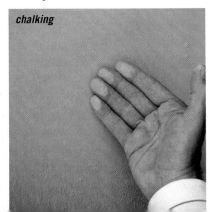

chalking

wrinkling

WRINKLING Wrinkling results when one coat of paint is applied over another that is not thoroughly dry or when a coat is applied too heavily. To treat, allow the paint to dry thoroughly, sand off the wrinkles, and repaint.

ALLIGATORING Alligatoring can result from a hard finish coat applied over a soft primer or from the loss of flexibility in thick layers

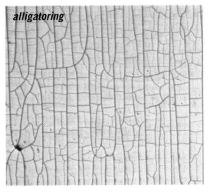

alligatoring

of paint on wood surfaces. To treat, scrape and sand off all the old paint and then repaint the area with a primer and two finish coats.

MULTIPLE-COAT PEELING Structures that have been painted over many times, especially those finished with oil-based paints, sometimes will show paint failure down to the

bare wood. This happens when the paint layers become brittle and then crack as the wood below expands and contracts with temperature changes. These cracks allow moisture to enter and cause peeling. To treat, strip the surface down to bare wood and prepare the area as you would new wood before you repaint.

multiple-coat peeling

BLISTERING Blistering can be caused by moisture invading the subsurface of paint because there is no vapor barrier behind the siding or because of cracked boards or poor caulking. Blistering also results when oil-based paints are applied in hot weather, which can trap solvents. In any of these cases, scrape and sand the blistered paint and seal any sources of moisture. Then repaint in cooler weather.

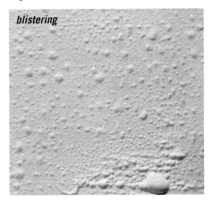

blistering

⌁ AMERISPEC® TIP | **RUSTY NAIL HEADS**

If you have nails that show or even drip rust stains, spray or dab them with a rusty-metal primer, then standard primer, before applying the finish coat.

COMMON WOOD SIDINGS

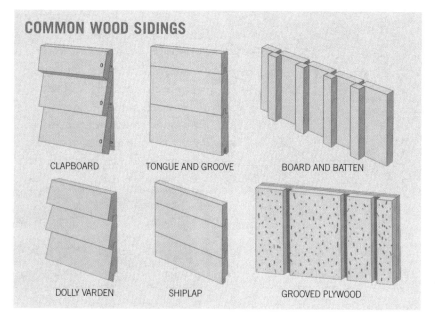

CLAPBOARD

TONGUE AND GROOVE

BOARD AND BATTEN

DOLLY VARDEN

SHIPLAP

GROOVED PLYWOOD

wood siding

With annual upkeep, wood siding should last as long as the house. To prevent deterioration, repair simple surface problems—holes in the wood, split or warped boards, and damaged paint—as soon as they appear. Severely damaged siding will need to be replaced.

Be sure to determine the cause of any serious damage before replacing siding. If moisture is the culprit, find the source by checking for deteriorating roofing (page 120), leaking gutters or downspouts, and poor drainage. Consult a professional if you can't locate the source. If after removing damaged siding you see evidence of dry rot or insect infestation, call in a professional.

REPAIRING HOLES Small holes in board siding can be filled with exterior-grade wood putty. To conceal a small hole, fill it with putty and allow it to dry completely. If the hole is deeper than ⅜ inch, mix and apply two-part epoxy wood filler or auto body filler. When the final layer is dry, sand the surface smooth. Then prime and paint or apply another finish.

REPAIRING WARPED BOARDS Warped or buckled boards usually show up where they have been fitted too tightly during installation. If a board has nowhere to expand when it swells with moisture, it warps or buckles.

To straighten a warped or buckled board, try to pull it into line by drilling angled pilot holes and driving long screws through it and into the wall studs. Cover the screw holes with wood putty.

If that doesn't work, you'll have to shorten the board to give it more room. Pull out the nails within the warped area. Continue removing nails to the nearest end of the board. Pull the end outward, then carefully file or cut it to fit. Renail the board.

AMERISPEC® TIP | A ROTTING BOTTOM ROW

If the bottom row of siding is rotting, chances are it is too close to the ground. Dig away soil or sod so it is at least 8 inches below the siding at all points. If the siding is rotten only in spots, apply wood hardener, then primer, and cover with two coats of paint. If the siding is very rotten at the bottom only, you may be able to cut a straight horizontal line to remove the rot. Otherwise, you will need to replace the bottom boards.

Repairing a split board

1 Carefully pry the damaged board apart at the crack and liberally coat the two split edges with exterior glue.

2 Push the edges tightly together, drill pilot holes, and drive nails or screws into the sheathing.

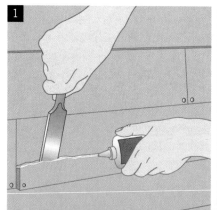

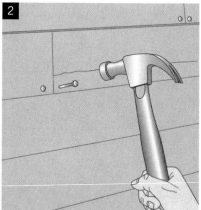

REPLACING DAMAGED BOARDS, SHINGLES, AND SHAKES

Sometimes a board is so badly damaged that you must replace it. A damaged shingle or shake should also be replaced.

The approach to replacing board siding depends on the milling of the boards (common types are shown on the opposite page) and how they're nailed. Often the trickiest part of the job is finding a replacement that matches the original.

No matter what type of siding you're replacing, you'll have to cut the damaged piece and remove the nails in order to pry it out. Pull nails with a nail puller, or cut off nail heads with a hacksaw blade. Repair any damage to the building paper with roofing cement, then cut the new piece of siding so it will fit snugly but not too tightly. For best results, cut out and replace a section that spans at least three studs.

TONGUE-AND-GROOVE SIDING
Because the boards are locked together, the damaged piece must be split lengthwise and cut at the ends (as shown on page 110) before it can be removed. It's easiest to make the cuts with a circular saw. Set the blade depth just shy of the thickness of the siding. Finish the cuts using a hammer and chisel.

OVERLAPPING SIDINGS
Clapboard, Dolly Varden, shiplap, and other lap styles are face-nailed to studs or sheathing. Though the boards overlap, you can replace a damaged piece without removing the surrounding boards. You may need to pry up the board above the one you're replacing to free the last pieces of damaged board. To replace all types of lap siding, follow the directions shown at right.

To provide a solid nailing base for the replacement board, try to center the end cuts over studs. You can use a backsaw to cut clapboard, bevel, and Dolly Varden siding. Make the cuts with a circular saw, as described for tongue-and-groove siding on page 110. If nails are in the way of your saw cuts, pull them out.

BOARD-AND-BATTEN SIDING
To remove board-and-batten siding, pry up the battens on each side of the damaged board far enough to raise the nail heads. Then pull out the nails. Repeat this process until you can remove the damaged board.

SHINGLES AND SHAKES
When a shingle or shake splits, curls, warps, or breaks, you'll have to replace it. The technique depends on whether the shingles or shakes are applied in single or double courses.

In a single-course application, each row overlaps the one below by at least half a shingle or shake length. The nails are concealed under the shingles or shakes of the course above. Replacement procedures are the same as for a shingle or shake roof (see pages 124–125).

Double-coursing calls for two layers of shingles or shakes. Here, the nail heads are exposed. To replace a damaged shingle or shake, simply pull out the nails, remove the damaged piece, slide in a replacement, and nail it.

Patch any cuts or tears in the building paper with roofing cement. Replace the damaged board and batten with identically sized new ones. Seal all joints with caulking compound, then stain or paint.

Replacing lap siding

1 Mark for cuts at each end of the damaged section. Drive shims up under the board directly above the damaged one on each side of the two marked lines. Using a keyhole saw, make straight cuts across both ends of the damaged board.

2 Use a small hacksaw to cut off any nails holding the damaged piece in place. Alternatively, you can split the damaged section with a chisel, pull out the pieces, and then pry out the nails. Repair any tears in the building paper with roofing cement.

3 Cut the replacement piece to fit and tap it into place with a hammer and a scrap of wood. Nail the new piece through the existing nail holes and along the bottom edge. Fill the nail holes and the board ends with wood filler. Then sand and paint it.

WOOD-BORING INSECTS

To detect damage by termites and other wood-eating insects, probe the edges of wood siding with a knife and look for soft, spongy spots. Pay special attention to any part of the siding that's close to or in contact with the ground.

In a primary infestation, the insects and their reproductive queen live in the ground near the house and make round trips into the walls to get food. In this case, the solution is to poison the colony and then make it difficult for future colonies to get into your house. In a secondary infestation, a smaller colony lives inside the wood. Here the solution is simply to destroy the bugs where they live.

Check for visible evidence of termites. Look for their translucent ½-inch-long wings or the mud tubes they sometimes build, which are usually visible from under the house. If you find evidence of dry rot or termites, consult a licensed termite inspector or pest control professional.

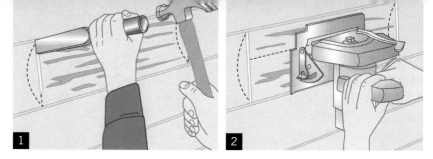

Replacing tongue-and-groove siding

1 Pull out all exposed nails in the area to be repaired. Mark the end cut lines, then cut with a circular saw almost to the bottom and top of each mark. Finish the cuts with a hammer and chisel.

2 Adjust a circular saw to cut just through the depth of the siding, then cut along the center of the damaged section, almost to the end cuts. Complete the cuts at both ends with a hammer and chisel.

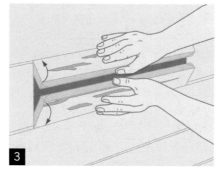

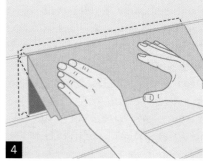

3 Cave in the board, then pull out the loosened pieces. If you find any cuts or tears in the building paper, repair them with roofing cement.

4 Remove the back side of the groove in the replacement board. Slide the board into place, drill pilot holes, and face-nail it. Fill the nail holes and ends, then finish.

Replacing a siding shingle

1 Pry out the shingle above slightly, insert a small hacksaw or a hacksaw blade (or a reciprocating saw), and cut away any nails that are holding the damaged shingle.

2 Use a hammer and chisel to split the shingle in two or three places. Pull the pieces out and repair any damaged building paper with roofing cement.

3 Cut a new shingle ¼ inch narrower than the opening. Slide it up until it is ½ inch too low, then drive nails just below the shingle above at a 45-degree angle.

4 Tap the shingle up into alignment using a scrap of lumber to protect it from damage. The nails will straighten when you do this.

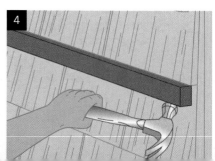

aluminum and vinyl siding

Aluminum and vinyl siding panels have interlocking flanges along both edges. The panels are nailed to the sheathing through slots along one flange, and the other flange interlocks with the adjacent panel.

REPAIRING ALUMINUM SIDING To remove a dent, drive a screw into its center. Gently pull on the screw head with a pair of pliers. Remove the screw and fill the hole with auto body filler. When the filler is dry, sand it smooth and touch it up with matching paint.

Conceal scratches in aluminum siding with metal primer. When it is dry, coat it with acrylic house paint.

Clean corroded areas with fine steel wool. Then treat the area with rust-resistant metal primer made specifically for aluminum, and cover it with acrylic house paint.

If a section is damaged beyond a simple surface repair, replace it as shown below.

REPAIRING VINYL SIDING If vinyl siding is cracked or punctured, you must remove the entire damaged section and install a replacement. To do this, use a special "zipper" tool to separate the interlocked panels. Work during warm weather, when the vinyl is pliable.

Using the zipper tool, unlock the panel adjacent to or above the damaged one and lift it up to expose the nails securing the damaged panel. Pry out the nails. Mark cutting lines on each side of the damaged area

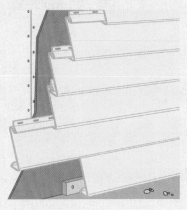

TYPICAL ALUMINUM OR VINYL SIDING

using a carpenter's square and a pencil. With tin snips or a backsaw, cut the panel along the lines and remove the damaged section.

Cut a replacement piece 2 inches longer than the section you just removed. (Cut the piece only 1 inch longer if the damaged section ends at a corner or joint.) Snap the top edge of the new section into place and nail it with aluminum box nails long enough to penetrate 1 inch into the studs. Using the zipper, snap in the other edge.

➤ AMERISPEC® TIP   REATTACHING VINYL SIDING

Sometimes vinyl siding just comes loose and the pieces disengage from each other. Shoehorn a zipper tool up under a popped-out section and slide it along as you push down, snapping the siding back into place.

Replacing a damaged section of aluminum or vinyl siding

1 Use a utility knife or tin snips to cut through the center of the panel to just beyond both sides of the damaged area. Make vertical cuts on both ends and then remove the lower half of the damaged section.

2 Cut the nailing strip off the replacement with a utility knife. The new piece should be 6 inches longer than the damaged section, or 3 inches longer if one end is at a joint or corner.

3 Generously apply polyurethane caulk or lap seal to the damaged panel. Press the new piece into place so that each end overlaps the existing siding by 3 inches. Hold or prop it there until the sealant is dry.

stucco siding

Stucco walls typically consist of three layers applied over spacers and wire mesh or wood lath. The final coat is either pigmented or painted, and it can be textured in a variety of ways.

Settling and poorly applied or poor-quality stucco can cause cracks and holes in stucco. To protect the house from moisture damage, repair damaged stucco right away.

The two keys to a successful repair job are slow curing of the patched stucco and careful matching of the color and texture of the patch to the existing wall.

CRACKS To fix large cracks, use a cold chisel and hammer to undercut the edges of the crack using the same technique as for interior plastered walls (see pages 18–19). Brush away loose stucco, then apply a liquid concrete bonding agent.

With a mason's trowel or putty knife, fill the crack with stucco patching compound and pack it tightly. Use a trowel or brush to approximate the surrounding texture. Cure the stucco by keeping it damp for about four days.

SMALL HOLES To repair a hole up to about 6 inches wide, use a hammer and chisel to remove loose stucco, and brush out any dust. If the wire mesh or wood lath is damaged, staple in a new piece of mesh. Dampen the area with a fine spray of water, pack the hole with stucco patching compound, and finish to match the surrounding area. To cure, keep damp for about four days.

LARGE HOLES Holes larger than 6 inches wide should be repaired with two or three coats of stucco—a scratch coat, perhaps a brown coat, and then a finish coat.

For the first and second coats, add ⅒ part lime to stucco mix for easier working. Mix with enough water to make a fairly stiff paste. For the final coat, purchase a stucco mix in the desired color (unless you will paint).

Prepare the surface as you would for a small hole. Apply liquid concrete bonding agent to the edges. Be sure to press the first coat well into the mesh for a good bond. When this coat is firm, scratch it all over with a nail to provide grip for the second coat. Tape a plastic

sheet over it to keep it damp and let it cure for two days. If needed to achieve the desired thickness, apply a second coat in the same way.

The final textured coat should be flush with the surrounding wall. Texture it to match while it's wet. To cure stucco, cover it with a plastic sheet and keep it damp for about four days. Wait a month before painting it.

Patching a medium-sized hole in stucco

1 Remove loose stucco from the damaged area with a cold chisel and hammer. Brush away dust, and dampen the area.

2 Mix stucco patch according to the label directions and apply it with a trowel. Press the patch into the wall as you smooth it.

3 Before the stucco sets up, use a whisk broom to match the wall's texture. If the wall is smooth, use a trowel.

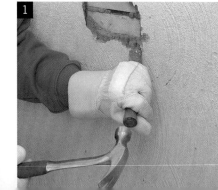

exterior caulking

Exterior caulk prevents water from penetrating. It will eventually dry out and need to be replaced, so check for cracked, loose, or missing caulking as part of your spring and fall maintenance inspections.

TYPES OF CAULK For most jobs, use latex-silicone or acrylic-silicone caulk—not cheap latex-only caulk, which will soon shrink and become brittle. Pure silicone caulk is more flexible and washable, but some versions come loose. A high-quality type that may be labeled "Silicone II" will likely stick well and last a

long time. If you plan to paint, be sure the caulk is paintable. Butyl and polyurethane caulks are very flexible, sticky, and durable, making them good choices for areas that will often get wet. However, they are difficult to work with. For gaps wider than ⅜ inch, use aerosol foam.

WHERE TO CAULK Generally, apply caulk to joints where different surfaces meet. For example:
■ Where one flashing meets another on the roof; between flashing and a roof or dormer surface; and where a chimney, flue, plumbing or electrical

pipe, attic fan, or skylight protrudes through the roof surface.
■ On siding where panels and trim meet at corners; around window and door frames; between badly fitting pieces of siding; where pipes and other protrusions pass through the siding; and where the siding meets the foundation, patio, or deck.

APPLYING CAULK Dig out the old caulk with a putty knife, a screwdriver, or a scraper. Use a wire brush to remove debris. Then wipe the surface with a cloth soaked with water or mineral spirits. Caulk on a warm, dry day when the temperature is between 50 and 80 degrees.

It will take practice to lay down a smooth, even bead of caulk. Gently press the nozzle of the caulking gun against the joint, pull the trigger until the caulk emerges, and slide the nozzle smoothly along, squeezing the trigger to keep the caulk flowing. Make sure the compound fills the crack completely and adheres to the surface on each side.

⅂ AMERISPEC® TIP | REPAIRING A CRACK IN STUCCO

Narrow cracks in masonry can be repaired with stucco caulk. Clean the area around the crack with a wire brush and then apply the stucco caulk according to the label directions. After the compound cures, the area can be finished with latex paint to match the wall.

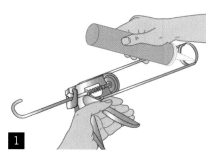

1

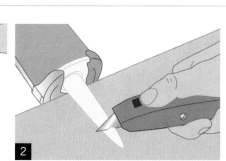

2

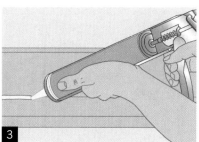

3

Using a caulk gun

1 To load the gun, pull the plunger all the way out. For the type of gun shown, insert the caulk tube top end first. For other types, insert the bottom end first. Push the plunger until it stops, then give one gentle squeeze of the trigger.

2 Use a utility knife to cut the nozzle. Some people prefer it at a 45-degree angle, while others prefer it nearly perpendicular. The closer to the tip you cut, the narrower the bead. With some tubes, you need to break a seal by poking it with a nail or coat hanger.

3 Holding the gun so the tip rests flat against the joint, squeeze the trigger until caulk starts to emerge, then slowly pull the gun along the joint as you continue to squeeze the trigger. After laying the bead, you may choose to wipe it smooth with your finger or a damp cloth.

brick veneer

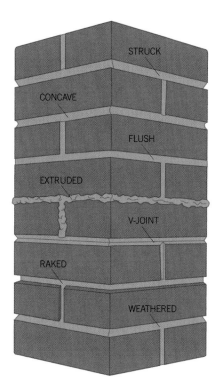

TYPES OF MORTAR JOINTS

(labels: STRUCK, CONCAVE, FLUSH, EXTRUDED, V-JOINT, RAKED, WEATHERED)

Brick-veneer siding is usually applied to a wood-frame wall over building paper. The mortared joints may be tooled, or finished, in a number of ways, as shown at left. Properly tooled joints are essential for strong, watertight walls.

REPOINTING Most problems develop at the mortar joints. Sometimes the mortar shrinks, causing the joints to open, and old lime-based mortar often crumbles. Freeze-thaw cycles in cold-winter climates, excess moisture, and settling also result in mortar problems. To repair cracked or crumbling mortar, you'll have to remove the old mortar and repoint the joints, as shown below.

Repointing a small area is not difficult, but if you have a large area to cover, consider hiring a pro, who can work quickly and neatly.

mortar samples

Repointing a brick wall

1 Grind while exerting moderate pressure. Work carefully, as a slip could cause you to damage a brick.

2 Use a raking tool, as shown, or a hammer and chisel to finish cleaning out the mortar.

3 The hand raking tool shown has a built-in depth gauge. Check that you have removed at least ½ inch at all points.

4 Mix a batch of mortar just stiff enough to stick to an upside-down trowel. Load a dollop of mortar onto a large trowel, press it against the wall, and push the mortar firmly into the joints with a repointing tool. Push more mortar into the joint than you'd like for the final result. Apply mortar to the horizontal joints first, then scoop more onto the tool and apply it to the verticals.

5 If the surrounding mortar joints are neatly tooled, smooth the joints using a striking tool (as shown below). If they bulge outward slightly, brush the new mortar to match.

Test to see that you have the right mortar color before you start. A masonry supply source will have samples (see opposite page) that you can compare with the existing mortar.

You can chip away mortar using only a chisel, but a grinder equipped with a masonry blade greatly eases the job. Wear long clothing, gloves, and protective eyewear.

REPLACING A BRICK If a brick has cracked or crumbled, use a grinder to cut away the joints as shown below and chip it out using a hammer and chisel. Clean out all the old mortar. Mix a small batch of color-matched mortar. Dampen the replacement brick and the opening. Apply a thick bed of mortar to the bottom of the opening and to the top and ends of the replacement brick. Holding the brick on a trowel, slip it straight into the opening. Scrape away excess mortar and tool the joints.

CHECK FOR MORE DAMAGE

If a fascia board is rotted, there is a good chance that the rafter ends are rotted as well. If a rafter end is only slightly rotten, you can apply wood hardener. If the rot is more extensive, you may be able to cut back all the rafters to the same length to reach solid wood. Otherwise, call in a carpenter or roofer.

If there is a horizontal board under the eave, also check it for rot. Gently lift up shingles to see if the roof sheathing is rotted as well. An under-eave board can usually be easily removed and used as a template for a replacement board. Replacing roof sheathing is more complicated; call in a roofer.

repairing fascia

Fascia boards take the brunt of harsh weather and often become damaged or badly worn. Repairs are relatively easy on a low single-story house if you are comfortable being on a ladder and have basic woodworking skills. If your home does not have eaves that are easy to work on, you will be better off hiring a professional.

You can repair small holes and areas of rot by chipping away loose material, applying wood hardener, and filling them with two-part epoxy wood putty.

Replacing a fascia board

1 Use a flat pry bar to pull the entire damaged fascia board loose from the eaves. Wear safety glasses and exercise extreme caution when working at the top of the ladder. After prying off the piece, cut the end of the existing fascia with a saw blade set at a 45-degree angle.

2 Use a circular saw set for a 45-degree angle to cut the replacement piece so it will join with the existing fascia. Use a square to mark the cutting line for the replacement piece and to guide the saw. It is important to make a straight cut that is perfectly perpendicular to the board.

3 Be sure the bottom edge of the new piece is in exact alignment with the rest of the fascia. If necessary, pull a string line across the bottom of the fascia and the board you are installing to check alignment. You may need to pull nails and adjust the angle of the existing fascia board.

4 Hold the piece in place and nail through the mitered ends and into the rafter ends with 8d (2½-inch) galvanized nails. For nails near the end of a board, drill pilot holes first. Caulk the joints before painting to match the existing fascia. Consider repainting the entire fascia for a better match.

preparing and painting siding and trim

Start prepping siding and trim by scrubbing. In many cases, simply washing the surface to be painted is not enough. Paint that has begun to fail must usually be completely removed to ensure that the new coat will adhere properly. For solutions to specific paint problems, see page 107. Prep work is tedious and time-consuming, but the reward is a great-looking, durable finish.

SCRAPING For scraping small areas of peeling paint, a paint scraper or putty knife is sufficient. To make sure you get all the loose material, scrape in all directions. Place two hands on the scraper and keep it flat to avoid gouging the wood.

POWER SANDING Power sanders can be used to smooth the edges of scraped areas or to clear an entire surface of paint. For big jobs, a

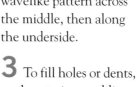

> **⚡ AMERISPEC® TIP ▏ FIXING MISTAKES**
>
> If you create gouges, fill them with a vinyl exterior spackling compound so they will not show through the new paint. If the paint that remains after scraping has high or rough edges, sand with coarse sandpaper to make them less noticeable.

commercial-grade 7-inch sander works best. You can buy one or rent one. Sand first with 60-grit paper, then use 100-grit.

Power sanding is a meticulous process that requires concentration. Make sure the sander is running at full speed before you touch the wheel to the surface. As you bring the sander into contact with the wall, lean on the tool slightly until you hear the motor slow. Keep moving it along the surface so you do not gouge the wood. Maintain the sanding wheel at a slight angle (5 to 10 degrees) to the wall. Otherwise, the wheel will spin out of control across the surface. Discard sanding disks as

they become clogged with paint so they will not burn the surface.

ALTERNATIVES TO SANDING Use liquid paint remover when stripping paint from ornate woodwork or hard-to-reach recesses. In especially difficult areas, try a heat gun. See page 25 for tips on these techniques.

PRIME Primer seals the surface and provides a base to which the paint can adhere. Slow-drying alkyd-based primers are your best bet. On partially bare wood, apply two coats of primer. To improve coverage, have your primer tinted with some of the finish color.

Preparing siding for paint

1 Begin by hosing down the siding, then scrub it with a stiff-bristle brush mounted on a pole. Clean the area with a solution of water and trisodium phosphate (TSP) or a nonphosphate substitute, following label directions. This solution is caustic, so do not use it on bare wood.

Also wear rubber gloves and safety goggles.

2 Scrape loose paint and, if necessary, use a power sander to remove large areas of paint or to smooth any roughly scraped surfaces. When using a sander, work in 3-foot sections. Move

horizontally across the top of a board, then in a wavelike pattern across the middle, then along the underside.

3 To fill holes or dents, apply exterior spackling with a putty knife or 6-inch taping knife. Use a matching wood-toned

filler if you intend to apply a semitransparent stain.

4 After the spackle has dried, use a sanding block or a vibrating sander with 100-grit sandpaper to sand each patch until it is smooth. Sweep away any residual dust or scrapings.

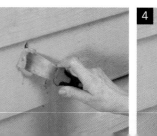

SIDING

Stripping and prepping a window

1 Remove paint from flat surfaces using a power sander. For other surfaces, blister the paint with a heat gun, then peel it away with a putty knife.

2 Use a hammer and chisel or an old screwdriver to tap out old window glazing compound that is cracked or brittle. Take care not to tap the glass.

3 Once most of the paint has been removed, power-sand the window-sills with a palm sander, graduating from rough to fine paper.

4 Fill cracks and holes with a vinyl exterior spackle and sand the surface when it is dry. Fill gaps in the glazing (see page 54).

PROTECT Before you paint, protect the area with thick cotton drop cloths or plastic sheeting. Use 3-inch tape to protect roofing or other surfaces from paint spatters.

PAINT For best results, paint in fair, dry weather above 50 degrees. Lower temperatures may cause poor adhesion. Apply paint after morning dew dries, and stop at least two hours before evening dampness arrives. Avoid painting in direct sunlight. If possible, follow the sun around the house. Do not apply oil- or alkyd-based paints to cool surfaces that will be heated by the sun in a few hours, as this may cause the paint to blister.

For best results, first brush on a coat of primer and let dry. Apply the finish coat with a high-quality brush. First paint the overhangs and gutters, then the main surfaces from the top down. Wait until the siding has dried completely, then paint the trim, shutters, railings, porch, and foundation. Apply masking tape to protect the siding from the trim paint and remove the tape immediately after finishing.

Painting a house's exterior

1 On lap siding, first brush the bottom edges of horizontal boards. Dip the brush no more than 1 inch into the paint. To prevent drips and lap marks, paint all the way across three or four boards.

2 To paint the face of the siding, dip the brush about 2 inches into the paint and tap it against the side of the bucket to clear paint from one side. Turn the brush parallel to the ground as you lift it. Quickly press the paint-heavy side of the brush against the siding, spreading the paint in a side-to-side motion on horizontal siding or up and down on vertical siding.

3 When painting windows, draw a lightly loaded tapered sash brush along mullions, allowing a slight bead of paint to lap onto the glass. This bead will help seal the window. To remove paint before it dries, use a rag wrapped around the end of a putty knife. You can remove dry paint with a razor blade.

4 To ensure good coverage on the face of the trim, first paint against the grain, then run the brush with the grain. When painting the sash of an operable window, open and close it several times so that it won't be sealed shut by paint.

5 Protect the abutting siding with painter's tape. First paint against the wood grain, then create an even surface by brushing with the grain. Turn the brush diagonally to the trim if it is wider than the trim. Or apply paint with a short trim roller and work it in with a brush, painting with the grain.

roofing

Knowing how your roof is constructed is the first step toward diagnosing problems. On page 120, you'll find a guide for inspecting your roof from the inside and outside. If you find problems, see pages 122–129 for the most common homeowner-friendly repairs.

UNDERSTANDING ROOF STRUCTURE

A roof protects a home and the people inside from the elements, especially water and sun. Roofs are designed to shed water and direct it away from the house.

A typical roof is supported by a framework of 2-by-4 rafters, a ridge board at the peak, and often hip rafters as well. Many newer roofs are made with trusses and other types of engineered framing, which combine smaller-dimensioned lumber and even plywood with special fasteners to create a structure that is straight and strong. Special pieces of framing hardware, such as H-ties and H-clips (sometimes generally called hurricane ties), add extra strength to critical junctures, such as where the rafters or trusses attach to the house's walls. They are required in many locales, especially where there is a fear of earthquakes or high winds.

CAUTION *Working on a roof is dangerous, so take special precautions (see page 121). Tile and slate roofs are especially slippery, and the materials break easily. Metal and plastic roofs are also slick. If your roof is slippery, icy, or wet, or if it is severely sloped, leave inspection and repairs to a professional.*

⚡ AMERISPEC® TIP **ROOF INSPECTIONS**

Most homeowners wait until something drastic happens to the roof, at which point they have to take immediate action. With periodic inspections, you can spot and correct minor problems before they become serious enough to cause damage.

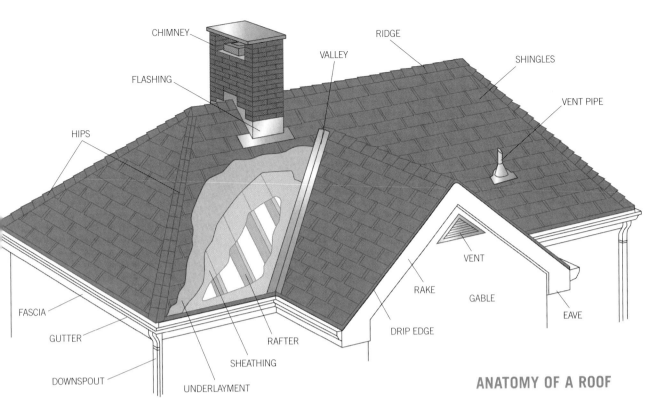

CHIMNEY   FLASHING   HIPS   VALLEY   RIDGE   SHINGLES   VENT PIPE   VENT   RAKE   GABLE   EAVE   DRIP EDGE   RAFTER   SHEATHING   UNDERLAYMENT   DOWNSPOUT   GUTTER   FASCIA

ANATOMY OF A ROOF

Sheathing is attached to the framing, and an underlayment is laid on the sheathing. Strips of metal called flashing are attached at the edges, along inside corners, and where the roof meets a vertical surface such as a chimney. The finish roofing material is nailed on top of the underlayment.

ROOF DECK Sheathing, the material that provides the nailing base for the roof surface material, is often made of plywood or oriented strand board (OSB). A prewar home may have sheathing made of 1-by-2 boards nailed closely together. If the roofing is wood shakes or shingles, the sheathing is likely a solid deck, but in some older homes it may be made of 1-by-2 boards with spaces between them.

Sandwiched between the sheathing and the surface material is the underlayment, usually roofing felt (tar paper), which resists water penetration yet allows moisture from inside the attic to escape.

ROOF SURFACE Sloping roofs are usually covered with overlapping layers of asphalt shingles or wood shakes. Less common roofing materials include clay tile (or imitation clay tile), slate, aluminum, and galvanized steel.

Flat or low-sloping roofs are often surfaced with alternating layers of roofing felt and asphalt or tar, sometimes with a layer of gravel on top. These are known as built-up roofs. Some flat roofs are covered with insulating polyurethane foam topped with a modified-bitumen membrane (often called rubber roofing).

FLASHING Flashing appears as the drip edge along the eaves of a roof, the collars around ventilation and plumbing pipes, the valleys between two roof planes, and the steps along a chimney. Less obvious flashing also protects other breaks in the roof, such as skylights.

At roof edges, gutters catch water runoff and channel it to the ground via downspouts, which direct water away from the house and into the soil.

inspecting a roof

Inspect and repair your roof in fall, before hard weather hits. Then check it in spring for any winter damage.

INSPECTING FROM INSIDE Begin in the attic using a strong flashlight, a thin screwdriver, a knife, and a piece of chalk. Examine the ridge beam, rafters, and sheathing. Look for water stains, dark-colored areas of wet wood, moisture, and soft spots that may indicate dry rot. If you see mold or mildew, the attic is not properly ventilated; call in a roofer or carpenter. Mark the wet spots with chalk so you can find them easily later on.

Turn off any lights. If you see sunlight coming through holes, drive nails or poke wire through them so they'll be visible from the roof's surface. (On a wood shingle roof, light coming in at an angle indicates cracks that may shut when the shingles are wet.)

INSPECTING FROM OUTSIDE To check the structure, stand back from the house and look at the lines of the ridge and rafters. They should be reasonably straight along the plane of each roof section. If either sags significantly, your house may have a structural problem. Call in a professional roofer or carpenter for an assessment.

Next, inspect the surface. Before climbing up on your roof, read the safety tips on the next page. If you're at all nervous, make the inspection from a ladder using a pair of binoculars. Don't walk on the roof any more than is absolutely necessary, as you may damage it.

Inspect the flashings for corrosion and broken seals along the edges. If you have metal gutters and downspouts, look for rust spots and holes. Then examine the roof surface for signs of wear, loose or broken nails, or curled, broken, or missing shingles.

Poke with a screwdriver to test the boards along the eaves and rakes. If the screwdriver sinks in easily, indicating rot, replace the boards and finish them to match the existing areas (see page 115 for fascia repairs).

LOCATING A LEAK

Roof leaks usually appear during storms, when you can't make permanent repairs. But you can discover the source of the leak.

Generally, leaks begin at a roof's most vulnerable spots: at flashings, where shingles are damaged, in valleys, or at eaves. The water may show up far from its point of origin after seeping through layers of roofing and down rafters to collect in a puddle where you can see it.

During a storm, trace the course of water to find where it's coming through the roof. Drive a nail or wire through the hole so you can find the hole later when you get up on the roof.

Once the roof is dry enough, look for spots that indicate a source of the leak. Remember, the point where a nail or wire is poking through may be below the actual source. Make permanent repairs as described on the following pages.

If asphalt shingles or roll roofing sheets are generally losing their granular surface, cracking at corners, or curling, you may need new roofing. See page 124 for more information.

GENERAL MAINTENANCE

Cut tree limbs back so they cannot cause damage. If leaves collect on your roof, sweep or hose them away.

To combat moss, mildew, or fungus, prune trees so the roof can receive sunlight. If that does not solve the problem, nail a strip of zinc near the ridge. When it rains, zinc will leach out and kill the moss, mildew, or fungus. When replacing shingles on a roof that is often moist and shaded, purchase zinc-impregnated shingles, which solve the problem.

On a wood shake roof, use a pump sprayer to apply preservative once or twice a year to prevent the wood from drying and cracking.

MINIMIZING DAMAGE FROM A LEAK

If you find a leak in the attic, drive a nail or poke a wire up into it to direct water into a bucket below. Similarly, if water is coming through a ceiling, poke a nail or an awl into the center of the leaking area so all the water flows into a bucket below.

AMERISPEC® TIP   **PROTECT YOUR SIDING**

The ends of a ladder can dent or scratch siding or bend gutters. Consider purchasing hold-off arms, which keep the ladder a few inches away from the house. You can also slip ladder boots onto the ladder ends.

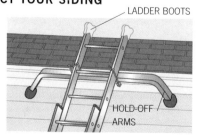

LADDER BOOTS

HOLD-OFF ARMS

working safely on the roof

Before climbing a ladder to repair roofing, siding, windows, or gutters, it's important that you know and observe the following safety precautions.

LADDER SAFETY

An extension ladder may be made of wood, aluminum, or fiberglass. Make sure all the rungs are in good shape. If the ladder sways alarmingly, do not use it. Here are some safety tips:

■ Place the base on firm, level ground at a measured distance from the side of the house.

■ Get on and off the ladder by stepping onto the center of the rung. Use both hands to grip the ladder rails, not the rungs. Reposition the ladder if it wobbles.

■ Keep your hips between the ladder rails. Don't lean out to reach an area. Reposition the ladder instead.

■ Make sure that only one person stands on a ladder at a time.

■ Install rubber safety shoes (available at home improvement centers) on the ladder feet if the ladder is to stand on a slick surface.

■ Don't stand on the top two rungs. If you're repairing a roof, at least two rungs should extend above the eaves so you can step directly onto the roof.

■ Be sure that the rung hooks of an extension ladder are locked in place and that no section is extended more than three-quarters of its length.

■ Pull materials up a ladder with a rope and have a place to put them at the top. Do not try to carry them up.

ROOF SAFETY

Working on a roof requires extra caution. The surface is usually slick, sloped, and well above the ground. Below are some precautions to observe when you need to make roof repairs.

■ Don't walk on a roof any more than is absolutely necessary, as you

POSITIONING A LADDER

1 Set the base against the wall.
2 Walk the ladder into an upright position.
3 Lean it against the house and move the base outward.
4 Set the base at a distance from the wall equal to one-quarter the ladder's length.

may damage it. Don't walk on tile and slate roofs at all, as they are slippery and breakable.

■ Let a professional make any repairs on a steeply pitched roof—one that slopes more than 25 degrees or rises more than 4 inches vertically for every 12 horizontal inches.

■ Wear loose, comfortable clothing and nonslip rubber-soled shoes with good ankle support.

■ Work on the roof only in dry, calm, warm weather. A wet roof can be treacherously slick, and a sudden wind can knock you off balance.

■ Never work on the roof when lightning threatens.

■ Be careful not to put your weight on brittle or old roofing materials, or rotted decking.

■ Stay well away from power lines and be sure neither your body nor the equipment comes into contact with them. Keep children and pets away.

Special safety equipment

These standard safety devices, which can be rented, help distribute your weight evenly and provide secure footing. Check with your local building department for safety requirements while working on a roof.

■ An angled seat board lets you sit on a level surface while working.

■ A metal ladder bracket allows you to hook a ladder over the ridge.

■ A pair of roof jacks hold a 2-by-6 to provide a safe support. To install a jack, lift up a shingle, slip the jack under, and drive two nails. The jacks have notches in them so they can be slipped off the nails. When you're finished, set and caulk the nails to avoid leaks.

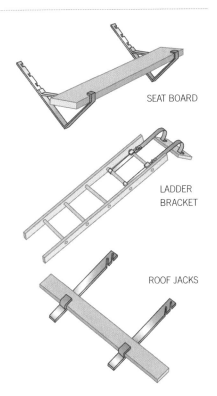

SEAT BOARD

LADDER BRACKET

ROOF JACKS

repairing flashing

Flashing protects the roof at its most vulnerable points: in the valleys, at roof and plumbing vents, around chimneys, along the eaves—anywhere water can seep through open joints into the sheathing.

Most flashing is made of a rust-resistant metal such as galvanized steel, aluminum, or copper, but flashing can also be made of roll roofing, roofing felt, or rubber. The flashing joints may be sealed with roofing cement or a special caulking compound. Cracked or crumbling roofing cement or caulking is often a major cause of leaks around flashing.

INSPECT FLASHING SEMIANNUALLY
Re-nail or replace loose nails, and cover all exposed nail heads with roofing cement. Look carefully for holes. You can plug pinholes with small spots of roofing cement. Patch larger holes with the same material as the damaged flashing, as shown at right. Old galvanized flashing that has developed a number of rusty spots should be replaced rather than patched. Check the all-important seals at the edges of the flashing, where it is attached to a vertical surface. If the roofing cement or caulking is cracked, dried, or crumbling, reseal the joints promptly.

TYPES OF FLASHING
■ Valleys require particularly sturdy flashing because they carry more water than any other individual roof plane. On most roofs, metal valley flashing is installed over a liner and under the underlayment and finish roofing material. On some asphalt shingle roofs, there

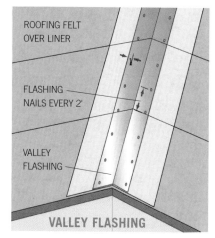

VALLEY FLASHING

ROOFING FELT OVER LINER

FLASHING NAILS EVERY 2'

VALLEY FLASHING

is no valley flashing; shingles span the valley instead.

■ Drip-edge flashing helps keep water from wicking back under the shingles. It is often installed at the top of a fascia board. Poor or damaged drip-edge flashing can lead to rotted sheathing, fascia boards, and even rafters. The flashing itself must be the right size and shape so water drips away from wood surfaces and does not seep under the shingles. In most cases, the flashing should be installed under the roofing felt. It should be shaped to resemble a "Z" in profile, so rainwater is directed away from the fascia.

■ Flashing around a chimney (see next page) can be complicated. Often there is a "cricket," made with two plywood triangles, to prevent water and snow from collecting behind the chimney. The cricket is topped with saddle and cap flashing. Step flashing pieces run along the side of the chimney,

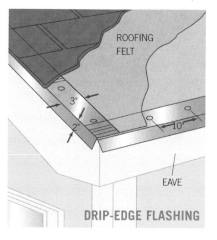

ROOFING FELT

3"

2"

10"

EAVE

DRIP-EDGE FLASHING

Patching a hole in flashing

1 Roughen the area around the hole with a wire brush or sandpaper, then clean the surface. Cut a patch of flashing material 2 inches larger than the hole on all sides.

2 Apply roofing cement, press the patch into place, and hold it for several minutes. Cover the patch with another generous layer of cement. If you find larger holes, seriously consider replacing the flashing.

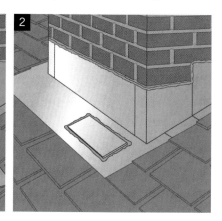

and the chimney front is sealed with base flashing.

■ Vent-pipe flashing is installed over the course of shingles directly below the pipe. The next courses of shingles will cover the flashing.

■ Skylights that are self-flashing have built-in flanges that sit on the roof deck. A skylight mounted on a wood frame attached to the deck requires flashing much like that for chimneys, installed around the frame.

■ Dormer flashing is similar to step flashing found on chimneys. It extends under the siding on the dormer and under the roof shingles at the base.

REPLACING FLASHING

Flashing must be installed in a precise manner or the roof will leak. Getting the flashing right is often tricky; even pros sometimes have trouble. If your roof leaks through a piece of flashing and the flashing is obviously damaged, replace it with a duplicate installed exactly like the old piece. If it leaks and you see no damage, or if you are not certain how to install a piece, call in a professional roofer.

Renewing flashing seals

CHIMNEY FLASHING Chip out old caulking along the cap flashing, then scour the area with a wire brush. Seal the joints between the flashing and chimney and between the cap and step flashing with roofing cement, which comes in a can or a caulk tube.

DORMER FLASHING First remove the old caulking and then apply new caulking to the joints between the flashing and siding or shingles, and between the flashing seams.

ALONG A VALLEY Seal shingles to valley flashing and to the courses below by lifting their edges along the flashing and spreading roofing cement beneath the shingles.

AROUND VENT-PIPE FLASHING Apply roofing cement to the joint between the flashing and the pipe. Lift the side and back shingles and apply roofing cement to the joints between the flange and shingles.

ALONG DRIP-EDGE FLASHING Lift the shingles and spread roofing cement on the top of the drip edge and the course below. Do not seal the drip edge along the eaves or against the fascia.

asphalt shingles

As shingles age, they can become brittle and crack, allowing water to penetrate. Some shingles can be repaired, but replacement is often necessary.

INSPECTING The first signs of aging are bald spots and a heavy accumulation of surface granules in the gutters. Check your roof's condition on a warm day, when the shingles should be flexible. Gently bend

SEALING A CRACK

Seal a small hole or crack with roofing cement, applying the substance with a putty knife or caulking gun. For tears or curls, liberally apply roofing cement under the pieces, press them down, and then secure them with roofing nails if necessary. Cover the nail heads with roofing cement.

several shingles back. If they appear gray and bloated, if the material crumbles easily, or if you see large bare spots or damaged areas, consider reroofing.

REPAIRS Cracked, torn, or curled shingles can often be repaired. If some shingles are badly worn or damaged, replace them using shingles that remain from the original roof installation, or buy shingles identical in brand, color, and size. Fasten the shingles with galvanized roofing nails that are long enough to penetrate all of the roofing layers and the sheathing.

Do not remove a damaged shingle that is on a ridge or along a hip. Instead, nail each corner of the shingle in place. Apply roofing cement to the bottom of a new shingle and set it on top of the defective one. Nail each corner and then cover the nail heads with roofing cement.

Repair asphalt shingles on a warm day, when the shingles are pliable. (On a cold day the shingles could crack, and on a hot day you could wear away the mineral coating.) Keep the roofing cement at room temperature.

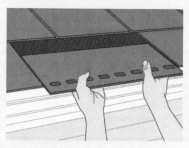

REPLACING A STARTER SHINGLE

A starter shingle runs along an eave, under a standard shingle. To make a starter shingle, use a knife or tin snips to cut off the tabs from a shingle. Apply a 3-inch-wide strip of roofing cement near the eave, then set in the starter shingle with the adhesive spots at the bottom. Drive four roofing nails about 3 inches from the eave. Install the replacement shingles on top of the starter shingle.

REROOFING Asphalt shingles generally last from 15 to 25 years, depending on the climate and type of shingle. If shingles are generally failing, call a roofer for assessment.

If the roof has only one or two layers, you probably have to pay only for adding a new layer. If you have three layers, you will need to pay much more for a "tear-off" job, in which all the old roofing is removed.

Replacing an asphalt shingle

1 To remove a damaged shingle, lift the shingle tab above it. With a flat pry bar, pull out both rows of nails holding the damaged shingle.

2 Slide the new shingle into place, taking care not to damage the roofing felt. If the corners stick, trim them with a knife or tin snips.

3 Nail on the new shingle. If you can't lift the tab above it enough to nail underneath, place a pry bar on the nail's head and a block, as shown, and strike the pry bar to drive in the nail.

wood shingles and shakes

Wood shingles are fairly smooth and ⅜ inch thick; shakes are rough-hewn and up to 1½ inches thick. Both are made of cedar in 18- or 24-inch lengths.

Shingles and shakes are laid in overlapping rows. Shingles are often installed on spaced sheathing and no roofing felt. Shakes are typically installed onto solid or spaced sheathing that has a continuous underlayment of roofing felt, plus strips of felt, called "interlayment," which overlap onto the upper portion of the shakes. Both are attached with galvanized shake nails.

Wood shingles and shakes should last from 15 and 25 years, depending on the slope of the roof and the climate. Inspect the roof for curled, broken, or split shingles and for any that have been lifted by wind. Also look for those that have thinned, especially around areas where an attic inspection reveals pinpoints of light (see page 120).

If only a few shingles or shakes are split or wind-lifted, you can repair them. But if the damage is extensive, consider having the entire roof replaced.

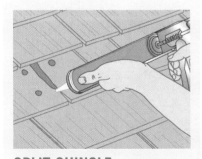

SPLIT SHINGLE

If a shingle is split, butt the pieces together, drill pilot holes, and drive nails in four places as shown. Cover the nail heads and the joint with roofing cement.

Replacing a wood shingle or shake

1 To remove a damaged wood shingle, use a hammer and chisel to split it apart along the grain and pull out the pieces. Be careful not to cut the roofing felt underneath. Cut the hidden nails as discussed below.

2 Hold the replacement shingle just below the spot where it will go, and mark its width. Then move your marks toward the center ¼ inch on each side (to allow for expansion caused by moisture) and cut.

3 Insert the replacement shingle so it protrudes 1 inch below adjoining shingles. Allow ¼ inch clearance on each side. Drive in two shake nails at an angle, as shown, just below the edge of the row above.

4 Drive the nails just flush. Do not sink the heads below the surface or the wood may split. Then nudge the edge of the new shingle even with the others using a hammer and woodblock as shown.

> **↗ AMERISPEC® TIP** | **REMOVING A HIDDEN NAIL**
>
> To remove the nails from a damaged shingle or shake that you are replacing, either rent a shingle ripper to cut them or use a hacksaw blade. To use the ripper, slide it under the shingle and around a nail (right). Then cut the shank of the nail by delivering a strong hammer blow to the ripper.
>
>

built-up roofs and roll roofing

An older built-up roof consists of several layers of roofing felt, each coated with hot- or cold-mopped asphalt. It may be topped with crushed gravel or rock. These roofs generally last from 10 to 20 years.

Newer modified-bitumen roofing, often called rubber, may be attached with a torch or may be laid in roofing cement. It can last 25 years or more.

Asphalt roll roofing is made of the same material as shingles, and has a lifetime of 5 to 15 years.

Leaks in a flat roof are usually easy to locate, as they tend to be directly above the wet area on the ceiling below. Leaks are also likely where weather and wear have caused blistered asphalt, separations between the roof surface and the drip edge, curling or splitting of exposed roofing felt, and cracks or holes in the roof material.

Repairs are the same for built-up and roll roofing. Fill cracks with roofing cement. Avoid using nails when repairing blisters and small holes as driving a series of nails may cause additional leaks.

Repairing a blister

1 Sweep away gravel and debris. Use a utility knife to slice through the blister. If water emerges, wait a day for it to dry. Use a putty knife or caulk gun to slip a generous amount of roofing cement well under.

2 Press the roofing into the cement. If needed, widen the slit so the roofing can lie flat. Apply roofing cement to the area, and lay a piece of fiberglass mesh in the cement.

3 Use a 6-inch taping knife to embed the mesh so there are no folds. Apply another layer of roofing cement over the mesh. Smooth the cement and feather the edges so water cannot puddle.

Patching a hole

1 Sweep away any gravel and debris. Use a straightedge and a utility knife to cut out a rectangle around the damaged area. Remove the piece and use it as a template for cutting a replacement.

2 Use a putty knife to smear roofing cement inside the cut-out rectangle. Also work cement several inches under all the cut edges. Set the replacement piece inside the rectangle and press it into place.

3 Cut another patch, 6 inches wider and longer. Apply roofing cement to the area, set the second patch on the cement, and apply yet another coat of roofing cement over the second patch. Feather the edges.

tile roof repairs

Tiles made of masonry or clay can last 50 years or more, but they can crack sooner if a branch falls on them. You may be able to handle small patches or replacements, but hire a professional roofer for major problems. A new masonry or clay tile roof is extremely expensive; newer imitation clay tiles reduce the cost and are actually more durable.

Patch small holes or cracks with asphalt roofing cement or butyl caulk, which may be available in a color that nearly matches. If a corner has cracked off, clean the area with a wire brush and glue the broken-off piece back on using butyl caulk or polyurethane glue. If the broken piece does not rest on another tile, support it with a dollop of roofing cement underneath.

The tiles that top a ridge or hip are often set in mortar, which is prone to cracking over time. If the crack is narrow and the tiles are still firmly embedded, seal the crack with roofing cement or a color-matched caulk. If the tiles are loose or the cracks are large, replace the mortar as shown above right.

If a crack extends above the overlap of the tile below, remove and replace the tile. Finding a replacement can be difficult. Be sure it is the same shape and attaches in the same way as the old tile.

To replace a tile laid directly on sheathing, gently pry up the tile or tiles in the course above and remove the old tile pieces. Spread roofing cement on the underside of the replacement tile and slide it into position.

Replacing mortar

1 Use a chisel and hammer to gently chip away the mortar until the ridge tiles break free. Set the tiles aside and chip away most of the remaining old mortar.

2 Mix a stiff batch of type N or S mortar and trowel it where the old mortar was. Soak the tiles in water, then set them in the mortar. Make sure all the joints are sealed.

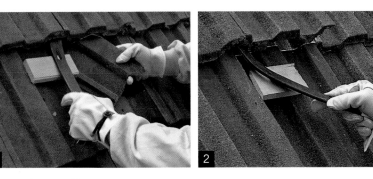

Replacing a tile

1 Pry up the concrete tile above the damaged one using a flat pry bar. Place a short woodblock beneath the pry bar for leverage and to protect the tile below. Pull out the broken pieces. If necessary, strike the tiles with a hammer to break them into smaller pieces. Wear safety glasses and gloves when doing this.

2 Repair any tears in the roofing paper underlayment with asphalt roofing cement. Lift the tiles in the course directly above the damaged tile's position using a pry bar, as shown. Spread roofing cement on the underside of the new tile and then slip the tile into place. Press the pieces firmly to embed the replacement tile in the cement.

☆ AMERISPEC® TIP **WORKING ON A TILE ROOF**

If tiles are brittle, walking on the roof can crack them. Whenever possible, work from a ladder leaning against the house rather than on the roof itself. If you must walk on a roof of tiles that are brittle, first place a large piece of plywood on top of the tiles and then stand or sit on the plywood.

gutters and downspouts

The gutter and downspout system carries the water away from the house. Most gutters and downspouts are made of galvanized steel, aluminum, or vinyl, though you may find some made of wood or copper.

Gutters are attached to the eaves of the house with strap, bracket, or, most commonly, spike-and-ferrule hangers. Downspouts are attached to the exterior walls with straps.

In order to work efficiently, gutters and downspouts must be in sound condition, must be sloped properly, and must be free of leaves and other debris.

GUTTER AND DOWNSPOUT MAINTENANCE Inspect the system in fall and spring. Clean out accumulated leaves and other debris. Check the slope of the gutters by running water through them. If drainage is slow, reposition for correct slope. Gutters should be tight against the fascias and should slope toward the downspouts at a rate of 1 inch for every 20 feet. Correct low spots by adjusting the hangers. For appearance, some gutters are hung level, so they need more downspouts.

Test for weaknesses in gutters, downspouts, and fascia boards by probing with a thin screwdriver or knife. Also look for flaking or peeling paint, rust spots, broken hangers, and holes or leaky joints.

REPAIRING GUTTERS AND DOWNSPOUTS If you find rotted fascia boards, repair them first (see page 115). Tighten loose hangers and replace broken ones. Check that downspout straps are secure and that elbow connections are tight.

KEEPING LEAVES OUT
A gutter screen (above) deflects leaves and twigs. A solid cover (below) allows rainwater but not leaves to enter the gutter. Check with a local roofer to find which product works best in your area.

Patch any leaking joints or holes, taking care to clean them thoroughly first. Pinholes can be sealed with a dab of roofing cement. To repair a larger hole, see below. If a whole section of your gutter system is badly damaged, call several gutter installers to find a good price and a good guarantee on a new system.

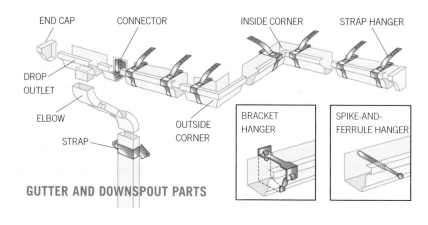

END CAP   CONNECTOR   INSIDE CORNER   STRAP HANGER

DROP OUTLET

ELBOW   OUTSIDE CORNER

STRAP

BRACKET HANGER   SPIKE-AND-FERRULE HANGER

GUTTER AND DOWNSPOUT PARTS

Repairing leaks

LEAKY JOINT Apply gutter or butyl caulk to seal the insides and outsides of seams between gutter sections.

HOLE Cover a hole with roofing cement and embed a sheet-metal patch or fiberglass mesh (see page 126) in the cement. Apply another coat of cement over the patch.

END CAP If a cap leaks or is loose, replace it. Apply gutter caulk to the groove and push it back into place. With some types, you also need to drive pop rivets (see next page).

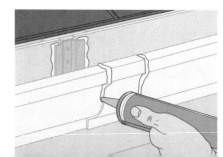

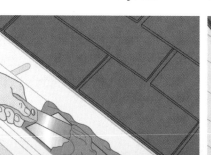

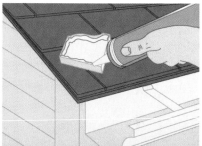

Supporting a gutter or downspout

SPIKE AND FERRULE If a sagging gutter is attached via a spike-and-ferrule system, hold the gutter sloped correctly and drive a new 7-inch screw or nail through an existing ferrule. Or drill a hole in the gutter's front lip and install a new ferrule and spike (above left).

BRACKET If the gutter hangs from brackets, purchase supplemental hangers. Hook a hanger onto the gutter's front lip and rear edge, hold the gutter sloped correctly, and drive a screw, if possible, into a rafter end as well as through the fascia (below left).

LOOSE DOWNSPOUT If a downspout is loose, fit a wall bracket around the elbow or the downspout and screw it into place (above right). Use galvanized screws long enough to penetrate solid wood by at least 1½ inches.

ATTACHING WITH POP RIVETS

Most metal gutter components are attached with pop rivets. You will need a pop rivet gun. Drill a hole of the required size, place a rivet in the gun, insert it, and squeeze the handle. Or fasten sections using sheet-metal screws.

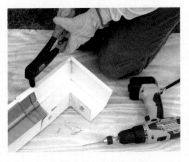

> **⌂ AMERISPEC® TIP | OTHER DRAINAGE OPTIONS**
>
> In some municipalities, a downspout can connect directly to the city's storm and sewage drainage system. Contact your local building department to find out how to do this. A downspout can also be attached to a flexible extender (see page 87). If you have an extreme drainage problem, run the downspout into a dry well—a hole in the ground at least 3 feet wide and deep that is filled with rocks or loose gravel.

EXTENDING DRAINAGE

To carry drainage from downspouts away from the house, extend them horizontally and add splash blocks at their bases. Water that is allowed to flow from the downspouts directly into the ground may end up in your crawl space or basement and can erode the soil along the house, causing settling.

Unclogging gutters and downspouts

1 Wearing gloves, remove leaves, twigs, and other debris from gutter troughs. Loosen dirt with a stiff brush. If the dirt is very hard, purchase a trowel made for cleaning gutters.

2 Clean a blocked downspout by spraying into it from above with a garden hose turned on full force. Or feed a plumber's snake into it and then flush all loosened debris with a hose.

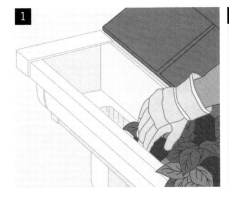

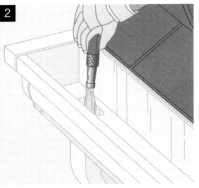

plumbing

When you're making plumbing repairs, it helps to understand the system hidden behind your home's walls and under its floors. To figure out what kind of pipes you have and where they go, look in the basement, attic, or crawl space for any exposed pipes. Often there is an access panel on the wall opposite a tub or shower, in an adjacent room or closet. A wider than usual "wet wall" contains the house's main vent stack.

In a typical system, three elements are at work: supply, drain-waste, and vent.

■ The supply system carries water from a utility or other source into your house, to all the fixtures (such as sinks, tubs, toilets), and to appliances (such as the dishwasher and washing machine).

■ The drain-waste system carries used water and waste out of the house into a sewer or an on-site disposal (septic) system.

■ The vent system carries sewer gases away and maintains atmospheric pressure inside the drainpipes, preventing toxic gases from entering your home.

SUPPLY SYSTEM

Water enters your house through a main supply pipe that is connected to a water utility main or to a source on the property. Usually, a meter monitors water usage from a utility. Newer homes may have a check valve to prevent backflow. A main shutoff valve, usually near where the supply pipe enters the house, turns the water on and off (see page 8).

Once inside the house, the main supply pipe divides into branches for hot and cold water. If there is also a water softener, it may be either on the main supply line before it divides or on the branch supplying just the water heater.

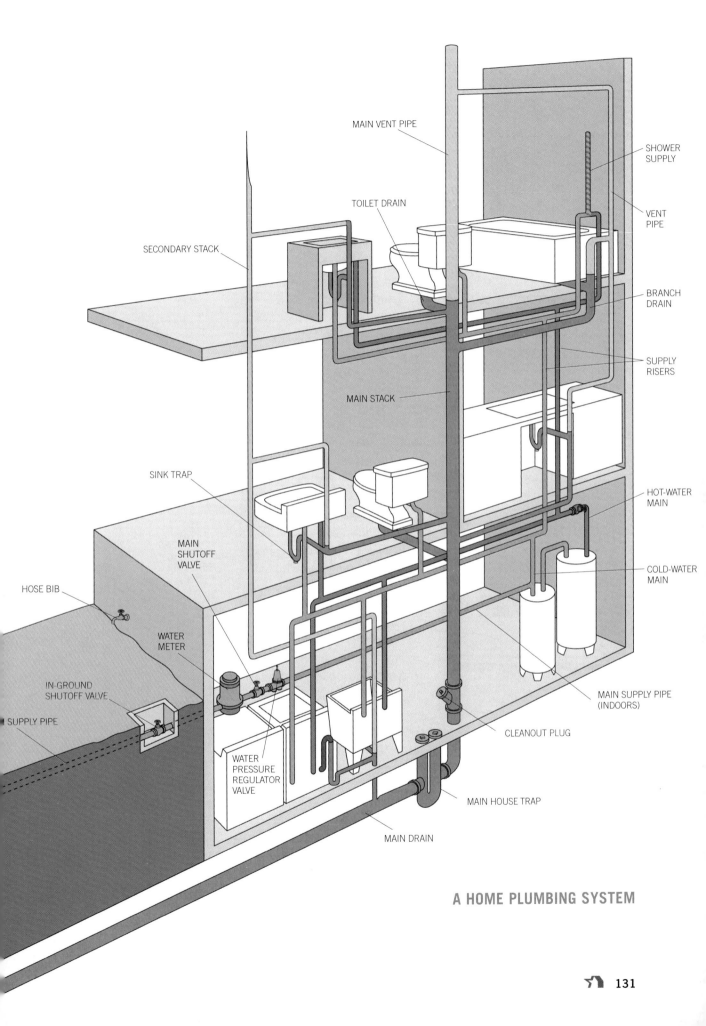

MAIN VENT PIPE

SHOWER SUPPLY

TOILET DRAIN

VENT PIPE

SECONDARY STACK

BRANCH DRAIN

SUPPLY RISERS

MAIN STACK

SINK TRAP

HOT-WATER MAIN

MAIN SHUTOFF VALVE

COLD-WATER MAIN

HOSE BIB

WATER METER

IN-GROUND SHUTOFF VALVE

MAIN SUPPLY PIPE (INDOORS)

SUPPLY PIPE

CLEANOUT PLUG

WATER PRESSURE REGULATOR VALVE

MAIN HOUSE TRAP

MAIN DRAIN

A HOME PLUMBING SYSTEM

For most of their distance, hot- and cold-water pipes run parallel and horizontally until they reach the vicinity of fixtures and appliances. Vertical branches called risers connect fixtures and appliances to the water system. Risers are usually concealed inside walls. Horizontal pipes can be inside walls, fastened to floor joists with pipe straps, or buried under a concrete slab.

Most houses built before 1945 have supply pipes made of galvanized steel, which is usually a dull gray color. These pipes are likely to develop leaks due to rust. They also tend to get clogged with mineral deposits, causing decreased water pressure. Whenever possible, have a plumber replace galvanized pipe with newer copper or plastic pipe, which remains virtually corrosion-free for many decades.

Solid copper pipe is joined to fittings by soldering, or "sweating." A good soldered joint is just as strong as the pipe itself. Copper lasts for

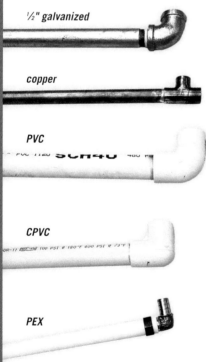

½" galvanized

copper

PVC

CPVC

PEX

many decades without degrading or building up mineral deposits.

Some newer homes have rigid plastic supply pipes. In some areas, they used to be allowed, but they are no longer allowed by code. White PVC pipes tend to come apart at the joints, while gray CPVC pipes are more reliable. Check with your building department to make sure your plastic pipes will be durable.

Flexible PEX is growing in acceptance throughout the country. It can be used for both hot- and cold-water supply lines. PEX is very easy to install, since it can curve to make turns in walls and so requires fewer fittings. The best fittings are made with brass ribs that are sealed with a special crimping tool. Many local codes require that all PEX fittings be accessible rather than hidden in a wall. If you want to replace old galvanized pipes, check to see whether PEX is allowed by your local building department. If so, it may be the least expensive and most durable replacement.

Some fixtures and water-using appliances have their own shutoff valves, often called stop valves. To be prepared for an emergency, everyone in the household should learn how to turn off the water supply both at the individual fixtures and at the main valve (see page 8).

A new method of installing supply pipes is to use control centers called manifolds. Typically, there are two manifolds, one for hot and one for cold water. Water enters the manifold from the main line, and a separate pipe (usually PEX) runs from the manifold to each fixture. This maintains even water pressure throughout the house, and eliminates that annoying change in shower temperature when another

faucet or appliance is turned on.

Excess water pressure—anything over 80 psi—can damage faucets and appliances. In areas where too-high water pressure is a possibility, there should be a pressure reducer valve located just after the main shutoff valve. It reduces excess pressure to a safe 40 to 70 psi. Once a year, follow the manufacturer's instructions to test this valve, or have it tested by a plumber.

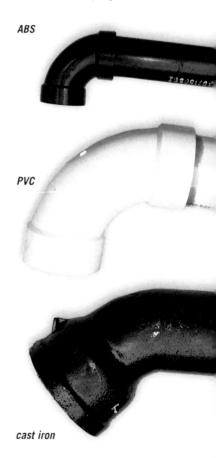

ABS

PVC

cast iron

DRAIN-WASTE SYSTEM

The drain-waste system uses gravity to channel wastewater and solid waste to the sewer line. Drainpipes lead away from all fixtures at a slope of at least ¼ inch for every horizontal foot of pipe.

The workhorse of the drain-waste system is the soil stack or main stack, a vertical section of 3- or 4-inch-diameter pipe that

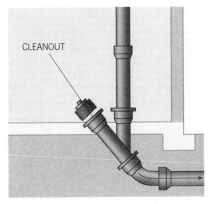

CLEANOUT

carries waste away from toilets and other fixtures and connects with the main drain under the house. From there, waste flows to a sewer or septic tank.

Since all types of systems will clog occasionally, cleanouts are placed in the drainpipes. A cleanout is usually a 45-degree Y fitting or a 90-degree T fitting with a removable plug.

Ideally, there should be one cleanout in each horizontal section of drainpipe. There should also be cleanouts in a main house trap, sometimes outdoors, for access to sewer or septic tank connections.

VENT SYSTEM

To prevent dangerous sewer gases from entering the home, each fixture's drainpipe must have a trap and must be vented. A trap is a bend of pipe that remains filled with water at all times to keep noxious gases from coming up the drain and into the house. A P-trap (see right) is the most common configuration. Some older installations have an S-trap (see below) instead. S-traps are no longer allowed by codes, because water can sometimes be siphoned

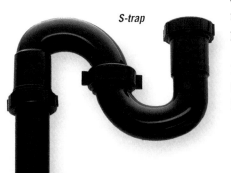

S-trap

out of the trap, leaving it dry and unable to trap gases.

The vent pipes in the drain-waste system are designed to get rid of sewer gases and to prevent pressure buildup in the pipes (see the illustration on page 131). The vents come off the drainpipes downstream from the traps and go out through the roof. This maintains atmospheric pressure in the pipes and prevents the siphoning of water from the traps.

Each plumbing fixture in the house must be vented. Usually, a house has a main vent stack (the upper part of the soil stack) with 1½- to 2-inch vent pipes connecting to it. In many homes, especially single-story ones, widely separated fixtures make it impractical to use a single main vent stack. In this situation, each fixture or fixture group has its own waste connection and its own secondary vent stack.

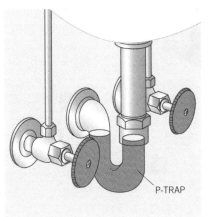

P-TRAP

An air admittance valve (AAV) is a cylindrical valve that in some situations may augment or even take the place of a vent pipe. It may be used to vent a single fixture or several fixtures. If you have AAVs, make sure they comply with local plumbing codes.

Drain and vent pipes in a pre-1945 home are likely made of cast iron, which often lasts for a very long time but sometimes rusts and

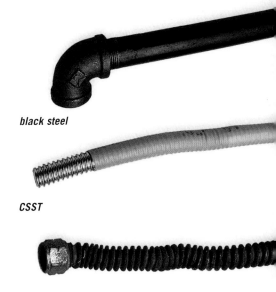

black steel

CSST

older brass flex line

newer coated stainless-steel flex line

leaks. A plumber may repair a damaged cast-iron pipe or replace it with plastic. In many areas, white PVC drainpipe is required by code, while in other areas black ABS is standard.

GAS LINES

In most areas, gas pipes are made of "black" (usually dark gray) steel with threaded fittings. Some steel gas pipes are tinted green. Copper pipe or tubing is also sometimes used. Newer corrugated stainless-steel tubing (CSST) is widely considered to be the most durable and reliable gas pipe.

An appliance or fixture is sometimes "hard piped," meaning that standard gas pipe runs all the way to it. In other cases, a flexible brass gas line is used for the final two feet or so. An older brass flex line should be replaced with a teflon-coated or stainless-steel line, which is more reliable and less likely to leak.

repairing sink faucets

I f you have a leaking faucet, it is often easy to fix. If water flow is sluggish, first try removing and cleaning or replacing the aerator (see page 138).

For most repairs, it is essential that you first shut off water to the faucet, preferably by turning off two stop valves under the sink. If there are no stop valves, you will need to shut off water to all or part of the house (see page 8). After turning off the water, open the faucet to drain the pipes.

If possible, find the manufacturer's name and purchase a repair kit made for your faucet. If you can't find the brand, take parts with you to a home center or plumbing supply source and ask a salesperson for replacement parts. If parts are hard

to find, or if you don't like the faucet anyway, you are likely better off replacing it (see pages 140–141).

LEAKING BALL FAUCETS

Inside a ball faucet is a slotted metal ball atop two spring-loaded rubber seals. Water flows when openings in the rotating ball align with hot- and cold-water inlets in the faucet body. A repair kit will likely include a new cam and washer, seals and springs, and small tools for removing the setscrew and tightening the adjusting ring. You may also need a new ball.

If the handle of a ball faucet leaks, use a hex-head wrench to loosen the setscrew, then remove the handle. Use an adjusting-ring wrench to tighten the adjusting ring.

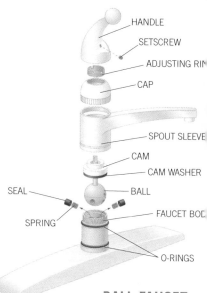

BALL FAUCET

If the leak persists, shut off water to the faucet and make repairs as shown at right. If the leak is at the spout, you may need to replace the cam above the ball and/or the inlet seals and springs. If the leak is under the spout sleeve, replace the O-rings or the ball itself. If water flow is sluggish, you may need to flush out debris collected in the faucet body.

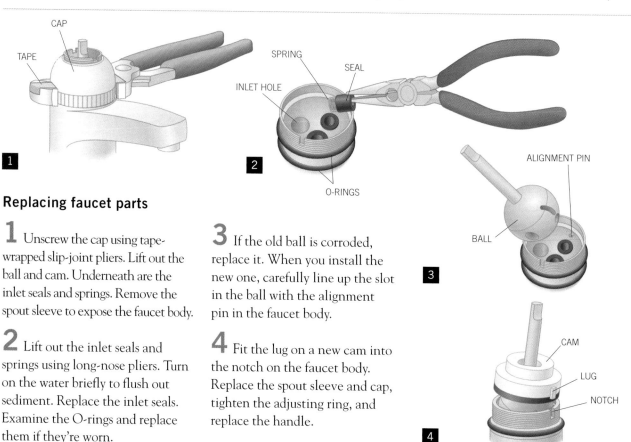

Replacing faucet parts

1 Unscrew the cap using tape-wrapped slip-joint pliers. Lift out the ball and cam. Underneath are the inlet seals and springs. Remove the spout sleeve to expose the faucet body.

2 Lift out the inlet seals and springs using long-nose pliers. Turn on the water briefly to flush out sediment. Replace the inlet seals. Examine the O-rings and replace them if they're worn.

3 If the old ball is corroded, replace it. When you install the new one, carefully line up the slot in the ball with the alignment pin in the faucet body.

4 Fit the lug on a new cam into the notch on the faucet body. Replace the spout sleeve and cap, tighten the adjusting ring, and replace the handle.

REPAIRING COMPRESSION FAUCETS

If your faucet has separate hot- and cold-water handles that come to a spongy stop, it's a compression faucet (or a two-handled disk faucet; see page 136). A compression faucet has a rubber seat washer secured to the base of a coarse-threaded stem. When you turn the handle to shut off the faucet, the stem screws down, compressing the washer against the valve seat in the faucet body. At the same time, a packing nut compresses the packing (either string packing, a washer, or an O-ring) against the stem and prevents water from leaking around it.

Leaks in compression faucets may occur around one of the handles or at the spout. Before beginning any repair work, turn off the water at the stop valves or the main house shutoff and open the faucet to drain the pipes.

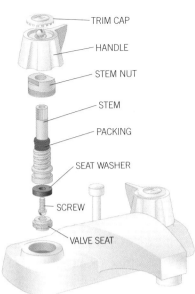

Labels: TRIM CAP, HANDLE, STEM NUT, STEM, PACKING, SEAT WASHER, SCREW, VALVE SEAT

COMPRESSION FAUCET

THREE PACKING OPTIONS

Labels: O-RING, PACKING WASHER, STRING PACKING

To replace worn packing, either remove the O-ring or packing washer and slide on a duplicate, or scrape off the packing string and wrap new packing clockwise around the stem.

To fix a leak around a handle, remove the handle and tighten the packing nut. If that fails, replace the packing. On some models, you can tighten the packing nut without removing the handle.

If the faucet leaks from the spout, either a washer is defective or a valve seat is worn or corroded. First find out whether the hot or cold side needs work by turning off the shutoff valves one at a time. If the spout still leaks when you turn off a valve, that's the defective side. Take off the corresponding handle and

remove the stem. If the washer is worn, replace it. If it looks fine or if it wears out in less than a year, the valve seat is damaged, either causing an imperfect seal with the washer or shredding it. On most compression faucets, the valve seat is replaceable. If the seat is built into the faucet, it can be smoothed with a valve-seat dresser, also called a seat grinder.

Before you reassemble the faucet, lubricate the stem threads with silicone grease. If the threads are worn or stripped, consider replacing the stem. If you cannot find a new stem, replace the faucet.

REPLACING A SEAT WASHER

To remedy a cracked or worn seat washer, remove the screw and washer and install a new washer. If the threads are too worn to hold a screw, snap in a swivel-head washer.

Labels: WASHER, SCREW, swivel-head washer, stem with washer, washers, seat

Working on a valve seat

REPLACE AN OLD SEAT

To exchange a removable seat, insert a valve-seat wrench into the valve seat and turn it counterclockwise until the seat lifts out. Buy a duplicate, slip it onto the wrench, and carefully screw it in.

Label: VALVE-SEAT WRENCH

DRESS A NONREMOVABLE SEAT

To recondition a valve seat, grind down its burrs with a seat dresser. Insert the tool and turn it clockwise once or twice until the seat is smooth. Remove metal filings with a damp cloth.

AMERISPEC® TIP   REVERSE-COMPRESSION FAUCET

If your two-handled faucet cranks upward rather than downward to shut off, you have a reverse-compression faucet. To repair it, purchase duplicates of the rubber washers and the metal sleeves that go over the washers. They will come in a kit.

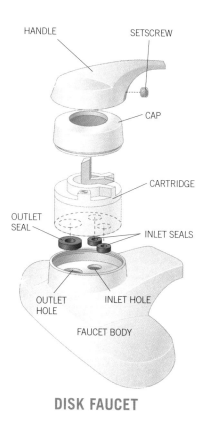

HANDLE   **SETSCREW**

CAP

CARTRIDGE

OUTLET SEAL

INLET SEALS

OUTLET HOLE   **INLET HOLE**

FAUCET BODY

DISK FAUCET

REPAIRING A DISK FAUCET

The core of a washerless disk faucet is a ceramic assembly, sometimes called a cylinder. Openings in the disk line up with inlet holes to allow the flow of water. The mix and flow of hot and cold water are controlled by two disks inside a sealed cartridge. Raising the faucet handle lifts the upper disk, controlling the flow. Rotating the handle turns the lower disk, controlling the mix.

Before doing any work on either type, turn off the water at the faucet valves or the main house shutoff (see page 8).

Disk assemblies seldom wear out, but if yours does, you'll need to replace the entire cartridge. More often, a worn inlet or outlet seal is the problem. If you have a leak at the base of the faucet, one seal may be worn. Take the faucet apart as shown on the opposite page and you'll find the set of seals under the cartridge. Replace them both with duplicates.

If water flow is sluggish, first check the faucet aerator for clogged holes (see page 138). If that's not the problem, the faucet inlet and outlet holes may be obstructed by sediment buildup. In this case, flush or scrape away any deposits.

REPAIRING TWO-HANDLE DISK FAUCETS

These operate the same way as single-handle models except that they have a pair of cartridges, or stem-unit assemblies, plus a single rubber or plastic seal and a small spring on each side. The cartridges may wear out and need to be replaced. More often, an inlet seal is the culprit.

If the faucet drips from the spout, the inlet seal and spring probably need replacing. If it leaks from the handle, the O-ring or stem-unit assembly needs replacing.

Working on a single-handle disk faucet

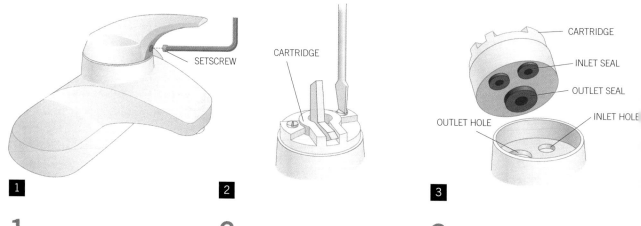

SETSCREW

CARTRIDGE

CARTRIDGE

INLET SEAL

OUTLET SEAL

INLET HOLE

OUTLET HOLE

1 Lift the handle as high as it can go and loosen—but don't remove—the setscrew with a hex-head wrench. Take off the handle and cap.

2 Loosen the two screws that fasten the cartridge to the faucet body. Then lift the entire cartridge unit straight up and off the body.

3 Check the rubber inlet and outlet seals in the bottom of the cartridge for signs of wear. Replace any worn ones. Aligning the seals on the cartridge with the holes, replace the cartridge, then the cap and handle.

CARTRIDGE FAUCETS

These washerless faucets have a series of holes in the stem-and-cartridge assembly that align to control the mix and flow of water. Leaks usually occur because of worn O-rings or a faulty cartridge.

First look at the O-rings on the faucet body. If they're worn, replace them. If they're in good shape, remove the cartridge. If the cartridge is worn, replace it with an identical one.

If a faucet is hard to turn, lubricating the cartridge O-rings should fix the problem.

Before doing any work, remember to shut off the water (see page 8).

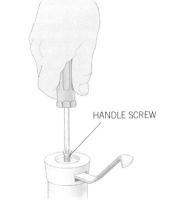

HANDLE SCREW

1

Taking a cartridge faucet apart

1 Loosen the handle screw with a screwdriver and lift off the cap and handle. Then remove the retainer nut.

2 Move the spout sleeve back and forth and gently pull it off the faucet body. Pull the retainer clip out of its slot in the faucet body using a screwdriver or pliers.

3 Grip the cartridge stem with pliers and pull it straight out. If it's stuck you might need to use a cartridge-pulling tool made for your faucet.

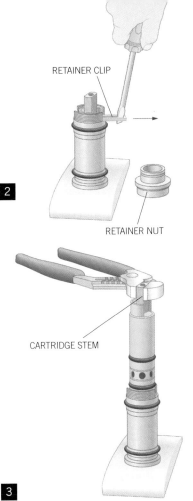

RETAINER CLIP

2

RETAINER NUT

CARTRIDGE STEM

3

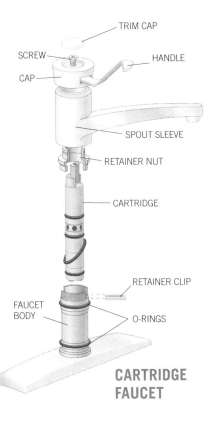

TRIM CAP

SCREW

HANDLE

CAP

SPOUT SLEEVE

RETAINER NUT

CARTRIDGE

RETAINER CLIP

FAUCET BODY

O-RINGS

CARTRIDGE FAUCET

Making cartridge repairs

CHANGING AN O-RING Examine the O-rings in the cartridge and replace them if they show signs of wear (A). Apply silicone grease to the new O-rings before installing them.

REPLACING THE CARTRIDGE If the O-rings are in good shape, replace only the cartridge. Buy a duplicate and push it down into the faucet body (B). If there's a flat side, be sure it faces forward. Reassemble the faucet, making sure to fit the retainer clip snugly.

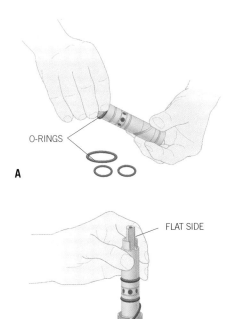

O-RINGS

A

FLAT SIDE

B

CLEANING A FAUCET AERATOR

If the flow from your faucet is sluggish, the trouble may be the aerator. This device, at the tip of most spouts, mixes air and water for a smooth flow. Minerals or dirt particles in the water sometimes build up on the screen and disk, blocking the flow. In an older home with galvanized pipes, it may be necessary to clean the aerators regularly.

If mineral deposits are present or if aerator parts are damaged, it's best to replace the aerator. But if dirt is the problem, you can simply clean the parts. Unscrew the aerator from the end of the spout and disassemble it. To loosen stubborn connections, douse them with penetrating oil. Clean the screen with a brush and soapy water and use a pin or toothpick to open any clogged holes in the disk. Or just soak the aerator in a small dish of vinegar.

FAUCET AERATOR

WASHER

PERFORATED DISK

SCREEN

BODY

KITCHEN SINK SPRAYERS

Sink sprayers are notorious troublemakers, either getting clogged or leaking from the handle, the spout, or the hose. Leaks may occur in three places: the spray head, the hose, or the diverter valve inside the base of the faucet that reroutes water from the spout to the sprayer. Before doing any work, remember to shut off the water supply (see page 8).

A sprayer on a cheap faucet may not be repairable. In this case, replace the entire faucet. The illustration above shows two common types of diverter valves. On a

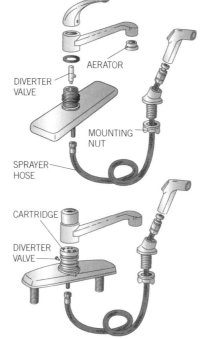

AERATOR

DIVERTER VALVE

MOUNTING NUT

SPRAYER HOSE

CARTRIDGE

DIVERTER VALVE

two-handle faucet, the valve is often a vertical piece just below the handle. On a single-handle model, it may be attached to the side of the cartridge.

SPRAY HEAD If the hose leaks at the spray head, try tightening the fitting at the base. If that doesn't solve the problem, unscrew the head from the fitting. If the washer under the head is worn, replace it, then flush out the hose.

HOSE If the hose leaks where it attaches under the sink, remove the fitting from the tip of the hose by

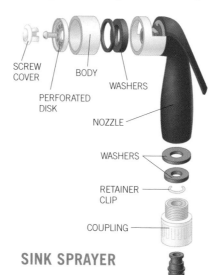

SCREW COVER

BODY

WASHERS

PERFORATED DISK

NOZZLE

WASHERS

RETAINER CLIP

COUPLING

SINK SPRAYER

first removing the retainer clip. Then unscrew the coupling nut under the sink using slip-joint pliers or a basin wrench (or unthread the hose if it connects directly into the base of the faucet without a coupling nut). Getting at the coupling nut can be awkward, as you'll need to lie on your back under the sink. If the hose is damaged, replace it with one of the same diameter. Nylon-reinforced vinyl is the most durable.

DIVERTER VALVE If the sink sprayer won't work or has reduced flow, the diverter valve may be clogged with deposits. Shut off water to the faucet and remove the spout to get at the valve. Take the valve apart and clean its outlets and surfaces with an old toothbrush and vinegar. Replace any rubber parts.

SHOWERHEADS

A showerhead simply screws off the shower arm, so replacing it or its internal parts is easy. If a showerhead is leaking or spraying wildly, unscrew it and tighten all connections with slip-joint pliers (wrap the jaws with tape to avoid damaging the finish on the head). If that doesn't work, replace the washer between the showerhead and the swivel ball.

SHOWER ARM

LOCKING COLLAR

ADJUSTING RING

SWIVEL BALL

WASHER

SHOWERHEAD

FACEPLATE

SCREW

SHOWERHEAD

Showerheads are put together in various ways. In many areas, codes require that they have flow restrictors to save water. If flow is sluggish, there's likely a clog in the screen or faceplate. Disassemble the unit and clean any clogged parts by soaking them in vinegar overnight. Or simply replace the head.

TUB AND SHOWER FAUCETS

Like sink faucets, tub and shower faucets can be compression, ball, or cartridge style. A three-handle compression faucet has a diverter valve that directs water to the faucet or showerhead. A single-handle faucet does not divert water; that is done by a little valve on the tub spout. (To replace a tub spout, see page 143.)

Make repairs much as you would for a sink faucet of the same type. Before taking a tub faucet apart, turn off the water. There may be shutoff valves in an access panel on the opposite side of the shower wall. Otherwise, shut off the main house valve (see page 8) and drain the pipes by opening a faucet that is lower than the level of the tub faucet.

To work on a recessed tub faucet, first unscrew the handle and remove the escutcheon. To access the stem nut in a compression faucet, you may need to chip away the wall's surface and then grip the nut with a deep shower socket wrench.

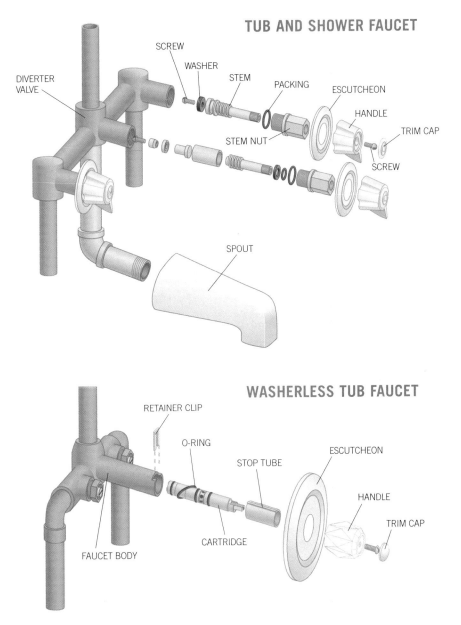

TUB AND SHOWER FAUCET

SCREW · WASHER · STEM · PACKING · ESCUTCHEON · HANDLE · TRIM CAP · DIVERTER VALVE · STEM NUT · SCREW · SPOUT

WASHERLESS TUB FAUCET

RETAINER CLIP · O-RING · STOP TUBE · ESCUTCHEON · HANDLE · TRIM CAP · CARTRIDGE · FAUCET BODY

MAINTAINING A WHIRLPOOL TUB

Most whirlpools have a pump that feeds water into flexible pipes, which lead to jets that point into the tub. Some models use channels in the tub itself rather than pipes. Do not let a whirlpool's motor run while it is dry, as you could damage seals or burn out the motor. To prevent scum from building up and clogging jets, minimize the use of soap and rinse the tub after using it.

To keep a whirlpool's jets, pipes, and other inner workings clear and free-flowing, do a thorough cleaning every month or so. Fill the whirlpool with water several inches above the jets. Add about 20 ounces of bleach plus two tablespoons of dishwasher detergent and then turn the pump on for 10 minutes. The cleaning solution

will circulate throughout the system. Empty the tub; run clear, cold water; and run the jets for another 10 minutes to rinse the system. If dark particles come out of the jets, you may need to clean the system several times using this method.

A whirlpool should be plugged into a dedicated GFCI receptacle or wired to a dedicated GFCI circuit breaker in the service panel. Every month or so, push the button to test that the GFCI is working. If water is leaking from the pipes or if the tub wobbles, call a plumber for an evaluation. Every few months, open the access panel and inspect the motor. Vacuum it if there is dust, and apply pump lubricant spray as directed by the manufacturer.

installing a new faucet

Hooking up a new faucet is not complicated, and instructions that come with the faucet will hold your hand through the entire process. The difficult part is usually gaining access to the connections. You may need to crawl into a tight cabinet under the sink and then turn nuts that are hard to reach. Unless the faucet is easy to reach with slip-joint pliers, purchase a basin wrench.

basin wrench

INSTALLING A KITCHEN FAUCET

A kitchen faucet—either a one- or two-handle type—covers the three holes on a typical kitchen sink. If your sink does not have stop valves for the supply tubes, it is a good idea to install them. Hire a plumber if you are not sure how to make the connections.

You may choose to install a "one-touch" faucet, which has a pullout spout that doubles as a sprayer. Installation is not very different from that of a standard faucet, but you will need to carefully thread the hose underneath so it can easily slide up and down.

To remove the old faucet, shut off the water, disconnect the supply tubes, and remove the nuts that hold the faucet to the sink. Pry the old faucet off and clean the sink deck where the new faucet will go.

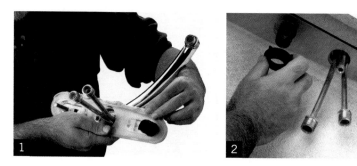

Installing a single-handle kitchen sink with sprayer

1 Roll a rope of plumber's putty between your hands. Shape it around the outside of the faucet body where it will rest on the sink.

2 Most faucets have one or more sets of nuts that secure the faucet to the sink at the side holes. There may also be a nut arrangement for the center hole. Hand-tighten plastic nuts, or use a wrench to tighten metal nuts.

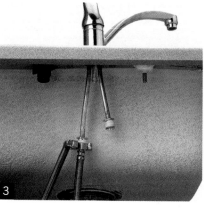

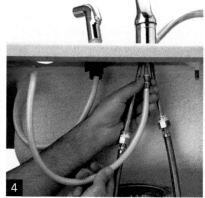

3 Run flexible supply tubes from the stop valves to the faucet's inlets. If you have integral copper supply tubes, as shown, take care not to overtighten them or you may twist the tubes. You may need to hold the copper tubes steady with another wrench.

4 Thread the sprayer's hose through the sink hole from above and then connect the hose to the faucet body below the sink. You may need to bend the supply tubes outward to access the spray-hose threads.

⚡ AMERISPEC® TIP **THE RIGHT SUPPLY TUBES**

Braided supply tubes make water hookups easy. Be sure that the tubes are long enough and that they will fit onto your stop valves, which may be either ⅜- or ½-inch.

INSTALLING A BATHROOM FAUCET

A lavatory faucet may have integral supply tubes like the kitchen faucet on the previous page. Or it may have inlets just below each handle, as shown in the steps below. You can also buy a spread-fit faucet, which fits a variety of sink-hole configurations.

In most cases, a bathroom faucet comes with a drain body and pop-up stopper assembly, which you install at the same time as the faucet. See page 142 for an illustration of how a pop-up assembly is put together.

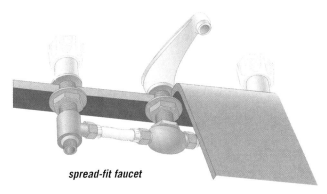

spread-fit faucet

Installing a two-handle bathroom faucet

1 Roll a rope of plumber's putty and apply it to the underside of the faucet as shown in Step 1 on the previous page. Slip the faucet into the sink's mounting holes. Align the faucet and press it down.

2 Working from below, thread the mounting nuts onto the sink's inlets or mounting bolts. Tighten plastic wing nuts by hand, or use a wrench for metal nuts.

3 Run flexible supply tubes from under-sink stop valves to the faucet's inlets, as shown, or to integral supply tubes, as shown on the previous page. Tighten the nuts with a basin wrench, slip-joint pliers, or an adjustable wrench.

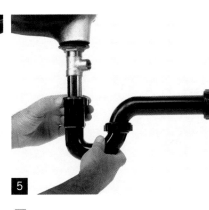

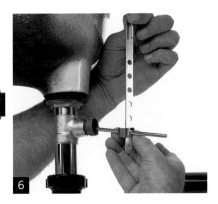

4 From above, apply a rope of plumber's putty to the underside of the sink body's flange and then press the faucet's body down through the hole. From below, secure the drain body with a rubber gasket, metal washer, and locknut. Tighten the locknut with slip-joint pliers.

5 You will most likely need to screw a tailpiece onto the drain body. Slip one end of the P-trap onto the tailpiece and make the trap connections as shown on page 144.

6 Install the pop-up. Slip the stopper down through the flange from above, insert the pivot rod, and secure it with the nuts. Attach the rod to the clevis and secure it with a spring clip. Secure the clevis to the lift rod that extends up through the faucet body.

sink and tub pop-ups

A bathroom pop-up has a lift rod that slides up or down to open or close the drain. The lift rod connects to the pivot rod to raise and lower the stopper. A bathtub's pop-up assembly (see opposite page) is not visible, but it's not mysterious and is usually relatively easy to access and repair.

REPAIRING A SINK POP-UP

Although a sink pop-up assembly is simple, its several moving parts need adjusting every so often. If the stopper doesn't open far enough for proper drainage, loosen the thumbscrew and retighten it lower on the lift rod. If there's not enough room left on the rod, you'll need to move the spring clip and pivot rod to a lower hole.

If the pop-up stopper doesn't seat snugly, remove it. The unattached type (see below) must be pulled out. The slotted type must be twisted to be freed. For the attached type, you'll need to undo the spring clip, unscrew the pivot nut, and pull out the pivot rod to remove the stopper. Clean the stopper of any hair or debris. Check its rubber seal; if it's damaged, pry it off and slip on

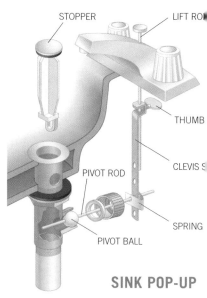

SINK POP-UP

a new one. If the pop-up still doesn't seat correctly, loosen the thumbscrew, push the stopper down, and retighten the screw higher up. When the drain is closed, the pivot rod should slope downhill from the clevis to the drain body.

If the pop-up is seating properly but water is still leaking out of the basin, try tightening the retaining nut that holds the ball in place. Still leaking? Replace the washer behind the ball, then adjust the pivot rod so the pop-up seats properly.

TYPES OF SINK POP-UPS

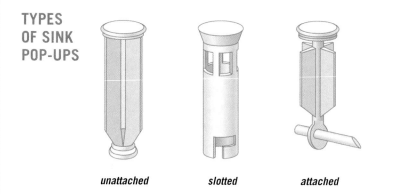

unattached   *slotted*   *attached*

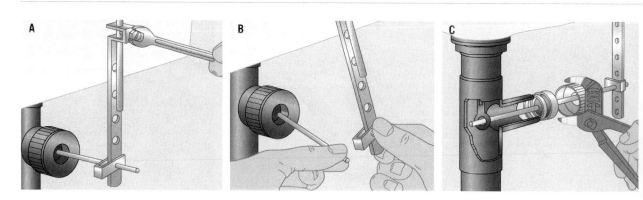

Adjusting a sink pop-up assembly

If a sink pop-up doesn't seat tightly, loosen the clevis screw with a wrench, push the stopper down, and retighten the clevis screw (A). When the drain is closed, the pivot rod should slope slightly uphill from the clevis to the tailpiece.

If the sink stopper is so tight that it impedes drainage and adjusting the clevis screw doesn't help, reset the pivot rod. Squeeze the spring clip and free the pivot rod (B). Move the clip up to the next clevis hole and insert the rod.

If water drips from around the pivot ball, use tape-wrapped slip-joint pliers to tighten the retaining nut that holds the ball in place (C). If the leaking continues, replace the gasket or washer (or both) inside the ball-and-rod assembly.

TUB POP-UPS

There are two basic types of tub overflow-and-stopper assemblies. In a stopper-type pop-up, a rocker arm is attached via linkage and a spring to the tub's stopper, so the arm can move the stopper up and down. In an internal plunger pop-up, a brass plunger inside the drain body moves up and down to open or close the drain.

If you have a stopper-type unit and the stopper doesn't seat properly, or if water drains slowly, remove the stopper and rocker arm by pulling the stopper straight up. Then unscrew and remove the tub's overflow plate and pull the entire assembly out through the overflow. For a stopper that isn't seating well, loosen the adjusting nuts and slide the middle link up to shorten the striker rod. The striker spring rests unattached on top of the rocker arm. For a sluggish drain, lower the middle link to

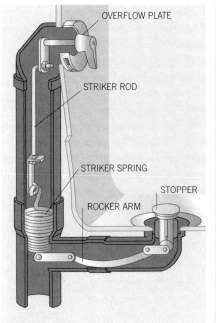

STOPPER-TYPE POP-UP

OVERFLOW PLATE

STRIKER ROD

STRIKER SPRING

STOPPER

ROCKER ARM

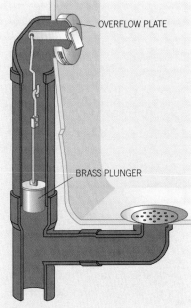

INTERNAL PLUNGER POP-UP

OVERFLOW PLATE

BRASS PLUNGER

lengthen the assembly. Before reassembling, clean the pop-up stopper.

If you have an internal plunger, the adjustments to the lift mecha-

nism are the same as for a stopper-type assembly. You may need to pull the plunger out through the overflow hole and clean away hair and debris.

REPLACING A TUB SPOUT

If a bathtub spout's diverter valve does not fully divert water to the showerhead, or if you don't like the way it looks, replace it. Doing so is usually a simple job.

A bathtub spout may be twisted onto a threaded pipe, which may barely extend past the wall or may protrude 6 inches or so. Or the spout may be attached to an unthreaded copper pipe by means of a setscrew. Before attempting to twist a spout off, first check underneath the

spout for a setscrew. If there is one, loosen it before proceeding (see below left).

If you will reuse the spout, wrap it with rags before using slip-joint pliers or a pipe wrench to twist it off (see below middle). With some spouts, you can insert a wood dowel into the spout's opening and twist it off.

Before installing the new spout, wrap the threads with Teflon plumber's tape to prevent leaks (see below right).

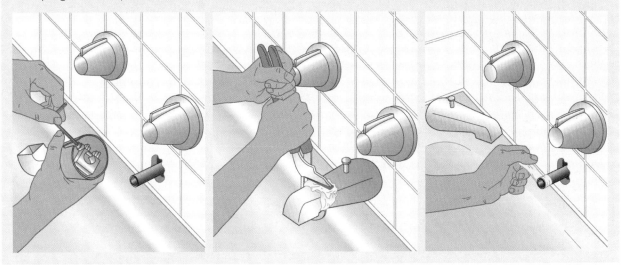

clearing clogs

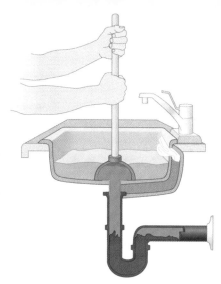

Dealing with clogged sinks, tubs, showers, and toilets is one of life's unpleasant necessities. The ideal is to prevent clogs entirely. But as this isn't usually possible, at least be alert to the warning signs of a sluggish drain. It is easier to clear a drain that is slowing down than one that has stopped completely.

Usually a clog will be close to the fixture. To determine its location, you can check the other drains in your home. If only one fixture is blocked, then you are probably dealing with a clog in its trap or drainpipe.

If more than one drain will not clear, something is stuck farther along in a branch drain, the main drain, or the soil stack, causing all the fixtures above the clog to stop up. If there is a blockage in the vent stack, waste drains slowly and odors from the pipes become noticeable in the house.

PREVENTING CLOGGED DRAINS A kitchen sink usually clogs because of a buildup of grease and food particles, so avoid disposing of grease or coffee grounds down the drain. Keep kitchen drains clear by pouring a gallon of boiling water down them monthly. If you have plastic drainpipes, use hot water that's not boiling.

Hair and soap scum are usually at fault in bathroom drains. Clean out strainers and pop-ups regularly. A solution of equal parts baking soda and vinegar can help prevent soap and hair clogs. Pour some down the drain every month or so, let it fizz, and then flush the drain with hot water.

UNCLOGGING STRATEGIES If a dose of scalding water doesn't eliminate a clog, the next step is to use a plunger or to dismantle and clean out the trap—whichever is easier in your situation. If these simple measures fail, you will need to use an auger.

PLUNGING

Use a plunger with a suction cup that is large enough to cover the drain opening completely. Fill the clogged fixture with enough water to cover several inches of the plunger cup. Then use wet cloths to block off all the other outlets (the overflow vent, the second drain in a double sink, and adjacent fixtures) between the drain and the clog. Insert the plunger into the water at an angle so that a minimum of air remains trapped under it.

Don't make the typical mistake of pumping up and down only two or three times, expecting the water to whoosh down the drain. Holding the plunger upright, use 15 to 20 forceful strokes. You should feel a definite suction. If you don't, try coating the rim of the plunger's cup with petroleum jelly for a tighter seal. The plunger may push the blockage through, or it may pull it up into the sink. Repeat if necessary.

DISMANTLING A TRAP

Taking apart a trap is not difficult, but be aware that an old chrome one may crumble or crack as you

plastic trap

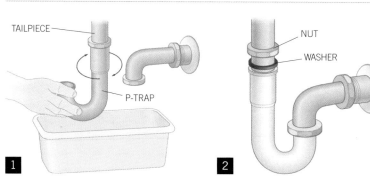

Removing and replacing a trap

1 Position a pail to catch water. Use slip-joint pliers to loosen the nuts at the tailpiece and the waste arm, then slide the nuts up or to the side. Pull off the trap and clean it of any collected debris.

2 To replace or reinstall the trap, first slide on new nuts, then washers. Slip the trap into place, slide the washers into position (make sure they are not twisted), and tighten the nuts. Test for leaks.

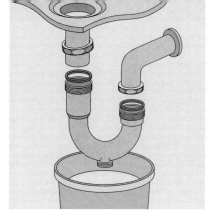

work on it. The rubber and plastic washers will likely need to be replaced. If you need to replace the trap, consider using plastic, which is more durable and is easier to install and dismantle.

AUGERING

If your sink has a garbage disposer and the disposer drainpipe clogs, turn off the electricity to the disposer. Disassemble the trap and then thread an auger into the drainpipe. If both basins of a double sink clog, feed an auger down the one without the disposer. If only the basin with the disposer is clogged, you will have to remove the trap to dislodge the blockage. If augering the sink drainpipe does not work, turn your attention to the main drain (see pages 146–147).

If the sink has a pop-up drain assembly, remove the stopper and the pivot rod (see below left).

Feed the auger (also called a snake) into the drain, trap, or pipe until it stops. If there is a movable handgrip, position it about 6 inches above the opening and tighten the thumbscrew. Rotate the handle clockwise to break the blockage (see below right). As the cable

☝ AMERISPEC® TIP   USING CHEMICAL DRAIN CLEANERS

Never use a chemical cleaner on a drain that has stopped completely, especially if the fixture is filled with water. It won't clear the blockage, and you'll face the problem of how to get rid of the caustic water that's become trapped. However, a drain cleaner may solve the problem of a sluggish drain. Take these precautions:

■ Work in a well-ventilated room and do not place your nose directly over the chemicals you are pouring in. Wear heavy-duty rubber gloves and a long-sleeved shirt and pants to protect your skin.

■ Never use a plunger if a chemical cleaner is present in the drain. You risk splashing caustic water on yourself.

■ Never use a chemical cleaner in a garbage disposer.

■ Read labels and match cleaners with clogs. Alkalis cut grease, while acids dissolve soap and hair. Never mix these two types together, as doing so can cause an explosion.

auger

works its way into the pipe, loosen the thumbscrew, slide the handgrip back, push more cable into the pipe, tighten again, and repeat. If there is no handgrip, push and twist the cable until it hits the clog.

The first time the auger stops, it probably has hit a turn in the piping rather than the clog. Guiding the auger past a sharp turn takes patience and effort. Keep pushing it forward, turning it clockwise as you go. Once the head of the auger hooks the blockage, pull the auger back a short distance to free some material from the clog. Then push the rest on through the pipe.

After breaking up the clog, pull the auger out slowly and have a pail ready to catch any debris. Flush the drain with hot water.

If the clog is beyond the trap, remove the trap and insert the auger into the drainpipe at the wall (see below) and work in the same way as for augering a sink.

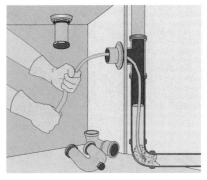

For a distant or particularly difficult clog, rent a power auger at an equipment rental supply, or call a drain-clearing company. They have powerful augers that can run long distances and cut through major blockages. Sometimes tree roots puncture through the main drain pipe and must be ground up to restore good drainage. Many companies use sewer cameras, which travel through drain pipes and pinpoint the blockages, so they can be cleared more efficiently.

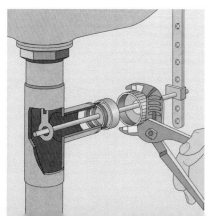

CLEARING CLOGS IN TUBS AND SHOWERS

Install a hair trap to help prevent clogs in tubs and showers. One type sits inside the drain, while another requires replacing the pop-up. Whenever a tub or shower drain does clog up, first find out whether other fixtures are affected. If they are, work on the main drain. If only the tub or shower is plugged, work on it.

Begin by plunging (see page 144), then remove the strainer or pop-up and clean it (see page 143). If this does not work, use an auger, a garden hose, or a balloon bag (see opposite page). To clear a clogged toilet, see page 148.

TUB WITH A P-TRAP To clear a tub P-trap, remove the stopper and rocker arm. Unscrew and remove the overflow plate and pull out the assembly.

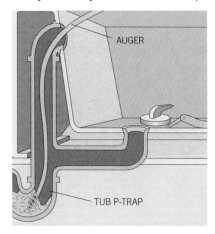

Feed the auger down through the overflow pipe and into the P-trap. If this does not clear the drain, remove the trap or its cleanout plug from below (if it's accessible) or through an access panel. Have a pail ready to catch water. Then insert the auger toward the main drain.

DRUM TRAP Instead of a P-trap, bathtubs in older houses may have a drum trap, recognizable by its round, usually chrome cover on the floor near the tub. To clear a clog, bail all water from the tub and unscrew the trap cover with an adjustable wrench. If the cover is rusted shut, you may have to tap it with a hammer and chisel; you will then need a new cover. Watch for any water welling up around the threads. Remove the trap's cover and rubber gasket and then clean out any debris. If the trap is still clogged, work the auger

through the lower pipe toward the tub and, if necessary, in the opposite direction.

SHOWER STALL Unscrew and remove the strainer of your shower drain if your auger cannot be threaded through it. Probe the auger down the drain and through the trap until it hits the clog.

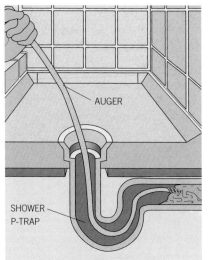

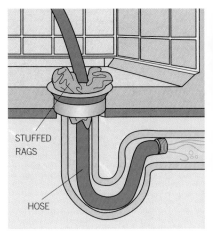

USING A HOSE You can also use a garden hose to clear a slow drain. Attach the hose to a faucet with a threaded adapter, or run it to an outside hose bib. Push the hose deep into the drain trap and pack wet rags tightly into the gap around it. Hold the hose in the drain and turn the hose water alternately on full force and then abruptly off. Alternatively, use the hose with a balloon bag (see "Single Cleanout Plug" below).

> **CAUTION** Never leave a hose in a drain. A sudden drop in water pressure could siphon raw sewage back into the fresh-water supply.

CLEARING THE MAIN DRAIN

If a clog is too deep in the pipes to access from a fixture, you can clean out the soil stack from below by working on a branch cleanout, the main cleanout, or the house trap. Cleaning the soil stack from below means working with raw sewage, so have rubber gloves, pails, mops, and rags on hand. Once you are finished, clean and disinfect all tools and materials.

SINGLE CLEANOUT PLUG Buy a balloon bag, or bladder, that matches the diameter of your drain. Attach the bag to a garden hose and then proceed as directed by the manu-

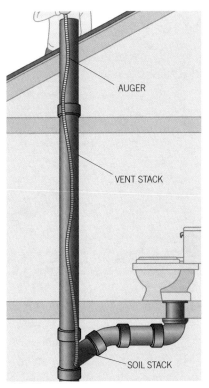

AUGER

VENT STACK

SOIL STACK

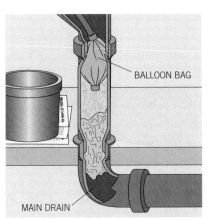

BALLOON BAG

MAIN DRAIN

MAIN HOUSE TRAP If the main drain has two closely spaced cleanouts, as shown below, you have a cleanout trap. Carefully unscrew one of the plugs. If sewage begins to seep out as you loosen it, retighten it and call a plumber, as sewage may be backed up into the main drain. Otherwise, work an auger down through the drain to get at the obstruction.

CLEANOUT TRAP

facturer. The balloon bag works by expanding in the drain and then shooting a stream of water into the pipe.

If a balloon bag does not do the trick, you can rent a large power auger made for main drains, but you are probably better off hiring a professional plumber or drain clearer.

WORKING FROM THE ROOF You can sometimes get at a clog in the main stack by working from the roof (see above). If you can work safely up there, thread an auger through the vent stack to the soil stack, moving it from side to side as you go.

MAINTAINING A SEPTIC SYSTEM

A good septic tank system does not require a great deal of care or call for many special precautions. But the maintenance it does require is crucial because a properly functioning septic system is much less likely to clog. You should have a diagram of your septic tank's layout, showing the locations of the tank, pipes, access holes, and drainage field.

Chemicals, chemical cleaners, and thick paper products should never be disposed of through the system. Chemicals may destroy the bacteria necessary to attack and disintegrate solid wastes in the tank. Paper products can clog the main drain, making the system useless.

Have your septic system checked once a year by a professional. The tank should be pumped whenever necessary, but it's best to have it done in spring if you live in a cold climate. If you have the tank pumped in fall, it may become loaded with solid waste that can't be broken down in winter, when bacterial action slows.

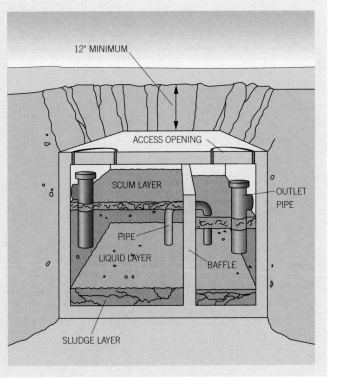

12" MINIMUM

ACCESS OPENING

SCUM LAYER

OUTLET PIPE

PIPE

LIQUID LAYER

BAFFLE

SLUDGE LAYER

A TYPICAL TOILET

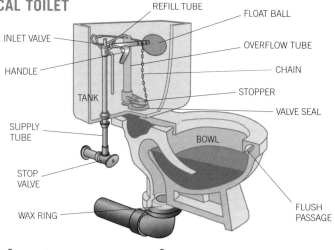

INLET VALVE

HANDLE

TANK

SUPPLY TUBE

STOP VALVE

WAX RING

REFILL TUBE

FLOAT BALL

OVERFLOW TUBE

CHAIN

STOPPER

VALVE SEAL

BOWL

FLUSH PASSAGE

toilet repairs

K nowing how a toilet operates is essential to troubleshooting. Two assemblies are concealed under the tank's lid: a flush-valve assembly, which controls the flow of water from the tank to the bowl, and an inlet-valve assembly, which regulates the filling of the tank. The toilet bowl includes a built-in trap. When someone presses the flush handle, a trip lever in the flush-valve assembly raises the chain or lift-rod wires connected to the flapper or stopper. As the flapper or stopper goes up, water rushes through the valve seat into the bowl via the flush passages under the rim of the toilet bowl. The water in the bowl yields to gravity and is siphoned out of the built-in toilet trap into the drainpipe.

As the tank empties, the float ball descends and the stopper drops into the flush-valve seat. The float ball trips the inlet valve open, letting a new supply of water into the tank through the tank-fill tube. As the water level in the tank rises, the float ball also rises until it gets high enough to shut off the flow of water. If the water fails to shut off, the overflow tube carries excess water into the bowl to prevent flooding.

A variety of inlet and flush valves

have been made over the years. In most cases, newer valves can be installed in old toilets. Your toilet may have a float-cup inlet valve, an all-plastic assembly with a cup that slides up to shut off water. An older toilet may have

a stopper attached to a lift wire (see below, right). This type of toilet often needs to have its handle jiggled to stop water from running into the tank. If you have this problem, consider replacing the stopper with a flapper.

The following pages provide instructions for making toilet repairs. Before beginning any toilet repair—unless you're simply adjusting the float arm—you'll need to shut off the water at the stop valve, flush the toilet twice to empty the tank, and sponge out any remaining water.

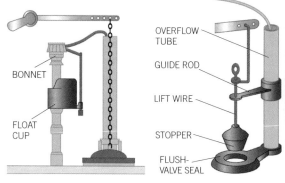

BONNET

FLOAT CUP

OVERFLOW TUBE

GUIDE ROD

LIFT WIRE

STOPPER

FLUSH-VALVE SEAL

Unclogging a toilet

PLUNGING If a toilet is clogged, bail out or add water so that the bowl is half full. Use a toilet plunger, which has a funnel-cup tip to fit the bowl. Pump the plunger up and down a dozen times, then pull off sharply on the last stroke. The alternate pressure and suction should loosen the obstruction.

AUGERING If the plunger doesn't work, use a toilet auger. It has a curved tip that starts the auger with a minimum of mess and a protective housing to prevent it from scratching the bowl. To maneuver the auger, simultaneously push it and turn the handle. The auger may push the obstruction through, or it may pull it up into the bowl.

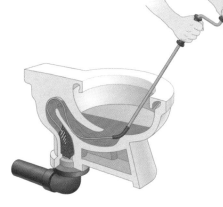

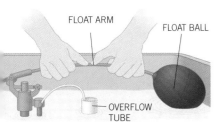

FLOAT ARM

FLOAT BALL

OVERFLOW TUBE

RUNNING TOILET

If water in your toilet tank trickles constantly or intermittently, you may need to adjust or replace the float mechanism or parts of the flush-valve assembly: the overflow tube, valve seat, tank stopper, guide rod, or lift wires. Or you may need to replace the entire assembly.

FLOAT MECHANISM If your toilet has a ball-cock inlet-valve assembly, bending the float arm downward (see left) may stop the water from running. If the float ball is filled with water, it should be replaced.

If you have a float-cup assembly, squeeze the clips and slide it down (see above right). If your valve has a pressure-adjusting screw, adjust it (see below right).

FLUSH-VALVE ASSEMBLY A defective or badly fitting valve seat or stopper may cause a toilet to run (see below for repairs).

If a metal overflow tube is cracked, replace it. If the toilet is still running, replace the entire flush-valve assembly.

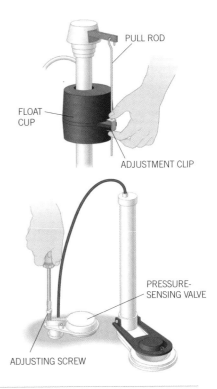

PULL ROD

FLOAT CUP

ADJUSTMENT CLIP

PRESSURE-SENSING VALVE

ADJUSTING SCREW

Working on a stopper and seat valve

1 If the stopper doesn't seat properly, loosen the adjustment screws and realign the guide arm and rod, or bend the lift wires.

2 If the valve seat is rough and pitted or covered with debris, scour it with fine steel wool or an abrasive pad to smooth its surface.

3 To replace a worn-out tank stopper, unscrew it from the lift wire and screw on a new one.

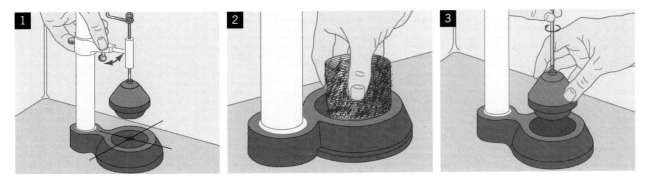

Replace a stopper with a flapper

1 To remove the old stopper, unhook the lift wires and loosen the screw on the guide arm. Lift off the guide rod and stopper.

2 To install the flapper, slide its collar to the base of the overflow tube. Position the flapper over the valve seat.

3 Adjust the length of the lift chain and hook it onto the tip of the trip lever, leaving about ½ inch of slack.

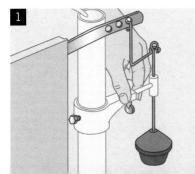

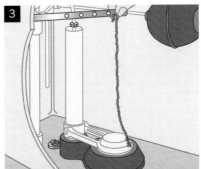

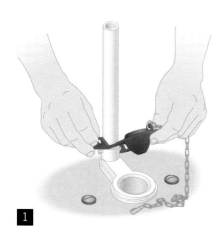

1

Replace a flapper

1 Some flappers have ears that attach to each side of the overflow valve. Others are designed to fit flush valves that are angled rather than flat. Take the old flapper when you buy a replacement, and ask a salesperson for advice if you're not sure.

2

2 Adjust the chain so that it lifts the flapper but does not tug on its ears or cause it to slide up the over-flow tube when the handle is turned. Test-flush several times to make sure the chain will not keep the flapper from seating properly.

NOISY TOILETS

If your toilet whines or whistles as the tank fills with water after flushing, the problem may be restricted water flow or a defective inlet-valve assembly.

First make sure the fixture shut-off valve is fully open. Still noisy? You may need to oil the trip lever or replace part or all of the inlet-valve assembly.

REPAIRING AN INLET VALVE

To stop ball-cock leaks, remove the retaining pins in the ball-cock lever and lift the float arm out. Remove the plunger from the ball cock and replace any defective washers. If you have a different type of inlet valve, remove it and take it to a plumbing supply source to find replacement parts. It may be easiest to replace the entire unit.

REPLACE A FLUSH VALVE

For a bowl-mounted tank, first remove the mounting bolts and gaskets and then lift the tank off. Unscrew the locknut under the tank after removing the spud

Replacing an inlet valve

1 Using pliers and a wrench, loosen the locknut holding the inlet-valve assembly to the tank. Unclip the bowl refill tube. Holding on to the base, remove the inlet-valve assembly.

2 Install the new inlet-valve assembly according to the manufacturer's instructions. Position the bowl refill tube in the overflow pipe.

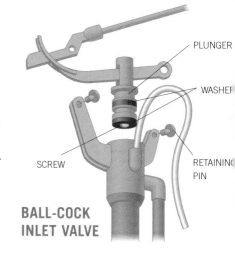

PLUNGER

WASHER

SCREW

RETAINING PIN

BALL-COCK INLET VALVE

washer. Remove the conical gasket and flush-valve assembly. To install the replacement, assemble the conical gasket and locknut. Then position the overflow tube and tighten the nut.

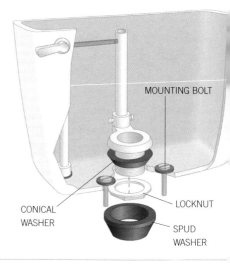

MOUNTING BOLT

CONICAL WASHER

LOCKNUT

SPUD WASHER

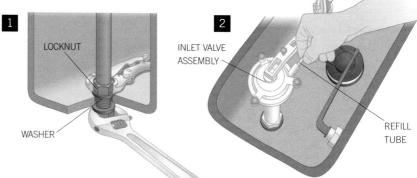

1

LOCKNUT

WASHER

2

INLET VALVE ASSEMBLY

OVERFLOW TUBE

REFILL TUBE

LEAKS AND FLUSH PROBLEMS

Other toilet problems you may need to repair include leaks, tank sweating, and certain flush problems. Some repairs require an empty tank. When this is the case, turn off the water at the fixture valve, flush the toilet twice, and sponge the tank dry before making the repair.

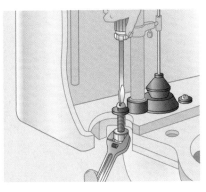

LEAKS To stop a leak between a tank and bowl, tighten the mounting bolts in the tank or replace the bolt gaskets (see above). If there's still a leak when the toilet is flushed, remove the tank and replace the spud washer on the bottom of the flush valve.

When a bowl leaks around its base, first try tightening the hold-down bolts that anchor it to the floor. If that doesn't stop the leak, you'll have to remove the bowl and replace the wax ring that seals the bowl to the floor (see above right).

FLUSH PROBLEMS A loose handle or trip lever may cause an inadequate or erratic flush cycle. Adjusting a setscrew (see above) or a mounting

nut on the handle, or replacing the handle, often solves the problem. Clogged flush passages under the bowl's rim may also restrict water flow. Clean obstructed passages with a piece of wire (see above).

SWEATING TANK This problem occurs most often when the weather is warm. Cold water from the tank cools the porcelain, and warm, moist air condenses on the outside.

Tank sweating encourages mildew, loosens floor tiles, and rots subflooring.

An easy solution is to insulate the inside of the tank by first draining and drying it. Then glue to the inside walls a special liner (see below) sold at plumbing stores or one made of foam rubber or polystyrene pads. A more costly remedy, and one that will add to your energy costs, is to install a tempering valve that mixes hot water with the cold water entering the tank.

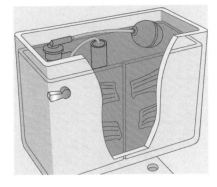

REPLACING A WAX GASKET

(labels: WAX RING, HORN, FLOOR FLANGE, HOLD-DOWN BOLTS)

⚐ AMERISPEC® TIP **LEAK OR NO LEAK?**

If you can't tell whether your toilet is leaking around the tank bolts or just sweating, add food coloring to the tank water. Wait an hour, then touch the bolt tips and nuts under the tank with white tissue. If the tissue shows coloring, you have a leak. If it doesn't, the moisture is just condensation.

water heater repairs

When a hot-water faucet is turned on, water is drawn from the top of the heater's tank. The tank is refilled with cold water that is carried to the bottom via a dip tube. When water temperature drops, a thermostat activates the heat source—a burner in a gas heater or the heating elements in an electric unit.

A standard gas heater has a flue running up the center and out the top to vent combustion gases outdoors. An electric heater produces no gases, so it does not require venting. In both types, a special anode rod attracts corrosive minerals in water that might otherwise attack the tank's walls.

A gas water heater may have a pilot light and a thermocouple, much like the gas burner in a furnace or boiler. See pages 164–165 for instructions on maintaining the burner, lighting the pilot, and replacing a thermocouple.

Twice a year, inspect the flue assembly to be sure it's properly aligned and its joints are sealed. Then check the flue by lighting a match, blowing it out, and placing it near the draft diverter with the burner on. If the smoke does not

GAS WATER HEATER

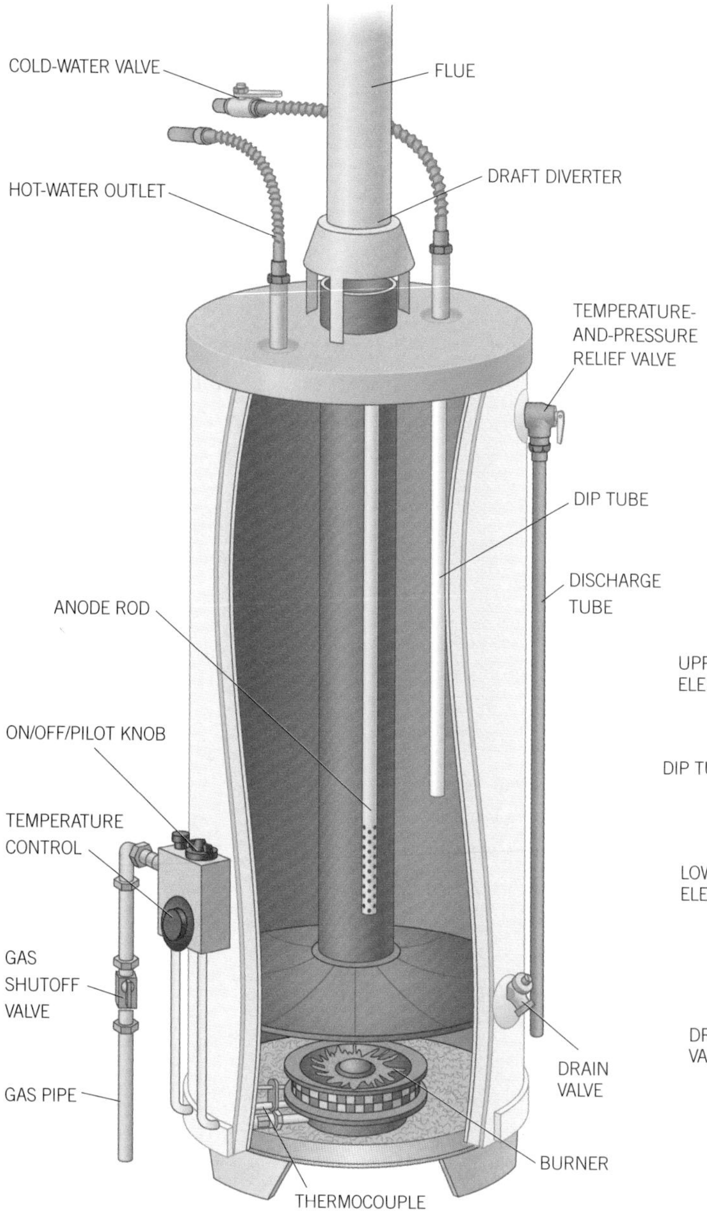

COLD-WATER VALVE
FLUE
HOT-WATER OUTLET
DRAFT DIVERTER
TEMPERATURE-AND-PRESSURE RELIEF VALVE
DIP TUBE
DISCHARGE TUBE
ANODE ROD
ON/OFF/PILOT KNOB
TEMPERATURE CONTROL
GAS SHUTOFF VALVE
GAS PIPE
DRAIN VALVE
BURNER
THERMOCOUPLE

ELECTRIC WATER HEATER

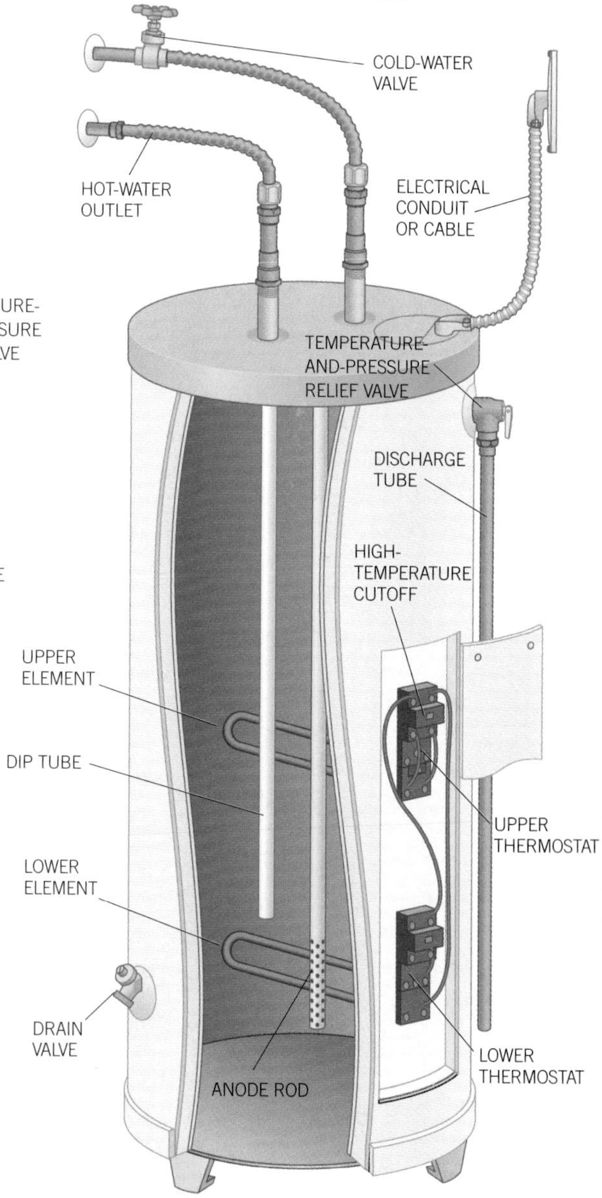

COLD-WATER VALVE
HOT-WATER OUTLET
ELECTRICAL CONDUIT OR CABLE
TEMPERATURE-AND-PRESSURE RELIEF VALVE
DISCHARGE TUBE
HIGH-TEMPERATURE CUTOFF
UPPER ELEMENT
DIP TUBE
UPPER THERMOSTAT
LOWER ELEMENT
DRAIN VALVE
ANODE ROD
LOWER THERMOSTAT

draft up into the flue, there is an obstruction, which should be removed immediately. If you cannot find the source of the problem, call for service.

Electric water heater problems are usually caused by the heating elements, their thermostats, and the high-temperature cutoff. The two heating elements are controlled by the thermostats and the cutoff, a device that shuts off the elements should the water get too hot. The thermostats and cutoff are concealed behind an access panel on the side of the water heater. After the panel is removed, insulation may need to be cut away to provide access. If the high-temperature cutoff has tripped, the solution may be as easy as pushing the reset button. Otherwise, to have the thermostats adjusted, the cutoff reset, or any of these components replaced, call for service.

MAINTENANCE To reduce sediment accumulation, open the drain valve every six months and let the water run into a bucket or through a hose to a drain until it looks clear.

At least once a year, test that the temperature-pressure relief valve, which guards against hazardous pressure buildup, functions properly. When you lift or depress

NEW FVIR WATER HEATERS

An older gas water heater can easily ignite vapors from flammable solvents and cleaners that are left nearby. For that reason, gas water heaters made after 2003 must, by law, be certified as flammable vapor ignition resistant (FVIR). An FVIR water heater keeps burning vapors inside its combustion chamber until they burn out. It has a sensor inside (above) that detects if it has ignited a flammable vapor from outside of the water heater, and then shuts off the gas to the burner and pilot light. If you buy a new water heater, make sure it's certified FVIR.

the lever, water should drain from the overflow pipe. If it does not, shut off water to the heater, drain some water (so the level is below the valve), let in air by opening a hot-water faucet in the house, and replace the valve.

ADJUSTING WATER TEMPERATURE
Water heaters are often set at 150 or 160 degrees Fahrenheit. By lowering the setting to about 120 degrees, you can save substantially on your fuel bills and keep water at a safe temperature for small children. Do not set the temperature lower than that, as you risk breeding bacteria. Lowering the temperature is also a wise safety measure. Dishwashers require higher temperatures to clean properly, but many models are equipped with their own water-heating device.

DRAINING AND FLUSHING A TANK
Turn off the gas or power, close the cold-water valve, and attach a hose to the drain valve to route water into a drain or outside the house. Open the drain valve and open one hot-water faucet somewhere in the house to let air in. When all the water has drained, turn the cold-water valve on and off until the water coming out of the valve runs clear. Then close the drain valve and the hot-water faucet, open the cold-water valve, and turn the power or gas back on.

THE TANKLESS OPTION

A tankless, or on-demand, water heater supplies nearly instant hot water (either electric or gas), and it does not waste energy by heating water that is not in use. A small tankless unit may be placed under a sink to supply hot water for the faucet above. A larger unit may supply hot water to several faucets or to an entire house. Even the larger units take up far less space than a standard water heater. And a tankless model will never run out of hot water, as a water tank will.

If the entering water is too cold, a tankless water heater may not be able to raise the temperature sufficiently. If you live in an area with cold winters, make sure that the unit you buy will be up to the task on even the coldest of days. Tankless units need to be properly connected to a flue that leads outside.

pipe repairs

epoxy putty

pipe-wrap tape

hose clamps

sleeve clamp

A higher than normal water bill may be the first indication that you have a leaking pipe. Or you might hear the sound of running water even when all the fixtures in your house are turned off.

FINDING A LEAK If you suspect a leak and don't see spraying water, first check all the fixtures to make sure the faucets are tightly closed. Then go to the water meter if you have one. If the lowest-quantity dial on the meter is moving, you're losing water somewhere.

To find the source of a leak, try listening through walls and ceilings with a stethoscope, or look for stains. If water has stained the ceiling or is dripping down, the leak will probably be directly above. Sometimes, however, water may travel along a joist and then stain or drip at a point some distance from the leak. If water stains a wall, it means there's a leak in a vertical section of pipe. The stain is most likely below the actual leak, so you'll probably need to remove a large section of wall to get at the pipe.

If you don't hear running water or see drips or stains, the leak is likely under the house in the crawl space or the basement. Search with a flashlight.

FIXING A LEAKING PIPE Once you spot the leak, turn off the water immediately (see page 8). If the leak is small, you may install a simple temporary solution until you have time for the replacement job.

A sleeve clamp is the best temporary solution for a leak in a straight section of pipe. A hose clamp with a rubber sleeve and pipe-wrap tape are both less secure. For a leak at a fitting, two-part epoxy putty is often the only possible temporary solution, but don't expect it to last long.

Eventually, a leaking pipe or fitting should be replaced. Arrange for a plumber to do the work as soon as possible.

FROZEN PIPES

A faucet that won't produce water is the first sign of frozen pipes. If your pipes freeze during a severe cold snap, warm them as quickly as possible to prevent them from bursting. Then take steps to prevent future freezings.

WARMING FROZEN PIPES If a pipe freezes, first shut off the main water supply (see page 8) and open the faucet nearest the frozen pipe. Cover the area with waterproof drop cloths. To warm a pipe, work from the faucet back toward the iced-up area. When using an electrical device to thaw a pipe, wear rubber gloves and plug the device into a GFCI receptacle to avoid getting shocked.

A hair dryer or heating pad will warm an exposed pipe gradually. If the pipe is hidden inside a wall, beam a heat lamp 8 inches or more

---

FROST-PROOF ANTI-SIPHON HOSE BIB

An old fashioned hose bib (also called a sill cock) is a simple valve that shuts off water just below the handle. This creates two possible problems: The pipe that attaches to the hose bib is very near the outside of the house, so water in it can easily freeze in the winter; and hose water can sometimes siphon back into the house, contaminating your drinking water. To solve both problems, have a plumber install a frost-proof anti-siphon hose bib. It has an extended stem, so it actually shuts off water a foot or so inside the house. It also has a built-in anti-siphon feature that keeps outside water from siphoning back into your water supply.

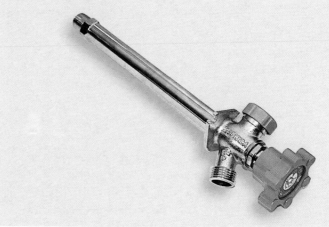

from the wall surface. In a pinch, wrap a pipe in rags and pour boiling water over it.

PREVENTING PIPES FROM FREEZING

During a severe cold snap, keep a trickle of water running from faucets throughout the house, or aim a small lamp or heater at exposed pipes. For a longer-term solution, wrap uninsulated pipes

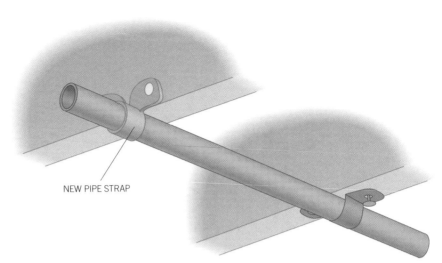

NEW PIPE STRAP

heat tape

with heat tape, then cover with foam insulation. Insulation helps heat tape operate more efficiently. By itself, though, insulation won't prevent pipes from freezing. The best heat tapes have a thermostat that turns the heat tape off when the temperature rises above freezing.

NOISY PIPES

Pipe noises range from loud banging to high-pitched squeaking, chatter, and resonant hammering.

WATER HAMMER The most common pipe noise, water hammer occurs when you quickly turn off the water at a faucet or an appliance. The water flowing through the pipes slams to a stop, causing a hammering sound.

Many water systems have short sections of pipe rising above each faucet or appliance, called air chambers, which act as shock absorbers. Over time, air chambers can get filled with water and lose their effectiveness. To restore air chambers, shut off the water supply

to your toilets and close the house's main shutoff valve. Open the highest and lowest faucets in the house to drain all water. Then close the two faucets and reopen the main shutoff and the toilet valves. This will empty any air chambers in your house.

BANGING, SQUEAKING, OR FAUCET CHATTER If you hear a banging noise when you turn on the water and it's not water hammer, check the way the pipes are anchored. Ideally, pipes should be held firmly in place but should not be right up against framing members or wall surfaces. Replace old hangers with new pipe supports (see above). Or wrap with a piece of pipe insulation and install a stirrup strap (see above right). You can also wrap the whole pipe with insulation. If a pipe rattles against a masonry wall, hold it away using wood blocks (see right).

Pipes that squeak are always hot-water pipes. As the pipe expands, it moves against the support and friction causes the squeak. To silence it, insert a piece of rubber or foam insulation

between the pipe and the support.

Faucet chatter is the noise you hear when you partially open a compression faucet. To correct the problem, tighten or replace the seat washer on the bottom of the faucet stem (page 134).

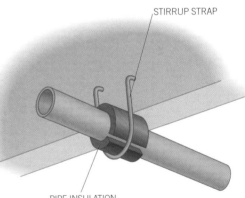

STIRRUP STRAP

PIPE INSULATION

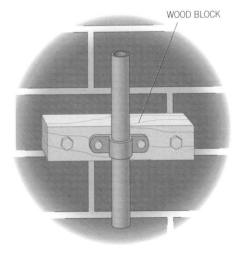

WOOD BLOCK

heating and cooling systems

Heating systems vary greatly, and it pays to get to know yours so you can talk knowledgeably with repair technicians. This chapter provides general overviews of the most common heating types. The unit that supplies heat to these systems may be a gas furnace or boiler, an oil boiler, or an electric device. Most homes today are heated by forced air or hot water. Steam heat, found in older homes, is rarely installed nowadays. Electric heat and heat pumps are sometimes the best choice in areas with mild winters.

UNDERSTANDING YOUR HEATING SYSTEM

Steam, hot-water, and forced-air systems have some basic similarities. Each is equipped with one or more temperature controls, a heat producer, a heat exchanger, and a heat distributor.

⚡ AMERISPEC® TIP **KNOW YOUR FUEL**

A furnace or boiler may be fueled with natural gas, liquefied gas (also called LP or propane), electricity, or oil. In most parts of the country, natural gas is the least expensive.

Know how to shut off the fuel in an emergency. Natural gas or LP usually has a shutoff valve near the boiler or furnace, or near the meter (see page 9). An LP tank has a shutoff on its top or on one end. A fuel oil tank, which may be in the basement or outside, usually has a shutoff near its bottom. If you have electric heat, learn how to turn off power at a switch near the heat source and at the service panel (see pages 9 and 173).

A thermostat signals a need for heat. The signal triggers the heat producer, usually a boiler or furnace. The heat warms the transfer medium—air, water, or steam—in the heat exchanger, which can be a furnace or boiler.

The transfer medium moves by gravity or is forced through ducts (warm air) or pipes (water or steam) to distributors in living areas. Heat distributors are registers in a forced warm-air system and convectors or radiators in a hot-water or steam system. In a hot-water radiant heating system, water moves through tubing concealed in the floor or ceiling.

Return ducts or pipes carry the medium back to the heat exchanger. When the temperature of the living area reaches the level that has been set on the thermostat, the thermostat automatically shuts down the system.

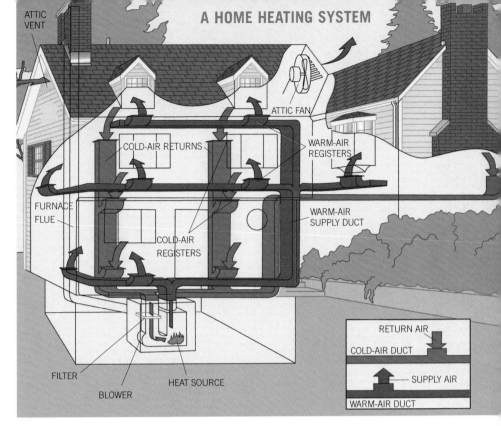

A HOME HEATING SYSTEM

ATTIC VENT

ATTIC FAN

COLD-AIR RETURNS

WARM-AIR REGISTERS

FURNACE FLUE

COLD-AIR REGISTERS

WARM-AIR SUPPLY DUCT

FILTER

BLOWER

HEAT SOURCE

RETURN AIR
COLD-AIR DUCT

SUPPLY AIR
WARM-AIR DUCT

CARING FOR YOUR SYSTEM

Heating systems can operate reliably for many years, provided they're carefully maintained. Most maintenance, minor repairs, and simple adjustments are well within the capabilities of a homeowner. But other repairs—those that are too dangerous or technical—require professional help.

Whether you're performing maintenance or trying to solve a problem, the following pages provide much valuable information as well as descriptions of the different heating systems and their major components, burners and thermostats.

USING ELECTRIC HEAT

In an area with warm winters or inexpensive electricity, electric heat often is a practical option. Here are the most common types:

BOILERS AND FURNACES In an electric boiler or furnace, the heating elements are immersed directly in the water or air to be heated. Many maintenance procedures are the same as for a gas-fired boiler or furnace. Repairs to electric heating elements should be left to a professional.

DUCT HEATERS These are installed in the ducts of an existing forced-air system. They may turn on at the same time as the blower, or they may be operated by a separate thermostat in an area that requires supplemental heat. Make sure the heaters don't turn on unless the blower is running.

BASEBOARD HEATERS These require no pipes or ducts, and they connect directly to the electrical system in the house. Baseboard heaters are often a good choice for a room addition or a hard-to-heat area. They typically have their own thermostats and safety thermal cutoff switches.

WALL AND CEILING HEATERS These are suitable for bathrooms or other small areas and are wired directly into the electrical system. Many units include a fan. Clean the heater occasionally. A defective unit usually should be replaced rather than repaired.

ELECTRIC RADIANT HEAT This option has grown in popularity. Electric heating panels or coils are installed in the floor or ceiling and are controlled by a thermostat.

FORCED-AIR HEATING SYSTEM

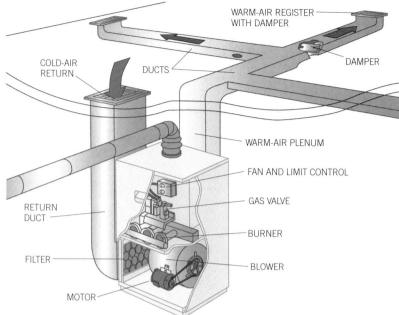

WARM-AIR REGISTER
WITH DAMPER

DAMPER

COLD-AIR
RETURN

DUCTS

WARM-AIR PLENUM

FAN AND LIMIT CONTROL

GAS VALVE

RETURN
DUCT

BURNER

FILTER

BLOWER

MOTOR

forced-air heat

Maintenance is critical for a forced-air system to perform well for a long time. Keep yours well tuned, in accordance with instructions in the owner's manual. The system should be inspected and tuned by a trained professional every year, but you can handle minor maintenance. Ask the professional how often you should clean or replace your filter; depending on your system and the amount of dust in your air this could be yearly or monthly.

Keep the system clean and make sure the thermostat (see page 163) works properly. For typical problems, see the troubleshooting information on the opposite page.

BASIC MAINTENANCE For trouble-free operation, service a forced-air system in the following ways:

■ If your furnace's cabinet contains a disposable filter, remove the old filter and replace it with one that's identical in size once every three months (see above).

■ If the filter is washable remove it, vacuum it (see left), then clean it with a hose or a hand shower. Let it dry completely before reinstalling it.

■ Brush and vacuum the heat exchanger surfaces annually. See the owner's manual for instructions.

■ Remove register covers and vacuum dirt and debris out of the boots

ZONED HEATING AND MULTIPLE FURNACES

Some forced-air systems built in the 1960s were zoned, with multiple thermostats that controlled mechanical dampers in order to raise or lower the heat in various parts of the house. Many of those systems had reliability problems, and so the dampers were often disconnected. Newer zoned systems use more reliable mechanisms, and offer an easy way to keep various parts of the house at different temperatures. (If you don't have zoned heating, you can simply close down a register to cool a room.)

Some homes have multiple furnaces, each of which has its own thermostat and supplies heat to a certain part of the house.

(the small chambers behind the covers). Get into the ducts as far as the vacuum attachments will reach (see below).

■ Clean the blower blades at the start of each heating season.

■ Vacuum debris and dust from the blower motor to prevent overheating which may lead to fire.

■ Examine the ducts annually for leaks. If you find any, seal them with professional-quality duct tape.

■ If the fan motor requires lubricating (typically twice a year), remove the access panel and squirt about

■ If the fan motor requires lubricat-

five drops of SA-30 motor oil into each port, or follow the instructions in your owner's manual.

■ If your unit includes a humidifier, you will likely need to remove its evaporative drum and clean or replace its pad at least once a year. You may also need to clean the tray below the drum.

BALANCING THE HEAT If some rooms are too hot or too cold, try adjusting the dampers in the registers and, if your system has them, the dampers on the warm-air ducts.

On a typical cold day, leave the thermostat at one setting and let the system run for three hours to stabilize the temperature. Open the dampers wide in the coldest rooms. Then adjust them until temperatures are balanced among the rooms. Wait half an hour or so after each adjustment before rechecking or readjusting.

In a home that is hard to heat, achieve maximum comfort by adjusting the blower so that it runs constantly at a lower level throughout the day. To do this, adjust the motor pulley of a belt-driven motor or, for a direct-drive blower, change the electrical connections (see the owner's manual) for a low blower speed that pro-

duces a 100-degree Fahrenheit temperature rise through the furnace while it is firing.

SETTING THE FAN CONTROL If you are chilled by a blast of cool air whenever the blower turns on, try adjusting the fan control (see below). Caution: If your furnace has a combination fan and limit control, do not touch the pointer on the limit-

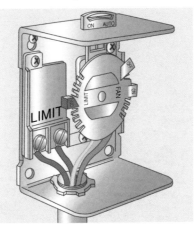

control side. This pointer turns off the furnace if the maximum allowable air temperature is exceeded.

As the blower turns on, hold your hand in front of the warm-air register farthest from the furnace. Your hand should feel neither cooler nor warmer. If it feels cooler, uncover the control and move the fan's ON pointer a few degrees higher. Adjust it as needed. To

increase fuel efficiency, check the air just before the blower shuts off. If your hand feels warmer, move the OFF pointer a few degrees lower.

TROUBLESHOOTING A FORCED-AIR HEATING SYSTEM

NO HEAT Check for power. See that the master switch is on and the circuit breaker is not tripped. If there is power, check the thermostat (page 163).

INSUFFICIENT HEAT Clean or replace the filter. Brush and vacuum the heat exchanger (see the owner's manual). Examine the ducts and seal any leaks with duct tape. If the blower is operating too slowly, adjust the speed. If you have a belt-driven blower, make adjustments as shown below.

BLOWER DOESN'T OPERATE Check for a broken belt. If the fan control is too high, adjust it. If the motor is not running, call for service.

NOISY BLOWER Oil the motor ports if there are any. Tighten or replace a loose or worn belt.

BLOWER CYCLES TOO RAPIDLY If the fan differential is too low, adjust it. If the motor itself is defective, have a professional replace it.

ROOM TEMPERATURE EXCEEDS THERMOSTAT SETTING See page 163 for servicing or replacing a thermostat.

ROOM TEMPERATURE DOESN'T REACH THERMOSTAT SETTING Check the thermostat (see page 163). Clean or replace any clogged filters. If the blower is operating too slowly, adjust the speed (see left). If the fan control is too low, adjust it.

Two adjustments for a belt-drive blower

CHECK THE MOTOR PULLEY ALIGNMENT Hold a straightedge against the pulley faces (A). If they're not aligned, loosen the mounting bolts and adjust the motor pulley.

CHECK THE BELT TENSION Push down on the belt. It should deflect ½ to ¾ inch. If it does not, turn the adjustment bolt and move the motor away to tighten the belt, closer to loosen it (B).

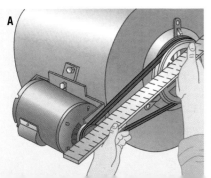

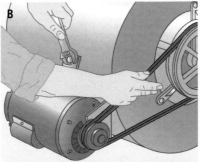

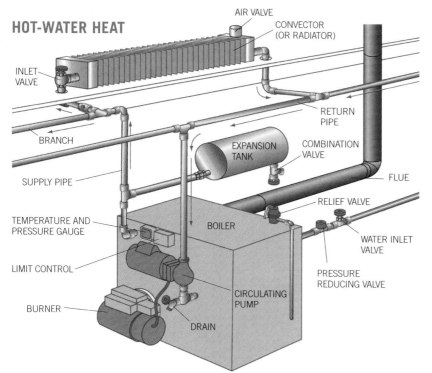

HOT-WATER HEAT

AIR VALVE

CONVECTOR (OR RADIATOR)

INLET VALVE

RETURN PIPE

BRANCH

EXPANSION TANK

COMBINATION VALVE

SUPPLY PIPE

FLUE

RELIEF VALVE

TEMPERATURE AND PRESSURE GAUGE

BOILER

WATER INLET VALVE

LIMIT CONTROL

PRESSURE REDUCING VALVE

BURNER

CIRCULATING PUMP

DRAIN

hot-water heat

In a home's hot-water system, water heated in a boiler travels through a network of pipes to radiators (in older homes) or to convectors (in newer homes) where the heat is given off. The cooled water then flows back to the boiler through return pipes.

In older homes, the movement of water is governed by gravity as warmer water rises. More modern systems employ a circulating pump to move the water under pressure.

ZONED HOT-WATER HEATING

Many hot-water systems that use convectors (rather than radiators) are zoned, meaning there are several thermostats throughout the house, each of which controls the heat for part of the house. Each thermostat controls one of the pumps that are located near the boiler. The thermostats tell the pumps when to send the hot water; a device called an aquastat tells the boiler when to come on or turn off.

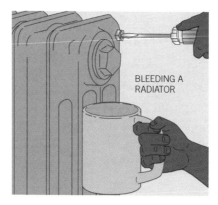

BLEEDING A RADIATOR

An aquastat governs the operation of the pump and burner.

An expansion tank, usually mounted above the boiler, contains air and water. The air acts as a cushion to maintain heated water at the proper pressure.

With proper maintenance, a hot-water system will give you many years of trouble-free service. Maintain the burner (see pages 164–167) as well as the thermostat (see page 163).

CONTROLLING THE HEAT In addition to adjusting thermostats, you can control the heat coming

from a radiator, and sometimes a convector, by turning its valve more open or closed.

BLEEDING CONVECTORS OR RADIATORS Convectors or radiators will not heat properly if air is trapped inside. If your units don't have automatic air valves, you'll need to bleed the air from them at the beginning of each heating season, whenever you add water to the system, or if a convector or radiator remains cold when it shouldn't.

Usually, the radiator or convector farthest from the boiler and on the top floor will need the most bleeding, so start there. Depending on the type of valve, use a wrench, screwdriver, or special key to open the valve. Hold a cup under it (see below left). You may hear air hissing or see water sputtering out. When the water flows without bubbles, close the valve.

RADIATOR LEAKS If a radiator leaks just under the handle at the packing nut, close the valve and try tightening the nut. If the leak is at the horizontal pipe going into the radiator, try tightening the two nuts using two pipe wrenches (see below). If a leak persists, a plumber may need to drain the system and replace the valve.

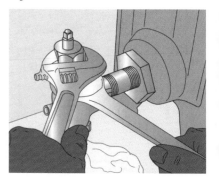

GETTING THE MOST OUT OF YOUR CONVECTORS A convector's cover is not just for show. It is configured so the right amount of cool air enters

HEATING AND COOLING SYSTEMS

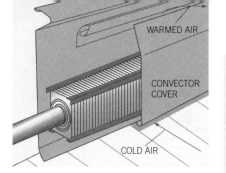

WARMED AIR

CONVECTOR COVER

COLD AIR

under the front plate to become heated and flow out the top (see above). Take care not to obstruct the cover or you will severely limit the convector's heat output. If you install new flooring in the room, you may need to raise the convectors so they work properly.

CHECKING THE GAUGES Mounted on the boiler are two gauges, one for water temperature and the other for pressure (sometimes they're combined in a single housing, as shown below). Water temperature is determined by the design of the system and the settings of the limit controls on the boiler. Adjusting the boiler temperature is a job for a professional.

The pressure gauge provides a check on the water level. The fixed pointer, set when the system was installed, is a reference point for water level. The moving pointer

TROUBLESHOOTING A HOT-WATER HEATING SYSTEM

NO HEAT Check that the electrical power is on (see page 9). Check the thermostat (see page 163). If the flame doesn't come on in a gas burner, relight the pilot or replace the thermocouple (see pages 164–65).

COLD CONVECTOR OR RADIATOR Bleed the convector or radiator.

LEAKING VALVE STEM Tighten nuts as shown on the previous page. To make other repairs (similar to those for a compression-step faucet, as shown on pages 134–35), you will need to drain the system first. Call in a professional.

LEAKING CIRCULATING PUMP Have a professional replace the pump or the seal.

NOISY CIRCULATING PUMP A professional should replace the pump coupling.

WATER DRIBBLING FROM RELIEF VALVE There is likely too much water in the expansion tank, so you'll need to drain it (see below).

indicates current water level and should align with the fixed one when the water is cold.

If the moving pointer reads higher, drain a little water from the expansion tank. If it's lower and you have no pressure-reducing valve, add water through the water inlet valve until the pointers are aligned.

In a system equipped with a pressure-reducing valve, the water level is maintained automatically. If draining the expansion tank doesn't work or if the water level is too low, consult a professional.

DRAINING THE EXPANSION TANK A pressure gauge that reads high or a tank that feels hot indicates there's too little air in the expansion tank. Draining some of the water from the tank, as shown at right, will restore the proper air-water ratio. You can do the job yourself unless you have a diaphragm tank. In that

case, call for professional service.

To drain the tank, turn off the power and the water to the boiler and let the water in the tank cool. Attach a hose to the combination valve and open it. Let water flow out until the pointers on the pressure gauge coincide. Close the valve, then restore power and water.

BALANCING THE SYSTEM If your system has zone controls, you can adjust the temperatures of various rooms simply by turning the thermostats up or down. If you do not have zones, you may need to

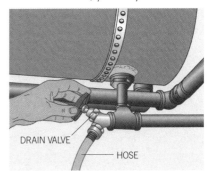

DRAIN VALVE

HOSE

balance your system to compensate for overly cold or warm rooms.

Turn on the system and let room temperatures stabilize. To adjust a convector or radiator, gradually open or close the valve. It may take several days of adjustments to bring the system into balance.

⚡ **AMERISPEC® TIP** | **REPLACING A RADIATOR HANDLE**

Most broken radiator valve handles can be replaced easily. Remove the screw holding the handle in place and take the broken handle parts with you when you buy a replacement. If the threads where the screw enters are stripped, buy a universal replacement handle, which attaches with setscrews driven horizontally into the stem.

steam heat

A hallmark of many older homes, steam heat begins in a boiler fueled by gas, oil, or electricity. The boiler turns water into steam, which rises through pipes to radiators or convectors. There the steam gives up its heat and condenses into water, which returns to the boiler.

To maintain a steam heating system in good working condition, periodically check the safety valve, steam pressure gauge, and water level gauge. Also regularly inspect the burner (see pages 164–165) and thermostat (see page 163).

Unlike a hot-water system, steam radiators get very hot, then cool off fairly quickly. During the heating season, avoid placing objects on or near steam radiators.

STEAM RADIATOR MAINTENANCE If a single radiator is not producing heat, shut off the valve at the bottom and unscrew the air vent at the top. Replace the air vent.

A steam radiator can usually only be turned completely on or completely off. To make a radiator heat-adjustable, turn it off at the bottom valve. Unscrew the air vent valve near the top and take it to a plumbing store to purchase an adjustable vent that fits. Screw the new vent in. You can now turn the radiator's heat up or down by turning a screw on the air vent.

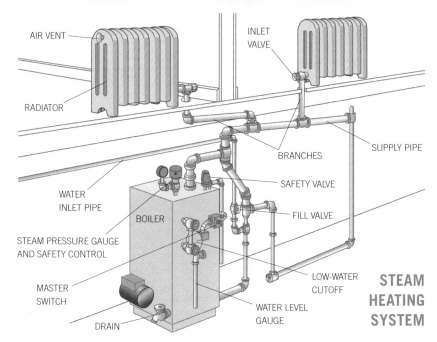

STEAM HEATING SYSTEM

AIR VENT

RADIATOR

INLET VALVE

WATER INLET PIPE

BOILER

STEAM PRESSURE GAUGE AND SAFETY CONTROL

MASTER SWITCH

DRAIN

BRANCHES

SUPPLY PIPE

SAFETY VALVE

FILL VALVE

LOW-WATER CUTOFF

WATER LEVEL GAUGE

SAFETY VALVE Located on top of the boiler, the safety valve allows steam to escape if the pressure in the boiler exceeds safe levels. Test the valve every month during the heating season by depressing the handle (standing clear of the valve pipe). If steam doesn't come out, have the valve replaced by a professional.

STEAM PRESSURE GAUGE Tap the gauge lightly to make sure it's not stuck and then see that the pressure of the steam in the boiler is within normal bounds—typically 2 to 10 pounds per square inch. If it's not, shut off the boiler and call for service.

WATER LEVEL GAUGE Once a month, open the valves at each end of the sight glass in the gauge. The water level should be in the middle of the glass. (Be sure to close the valves

after checking.) If water is not visible, immediately shut off the boiler and let it cool. Then add water by opening the fill valve on the water inlet pipe. If your system has an automatic water fill valve, call for service.

To remove the sight glass for either cleaning or replacement, shut off the valves and undo the collar nuts at each end of the glass. Install new gaskets when you reassemble the unit.

BOILER WATER LEVEL

A boiler for a steam radiator must have water at the correct level or it will burn out. Many boilers have an automatic feed that keeps the water at the proper level. If yours does not, check the water level every week or two during the heating season. If the level is low, open the valve to fill it.

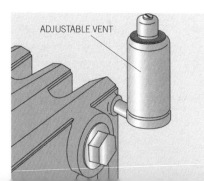

ADJUSTABLE VENT

⚡ AMERISPEC® TIP   KEEPING YOUR RADIATOR HAPPY

A SIMPLE WAY TO INCREASE HEAT Much of a radiator's heat is often misspent heating the wall just behind it. Purchase a piece of sheet metal and place it behind the radiator to direct more heat into the room.

STOP THE BANGING If a radiator makes a knocking sound, this may solve the problem: Place a level on top of the radiator. Shim the legs on the nonvalve side up so that the radiator tilts slightly toward the valve.

thermostats

Virtually all heating systems are equipped with one or more temperature controls. These thermostats occasionally need to be cleaned or adjusted. If a thermostat is defective, replace it.

Replacing a bimetal coil thermostat with an electronic model allows a greater range of programming options and results in cost savings.

HOW A THERMOSTAT WORKS A thermostat is a switch that is turned on by a temperature-sensitive device that in turn activates the switch controlling the operation of a boiler or furnace. The sensor contracts as it cools, tripping the switch to ON, and expands as it warms, tripping the switch to OFF.

The switch may have open contacts or a mercury-filled contact enclosed in an airtight glass tube. The anticipator prevents the living area from overheating by shutting off the boiler or furnace just before the desired temperature is reached.

CLEANING A THERMOSTAT Gentle cleaning helps ensure trouble-free operation. First remove the cover (it usually just pops off). First clean while the thermostat dial is in place, then remove screws and pull the dial off. Use a soft brush or a cotton swab to clean the heat sensor's bimetal coil (as shown below). Clean any switch contacts (which are shiny metal) with a cotton swab moistened with alcohol. If contact

points are nearly touching, you may need to use a thin piece of cardboard instead.

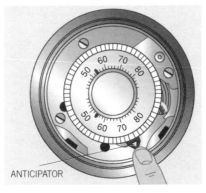

ANTICIPATOR

ADJUSTING AN ANTICIPATOR If the burner cycles on and off too seldom or too often, remove the thermostat cover. Move the anticipator pointer toward a longer or shorter setting.

JUMPER WIRE

TESTING A THERMOSTAT If there is no heat even when the thermostat is all the way on, remove the thermostat's cover. You may need to remove the dial as well. Using a short piece of wire with both ends stripped, connect the contacts marked W and R. If you hear the burner come on, the thermostat is not functioning. If cleaning does not solve the problem, replace the thermostat. If the burner does not come on, check the burner itself (see pages 164–165).

⭑ AMERISPEC® TIP   HOW MUCH JUICE?

Most thermostats run on just 6 to 20 volts carried by thin doorbell wires. There is no need to turn off the power when working on a low-voltage thermostat. However, if you see standard-thickness wires leading to a thermostat, it is a line-voltage type. Shut off the power before working on it (see page 9).

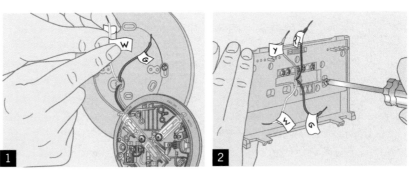

Installing an electronic thermostat

1 Remove the cover and detach the wires from their lettered terminals. Flag and label all wires to ensure that you hook them up to the correct terminals and that they do not slide back into their holes.

2 Attach the new base plate to the wall with screws, checking that it's level. Strip the wire ends. Wrap them clockwise around the terminal screws and tighten the screws. Mount the cover and follow instructions for programming.

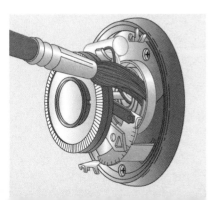

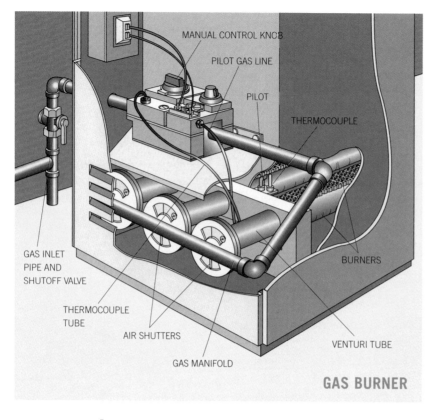

MANUAL CONTROL KNOB

PILOT GAS LINE

PILOT

THERMOCOUPLE

GAS INLET
PIPE AND
SHUTOFF VALVE

BURNERS

THERMOCOUPLE
TUBE

AIR SHUTTERS

VENTURI TUBE

GAS MANIFOLD

GAS BURNER

gas burner

Older gas furnaces, water heaters, dryers, and ranges all operate in a similar manner. When the thermostat calls for heat, the burner's automatic gas valve opens, allowing gas to flow into a manifold and then into venturi tubes, where it mixes with air. When the air-gas mixture emerges from the burner ports, the pilot ignites it and heat is created. A thermocouple adjacent to the pilot closes the gas valve when the pilot is not in use or is not working. Some newer units have electronic ignitions that light the flame with a spark rather than a pilot light.

Always turn off the gas and the electricity to the unit before making any type of repair. If in doubt about the proper procedures to take, call your gas company. Depending upon your locale, a service person may come out free of charge.

LIGHTING A GAS PILOT Use the manual control knob on the automatic gas valve to turn off the gas to the main burner and pilot. Allow at least five minutes for gas to dissipate. Allow ten minutes for LP gas, which does not dissipate readily.

Set the thermostat well below room temperature. Turn the manual control knob to PILOT and light the pilot, holding the knob there for a minute. Release the knob and turn it to ON. If the pilot does not stay on, replace the thermocouple (opposite page, bottom), adjust the pilot (opposite page, top), or call

the gas company. Remember to reset the thermostat once the pilot is relit.

ADJUSTING AND CLEANING THE PILOT ORIFICE The pilot flame should be blue and should cover the thermocouple. To adjust the pilot, turn down the thermostat. Turn the pilot adjustment screw (often under a cover screw) clockwise to reduce the flame, counterclockwise to increase it. Reset the thermostat.

If you have trouble lighting the pilot, the orifice may be plugged. To clean it, first shut off the gas supply. Disconnect the thermocou-

---

★ **AMERISPEC® TIP** **KEEP A THERMOCOUPLE HANDY**

Replacing a thermocouple is one of the most common household repairs. If you have a burner (or a water heater or dryer) that lights with a pilot, purchase extra thermocouples of the right length and keep them within easy reach so you can replace them quickly.

ple tube and the pilot gas line from the valve, and remove the bracket holding the pilot and the thermocouple.

Blow out the orifice using a flexible vinyl tube. Reattach the bracket, pilot gas line, and thermocouple tube. Turn on the gas and relight the pilot.

CLEANING THE BURNERS Clogged gas burners and ports heat inefficiently. Clean them at the start of the heating season. To reach the ports, shut off the gas valve and remove the bracket holding the thermocouple and pilot. Remove any screws holding the burners in place, then maneuver them out of the combustion chamber.

Scour the burners with a stiff wire brush, and poke a wire into the openings. Reassemble the burners in the combustion chamber. Then mount the bracket holding the pilot and thermocouple. Turn on the gas and relight the pilot.

TROUBLESHOOTING A GAS BURNER

BURNER DOESN'T OPERATE Check that electrical power is present (see page 9). See that the gas valve is turned to ON and that the pilot is on (if there is one) and relight it if needed. Check the thermostat (see page 163).

PILOT WON'T STAY LIT Make sure there is no draft that is blowing out the pilot. Clean the orifice or replace the thermocouple.

INSUFFICIENT HEAT Check the burner flame and adjust it as necessary. If flames are erratic, clean the burners and ports.

BURNER WON'T TURN OFF Immediately close the inlet valve, leaving electric power on, and call the utility company.

GAS ODOR Immediately get everyone out of the house, close the main gas supply to the house, and call the utility company from a neighbor's home or a cell phone.

ADJUSTING THE BURNERS For maximum efficiency, burners fueled with natural gas should burn with a bright blue flame that has a soft blue-green interior and no yellow tip. To correct the air–natural gas ratio, you will need to adjust the air shutters. Turn up the thermostat so the burners light, and then loosen the lock screws. Slowly open each shutter until the flames are bright blue. Then close the shutters gradually until yellow tips appear. Make sure the flame covers the tip of the thermocouple. Slowly reopen the shutters until the yellow tips just disappear, and then tighten the screws.

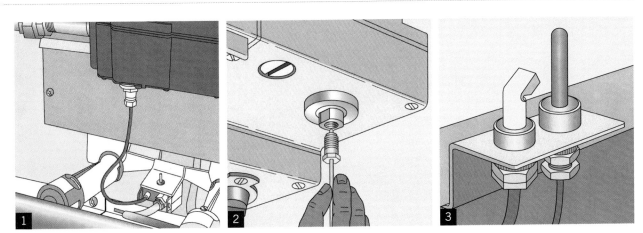

Replacing a thermocouple

1 Turn the manual control knob to OFF. Remove the cover and find out where the thermocouple is and where it travels. If it is difficult to get at the rear connection, it may be simpler to remove the burner unit before replacing the thermocouple.

2 Unscrew the nut that secures the thermocouple tube to the automatic gas valve. Pull it out.

3 Unscrew the nut holding the thermocouple to the bracket next to the pilot. Screw in a new thermocouple at both ends. Make sure the thermocouple's tip is positioned so that the pilot flame will touch it. Relight the pilot.

modern furnaces and boilers

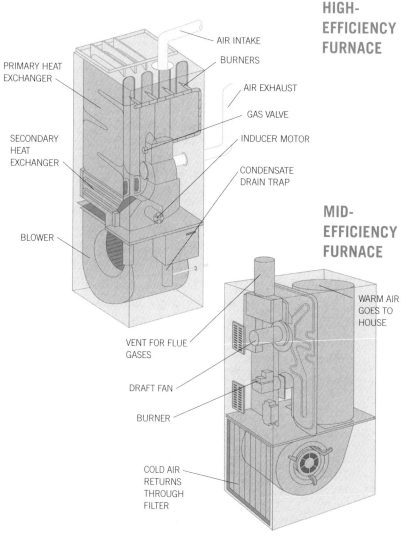

HIGH-EFFICIENCY FURNACE

AIR INTAKE

BURNERS

PRIMARY HEAT EXCHANGER

AIR EXHAUST

GAS VALVE

SECONDARY HEAT EXCHANGER

INDUCER MOTOR

CONDENSATE DRAIN TRAP

MID-EFFICIENCY FURNACE

BLOWER

WARM AIR GOES TO HOUSE

VENT FOR FLUE GASES

DRAFT FAN

BURNER

COLD AIR RETURNS THROUGH FILTER

An older furnace or boiler may run at only 60 percent efficiency, meaning that 40 percent of the heat is lost. Newer units aim for a more efficient use of energy.

"Mid-efficiency" furnaces and boilers typically have electronic ignitions rather than pilot lights, so they do not waste gas by burning when not needed. They also have high-quality burners, insulated walls, and an efficient heat exchange system that keeps heat from dissipating into the utility room. In an

older unit, natural convection draws fumes-and plenty of hot air-outside; because a mid-efficiency unit has greater heat exchange, it uses an exhaust fan to blow barely warm air outside. The result is energy savings of 20 percent or more over conventional gas furnaces and boilers.

"High-efficiency" furnaces and boilers, also called "condensing" units, achieve even greater efficiency. The process of extracting nearly all of the heat before it is exhausted results in water vapor due to condensation. So high-efficiency units

must use many stainless-steel parts to avoid corrosion, which makes them expensive. Instead of a wide flue, there are two relatively narrow pipes, often made of PVC plastic, that lead to the outside.

REGULAR MAINTENANCE AND INSPECTION A furnace's filter should be changed or cleaned monthly. Some systems have aluminum air intakes connected to a nearby chimney. See that the intakes are free of debris, so fresh air can flow freely through them.

There is often a drain line for removal of condensed water that collects in the heat exchanger. Clean it yearly by running water through it. Check the vent pipes for signs of corrosion or leaks.

HEAT-RECOVERY VENTILATORS
Newer homes tend to be tightly sealed and well insulated, which saves on heating costs. But the lack of airflow can lead to stagnant air, humidity, and perhaps even mold. For this reason, many newer homes in cold climates have heat recovery ventilators (HRVs, shown on opposite page), which provide ventilation without losing much heat or allowing significant cold to enter the house.

Basically, an HRV uses one fan to bring in outside air and another to blow out stagnant air. Air moving in both directions passes through a core unit, where the exhaust warms the cool incoming air. In summer, the system can work in reverse, so the air can stay fresh while the air conditioner is running with the windows closed. You can install a large HRV to ventilate the entire house or use a smaller version to air out a room or two.

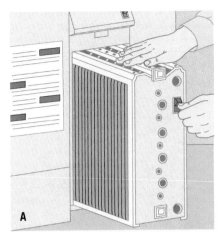

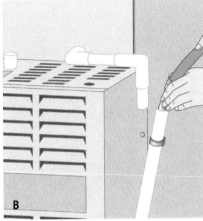

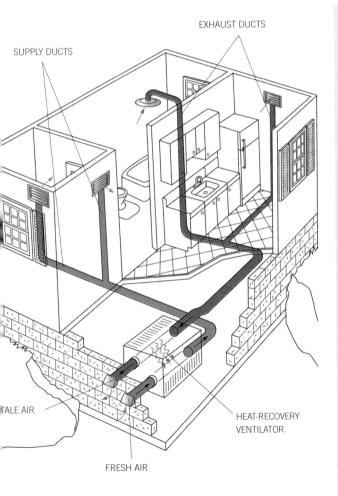

Three maintenance procedures

CLEAN THE FILTERS
Once a month, pull out the unit that holds the electronic filters (A) and follow the manufacturer's directions for cleaning them.

CLEAR THE DRAIN LINE
Loosen a clamp or a nut to disconnect the drain line. Run water from a garden hose through the line until you see the water running freely (B). Reattach the line.

CLEAR A BLOCKED AIR INTAKE
Clean away any dust, spider webs, or other material that might obstruct the free flow of air through the intake (C).

EXHAUST DUCTS

SUPPLY DUCTS

TALE AIR

HEAT-RECOVERY
VENTILATOR

FRESH AIR

HEAT-RECOVERY VENTILATOR

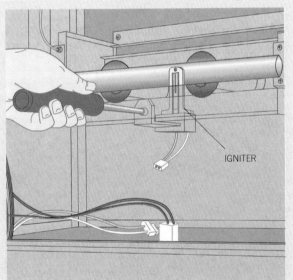

IGNITER

REPLACING AN IGNITER
If the furnace or boiler won't fire, have someone turn up the thermostat while you watch the igniter (there should be a little hole for observing). If the igniter does not glow, it likely needs to be replaced. Note: Never touch the igniter's heating element, as the oil in your fingers can shorten its life. Shut off power at the service panel, unplug the wires leading to the igniter, and remove it. Take it to a heating supply store and have it tested. If it tests faulty, replace it with an identical igniter. Reattach the wires, then screw the igniter in.

oil burner

The high-pressure, or gun type, is the most common oil burner. For greatest efficiency, call in a professional every year to service your burner. To keep repair and fuel bills low, inspect and clean the burner several times between service calls.

When the thermostat demands heat, the burner motor turns on, pumping filtered fuel oil under pressure through a nozzle and forming a mist. The burner's blower forces air through the draft tube, where it mixes with the oil mist. As the mixture enters the combustion chamber, it is ignited by a high-voltage spark between two electrodes at the end of the draft tube. If the oil fails to ignite, then the burner is turned off by a flame sensor in the burner or by a heat sensor on the stack control attached to the flue.

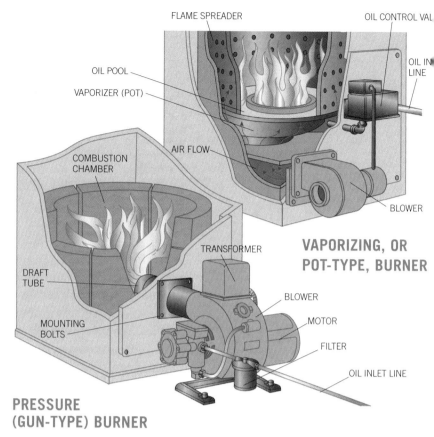

FLAME SPREADER OIL CONTROL VAL

OIL POOL

VAPORIZER (POT)

OIL IN LINE

AIR FLOW

COMBUSTION CHAMBER

BLOWER

VAPORIZING, OR POT-TYPE, BURNER

TRANSFORMER

DRAFT TUBE

BLOWER

MOTOR

FILTER

MOUNTING BOLTS

OIL INLET LINE

PRESSURE (GUN-TYPE) BURNER

Turn off the power to the burner before you begin cleaning it. Clean the sensors with soapy water as shown on the opposite page. Lubricate the motor and blower bearings by pouring oil into the oil cups, if the motor and blower are equipped with them. Clean the blower and oil strainer with mineral spirits or kerosene and, when necessary, replace the filter and gasket.

TROUBLESHOOTING AN OIL BURNER

BURNER DOESN'T OPERATE Check the master switch and the service panel for power. Check the thermostat (page 163). If the stack control motor relay or furnace limit control is tripped, reset it twice; call for service if that does not solve the problem. If the motor or motor relay is defective, call in a professional.

MOTOR SPINS BUT BURNER DOESN'T LIGHT This usually causes the system to automatically shut down. Check the tank level. Shut off the power and tighten any loose electrode wiring connections. If you see cracked electrode insulators or dirty electrodes, call in a professional. Clean or replace a dirty filter or strainer (see opposite page). If a nozzle is clogged, call a professional.

BURNER RUNS INTERMITTENTLY Clean or replace a dirty filter or strainer. If you often need to bleed and prime the pump, indicating air leaks, tighten connections and valve packings in the oil inlet line. Tighten the filter and strainer covers. If the dipstick indicates there is water in the oil, or if the flame is poor, call in a professional.

SMOKY FLAME Call a professional to adjust the air-to-oil ratio.

NOISY BURNER If there is air in the oil inlet, tighten all connections and valve packings in the inlet line. Tighten the filter and pump covers. If mounting nuts are loose, tighten them. Otherwise, call in a professional to realign the motor and pump or to replace the pump.

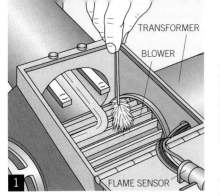

1

FLAME SENSOR

TRANSFORMER

BLOWER

Cleaning the blower, strainer, and filter

1 Turn off the power to the heating system. Remove the cover (the transformer may be attached). Clean the blower blades with a small brush.

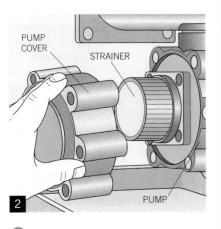

PUMP COVER

STRAINER

2

PUMP

2 To reach the strainer, unscrew the pump cover. Remove the strainer and clean it with mineral spirits or kerosene.

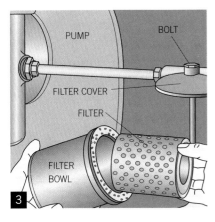

PUMP

BOLT

FILTER COVER

FILTER

FILTER BOWL

3

3 Shut off the valve between the filter and the tank. Then unscrew the bowl from the cover and change the filter and gasket.

HEAT PUMP

A heat pump is a refrigerated air-conditioning system in which the airflow is instantly reversible. In warm weather, the pump draws heat from the air inside the house, cooling it and transferring the hot air outside. During cool weather, the flow is reversed and heat extracted from the outside air heats the inside air.

Most heat pumps extract warmth from the air—amazingly, even air as cold as 30 degrees F. Water-based heat pumps use pipes submerged in a nearby pond or river. Geothermal heat pumps run a grid of pipes at least 6 feet underground, where a great deal of warmth is stored in winter. Water-based and geothermal heat pumps are much more efficient than air-based units, but they are also more expensive to install.

Once you set your thermostat to the desired temperature, the heat pump will automatically heat or cool your house as required. Where temperatures below zero degrees Fahrenheit are common, some other type of supplemental heat source is required. Because supplemental sources are normally electrical, heat pumps can be very costly to operate in particularly cold climates.

Maintenance is very similar to that for a central air conditioner and/or a forced-air heating system. Keep the outdoor portion of a heat pump free of snow and debris. Occasionally check the blower and filter in the air-handling unit indoors and replace the filter monthly during periods of heavy use.

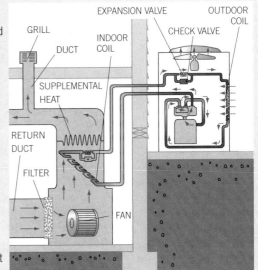

GRILL

DUCT

INDOOR COIL

SUPPLEMENTAL HEAT

RETURN DUCT

FILTER

EXPANSION VALVE

CHECK VALVE

OUTDOOR COIL

FAN

Cleaning the sensors

1 Lift the blower cover and clean the flame sensor with a soft cloth. If your flame sensor is at the end of the draft tube, leave this task to a professional.

2 Remove the stack control from the flue. Clean the heat sensor with hot, soapy water and a brush. Dry and replace the control.

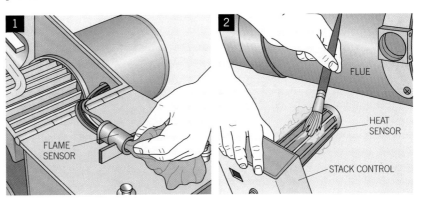

1

FLAME SENSOR

2

FLUE

HEAT SENSOR

STACK CONTROL

TYPICAL ROOM AIR CONDITIONER

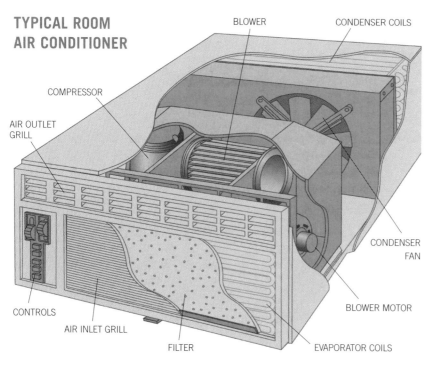

BLOWER

CONDENSER COILS

COMPRESSOR

AIR OUTLET GRILL

CONDENSER FAN

CONTROLS

AIR INLET GRILL

FILTER

BLOWER MOTOR

EVAPORATOR COILS

air conditioning

All refrigerated air conditioners, both room units and central systems, operate on the same principle. They extract heat and moisture from the room air, cooling and dehumidifying it, then return the air to the room. Refrigerant, the same substance that's used in a refrigerator, circulates through the system. A heat pump works on the same principle, except it is able to reverse itself during cool weather.

HOW REFRIGERATED SYSTEMS WORK

Inside a refrigerated air conditioner are a compressor, evaporator or cooling coils, a condenser, and connecting tubing. All are filled with refrigerant. Liquid refrigerant forced through a nozzle expands and partially vaporizes into a gas. The gas then flows through the evaporator coils, cooling the coils so they extract heat and moisture from the room air.

The warm gas then flows into the compressor, where it is heated by compression. From the compressor, the hot gas enters the condenser. There, the hot condenser coils dissipate heat to the outside and the gas condenses into a liquid, ready to repeat the cycle.

ROOM AIR CONDITIONERS

A room air conditioner is mounted in a window or wall, and most of the unit projects outside the house. A blower sucks warm room air through a filter protected by an inlet grille on the front of the unit. Cool, dehumidified air returns to the room through outlet grills. Water condensing on the evaporator coils drains outside, and a fan blows outside air around the condenser coils to dissipate heat.

During the cooling season, clean the filter and condenser coils every month and replace the filter as necessary. Regular cleaning will improve the unit's efficiency and prolong its life. You can reach the filter through a slot on either the

side or top or by removing the grill. To reach the condenser, remove the back of the outside housing. Any problems with the refrigeration system are best left to a professional.

Use a screwdriver to remove the front of the unit and lift off the cover. If the filter is washable, clean it in sudsy water, rinse it, and allow it to dry. Use an upholstery or floor brush attachment to vacuum off the refrigerant-filled coils. Use the vacuum's crevice tool to clean out all areas that you can reach. Then reassemble the unit.

CENTRAL AIR CONDITIONER

Central air conditioning is generally more efficient, quieter, and less costly in the long run than individual room units. Some systems use narrow ducts that can snake through wall cavities, so they can be installed in an older home without damaging the walls.

In a house without forced-air heat, a central air conditioner can be a single unit installed next to the house, or a split unit with the condenser and compressor outdoors and the evaporator and blower inside.

For a house heated with forced air, the most economical air conditioning installation is a split system. The evaporator is mounted in the plenum of the furnace, and the condenser and compressor are located outside the house.

To ensure efficient operation, clean the filter every month during the cooling season and replace it as necessary. Keep the area around the exterior condensing unit clear of leaves, bushes, and other obstructions. Vacuum and wipe the fan blades to keep them clean. Remove the coil guard, then clean the fins by spraying them with a garden hose from both the inside and the outside. Check that the condensate drain is clear and that the condenser and evaporator coils are clean. When you vacuum the coils, be careful not to damage the fins. Lubricate the motor as recommended by the manufacturer.

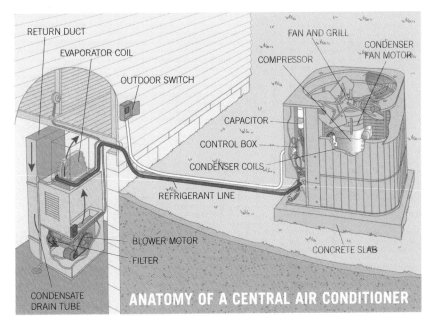

RETURN DUCT
EVAPORATOR COIL
OUTDOOR SWITCH
FAN AND GRILL
COMPRESSOR
CONDENSER FAN MOTOR
CAPACITOR
CONTROL BOX
CONDENSER COILS
REFRIGERANT LINE
BLOWER MOTOR
FILTER
CONCRETE SLAB
CONDENSATE DRAIN TUBE

ANATOMY OF A CENTRAL AIR CONDITIONER

13 SEER STANDARDS

SEER (Seasonal Energy Efficiency Ratio) is a measurement of efficiency for appliances. As of 2006, all new air conditioning and heat pump units in the United States must meet a tough 13 SEER standard, which is about 20 percent more efficient than most units previously built. If you have an older unit, you do not need to change. But if a repair person needs to replace a part, such as a condenser, you will need to install not only a 13 SEER condenser, but also other 13 SEER parts (perhaps the coil or air handler), because your older parts will not be compatible. It may be less costly to simply buy a new unit. On the bright side, 13 SEER regulations will save $3.4 billion in energy costs and avoid the construction of 150 power plants.

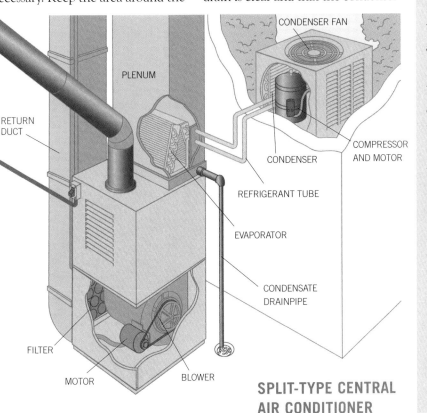

RETURN DUCT
PLENUM
CONDENSER FAN
COMPRESSOR AND MOTOR
CONDENSER
REFRIGERANT TUBE
EVAPORATOR
CONDENSATE DRAINPIPE
FILTER
MOTOR
BLOWER

SPLIT-TYPE CENTRAL AIR CONDITIONER

wiring

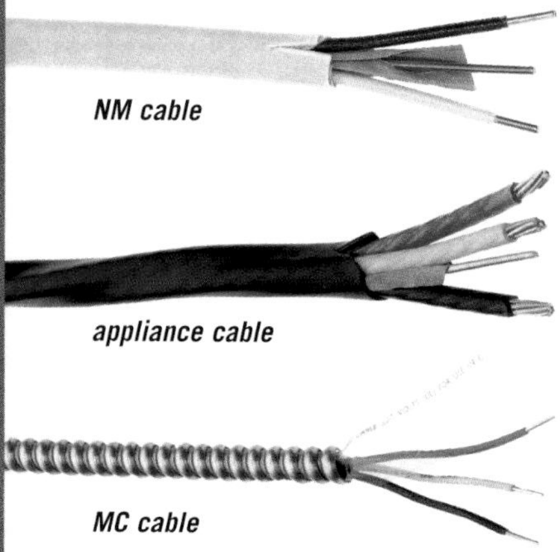

NM cable

appliance cable

MC cable

AFCI PROTECTION

If a lamp or appliance cord has damaged insulation, electricity can spark (travel in an arc) from one wire to another, creating the possibility of fire or shock. An Arc-Fault Circuit Interrupter (AFCI) circuit breaker detects the slightest arc and shuts off the circuit. It is now required that AFCIs be installed in circuits that control bedrooms. Ask an electrician if you can install this extra measure of protection in your service panel.

Your electrical system need not be a mystery. Even if you do not plan to work on it yourself, take the time to understand your home's wiring so you can speak knowledgeably with a repair person.

ELECTRICAL DISTRIBUTION As shown on the opposite page, electricity passes through a meter before it enters the service panel. Owned, installed, and serviced by the utility company, the meter measures the electrical energy consumed in kilowatt-hours. The service panel usually houses the main disconnect (the main fuses or main circuit breaker), which shuts off power to the entire electrical system, and the circuit breakers or fuses, which protect the individual circuits in the home.

Electricity travels in a circuit, moving from the service panel to the electrical user (such as a light, appliance, or receptacle) and back to the panel. Inside the panel, electricity is routed by cables to various branch circuits that carry power to different parts of the house. Each cable contains a number of wires, also called conductors. One or two hot wires carry current from the service panel to the electrical users. You can tell which wire is which by the color of the insulation, usually black or red. The white neutral wire carries current back to the panel.

In most homes built since 1945, there is also a ground wire (bare copper or coated with green insulation) which provides for grounding, an important safety feature (see pages 175–176).

THE SERVICE ENTRANCE Today, most homes have what is called three-wire service. The utility company connects three wires—two hot and one neutral—through a meter to your service panel. Each hot wire carries 120 volts, so two hot wires provide both 120-volt and 240-volt capabilities. One hot wire and the neutral wire combine to supply

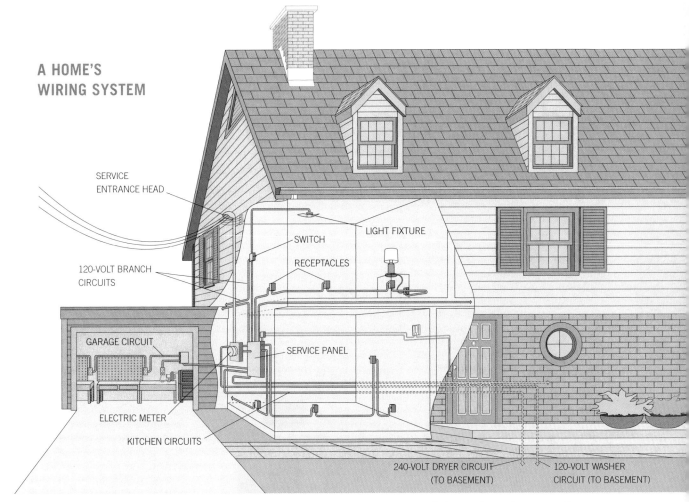

SERVICE
ENTRANCE HEAD

SWITCH

LIGHT FIXTURE

120-VOLT BRANCH
CIRCUITS

RECEPTACLES

GARAGE CIRCUIT

SERVICE PANEL

ELECTRIC METER

KITCHEN CIRCUITS

240-VOLT DRYER CIRCUIT
(TO BASEMENT)

120-VOLT WASHER
CIRCUIT (TO BASEMENT)

120 volts, the level that is used for most household applications, such as lights and small appliances. Both hot wires and the neutral wire form a 120/240-volt circuit used for larger appliances.

The system is rated for the maximum amount of current it can carry, measured in amperes. The service rating is usually stamped on the main fuses or circuit breaker and is determined by the size of the service entrance equipment. Today the minimum service rating of most new homes is 100 amps. Many of the newer and larger, or all-electric homes today have 200- or even 400-amp service. If you have an older home

that has not been updated, consult an electrician to see if you need to increase the amperage.

WIRES AND CABLES

You can usually get a good look at your cables and wires at your service panel. Most homes built after 1945 are wired with non-metallic (NM) cable, which has two or three insulated wires plus a bare ground wire. For appliances that use 240 volts, a similar type of cable, but with thick stranded wires, is often used. In some areas, MC cable is common. It houses the wires in a flexible metal sheathing and is often used where a cable must be exposed.

Solid metal or plastic conduit, through which individual wires are run, is used in some homes.

An older home may have BX cable, which is covered with flexible metal sheathing like MC cable but has no ground wire. The sheathing provides the ground path. Old homes may also have "knob-and-tube" wiring, in which individual wires are exposed and travel through ceramic knobs and tubes. Knob-and-tube wiring can last a long time if left undisturbed, but it is not grounded and is easily damaged. Some home insurance companies won't cover homes with knob-and-tube wiring.

shutting off power and working safely

Unless it is handled properly, electricity can cause dangerous, or even deadly, shocks and fires. But with a few precautions, you can work safely on your wiring. Before doing so, be sure to shut off the power; test to make sure power is not present; and make sure nobody will inadvertently turn the power back on while you are working.

Fuses and circuit breakers guard electrical systems from damage caused by too much current. Whenever wiring is forced to carry more current than it can handle safely (usually because of too many appliances on one circuit or a problem within the system), a circuit breaker will trip or a fuse will blow, immediately shutting off current.

SHUTTING OFF OR RESTORING POWER
For instructions on shutting off power to the entire house, see page 9. When replacing or testing an individual electrical user, you will probably want to shut off only one circuit. Ideally, a service panel will have an index on its door telling you which breaker or fuse goes with which receptacles. Otherwise, you will need to experiment to find out which breaker or fuse goes with

which user. (Or purchase a two-part circuit finder: Plug one part into the receptacle, and it will transmit a signal that the other part can read at the service panel.) Turn off the circuits one by one and have a helper communicate when the user has shut off.

If your service panel has circuit breakers, learn how to shut them off and turn them back on. With some

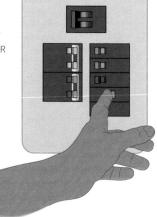

CIRCUIT BREAKER PANEL

breakers, you flip a switch to the left or right; with others, you push a button. If a breaker has tripped because of a circuit overload, it will tell you either by a switch that is partially thrown or with a button that pops out.

If you have a fuse box, you will

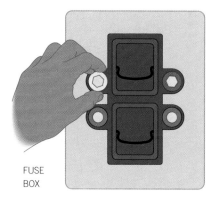

FUSE BOX

need to remove a large fuse block to shut off power to the house and unscrew a fuse to shut off a single circuit. Keep plenty of extra fuses on hand so you can replace them if they blow.

> **WARNING** *If a fuse blows often, resist the temptation to replace it with a fuse of higher amperage. Doing so could cause your wires to overheat—a dangerous situation. Call a professional.*

TESTING FOR POWER Purchase a simple voltage tester, as shown below. Test a receptacle by pushing the prongs into the slots. After removing a switch, receptacle, or fixture, test for power in several ways: With the prongs, touch the hot wire (black or colored) along with the neutral white wire; touch the hot wire along with the ground wire (bare or green); touch the hot wire

⚡ AMERISPEC® TIP **FOLLOW CODES**

Before beginning any electrical work, check with your local building department to see which, if any, permits and inspections may be required. Officials there can also inform you of any restrictions regarding the types of electrical wiring a homeowner is permitted to perform. In most cases, you can replace an existing fixture or device (switch or receptacle) without a permit. But any project that calls for running new cable will require a permit.

along with the box if the box is metal (as shown above). If there are two or more hot wires, test all of them.

TRACING A SHORT CIRCUIT

When a fuse blows or a circuit breaker trips, the cause is often easy to spot. Look for black smudge marks on switch or receptacle cover plates or for frayed or damaged cords or damaged plugs on lamps and appliances connected to the dead circuit. Replace a damaged cord or plug (see pages 180–181) and then replace the fuse or reset the breaker. If the circuit goes dead after an appliance has been in use for a short time, you probably have an overloaded circuit. Move some of the lamps and appliances to another circuit and replace the fuse or reset the circuit breaker for the first circuit.

If you find none of these signs of trouble, trace the circuit following the steps below. If these steps do not solve the problem, your wiring is faulty. In this case, call in an electrician to correct the problem.

■ Turn off all wall switches and unplug every lamp and appliance on the dead circuit. Reset the tripped breaker or install a new fuse.

■ If the circuit dies quickly after you turn it on, the problem may be a short circuit in a switch or receptacle. With the circuit dead, remove each cover plate and inspect the device and its wiring. Look and smell for charred wire insulation, a wire shorted against the metal box, or a defective device. Call in a pro to replace faulty wiring.

■ If the breaker does not trip or the new fuse does not blow right away, turn on each wall switch, one by one, checking each time to see if the circuit breaker has tripped or the fuse has blown.

■ If turning on a wall switch causes the breaker to trip or a fuse to blow, there is a short circuit in a light fixture or receptacle controlled by that switch, or there is a short circuit in the switch wiring. With the circuit off, inspect the fixture, receptacle, and switch for charred wire insulation or faulty connections. Replace the faulty switch, fixture, or wiring.

■ If turning on a wall switch does not trip the breaker or blow a fuse, the trouble is in the lamps or appliances. Test them by plugging them in one at a time. If the circuit does not go dead, it was

overloaded. Move some of the devices to another circuit. If the circuit goes dead just after you plug in a device, you have found the problem and should replace the plug or cord.

■ If the circuit goes dead as soon as you turn on the device, repair or replace the switch on the device.

GROUNDING

Current codes require that all circuits be grounded. Grounding ensures that all of the metal parts of a circuit that you might come into contact with are connected directly to the earth, maintaining them at zero voltage. This is a preventive measure. During normal operation, a grounding system does nothing. In the event of a malfunction, however, grounding protects you and your home from electric shock or fire.

The wiring method dictates how grounding is done. Most modern construction uses a separate grounding wire that runs along with the hot and neutral wires. When a home is correctly wired with older types of armored cable or metal conduit, the metal enclosure can serve as the grounding path.

Whichever method is used, the ground path must lead to the neutral or grounding bus bar in the service panel (see below). From there, it leads via a thick bare or green-insulated wire either to a grounding rod that extends deep into the earth or to a cold-water pipe, which is connected to other pipes that lead underground.

If a number of receptacles are ungrounded, check the connections where the thick ground wire attaches to a cold-water pipe or grounding rod outside the house. The connections should be very firm. If simply tightening a clamp does not solve the problem, call in an electrician.

Inside the electrical box, there are several possible methods for grounding. If you have a metal box and a ground wire, it is usually required that the ground wire be firmly attached to the box as well as to the service panel's bus bar (see below). If you have metal sheathing

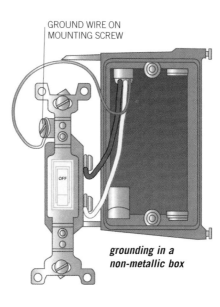

*grounding in a
non-metallic box*

or conduit and no ground wire, the metal itself must be firmly attached to the box and to the service panel (see above), and there should be no break in the line. If a receptacle analyzer tells you that a receptacle is not grounded, and if you cannot solve the problem by reattaching a ground wire or sheathing, call in a professional electrician.

TWO WAYS TO WIRE SWITCHES

There are two basic ways in which a switch and fixture are wired. With through-switch wiring, the cable

through-switch wiring

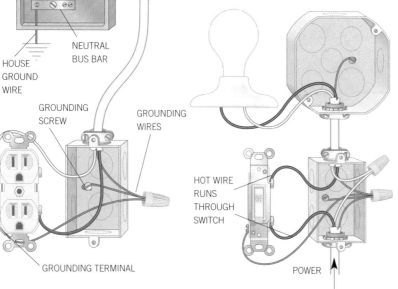

ALUMINUM WIRING

Some houses built in the mid-1960s to late-1970s were wired with aluminum rather than copper. Unfortunately, aluminum wires tend to come loose from terminals, so they were banned. If you have aluminum wiring, you don't have to replace it with copper wires, but have a professional electrician inspect your wiring. Usually, the wiring is safe as long as it connected to switches and receptacles labeled "CO/ALR." In some cases, the electrician will use special wire connectors to attach short copper wires (called "pigtails"), which then attach to the devices or fixtures.

switch-loop wiring

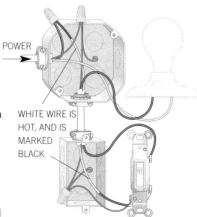

carrying power from the service panel runs to the switch box. Two cables enter the box. The two hot wires connect to the switch, and the neutral wires are spliced together. With switch-loop wiring, power runs to the fixture, then a single cable runs to the switch. Both the black and the white wires are connected to the switch, and the white should be marked black to indicate that it is hot.

grounding with NM cable

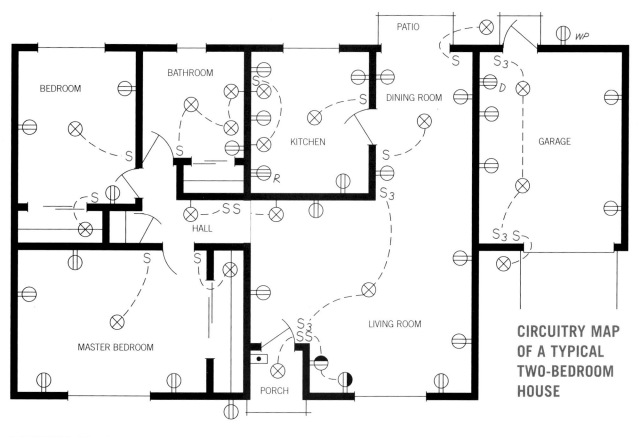

CIRCUITRY MAP OF A TYPICAL TWO-BEDROOM HOUSE

INDEXING OR MAPPING YOUR SERVICE PANEL

If your service panel does not have an index (typically taped to the inside of the door) showing which electrical users are on which circuit, make one so you can easily shut off or restore power to the correct circuit in an emergency or when you make an improvement. First make rough drawings of each room, indicating the location of each fixture, receptacle, switch, and hard-wired appliance. Assign a number to each circuit breaker or fuse.

Have a helper wander the house and tell you which electrical users are turned off when you turn off each circuit. (Communicate using cell phones or walkie-talkies, or by shouting.) Turn on all the lights in the house and turn off one breaker or unscrew one fuse. Note which lights have gone off. Also test receptacles and appliances and note them as well. Repeat this process for all the breakers or fuses, then make a chart indicating which users are controlled by which circuits.

CIRCUITRY SYMBOLS (SEE MAP ABOVE)

⊗	LIGHT FIXTURE
⊖	DUPLEX RECEPTACLE
⬒	SWITCHED RECEPTACLE
S	SINGLE-POLE SWITCH
S₃	THREE-WAY SWITCH
⊖R	240V RANGE RECEPTACLE
⊖D	240V DRYER RECEPTACLE
◓	SPECIAL RECEPTACLE
▫•▫	DOORBELL BUTTON
⊖ WP	WEATHER-PROOF RECEPTACLE
——	SWITCH WIRING

SAMPLE SERVICE PANEL LABELS

1. Range **(240 VOLT)**
2. Dryer **(240 VOLT)**
3. Kitchen & Dining Room Receptacles **(20 AMP)**
4. Kitchen & Dining Room Receptacles **(20 AMP)**
5. Washer **(20 AMP)**
6. Dishwasher **(20 AMP)**
7. Bath & Hall Lights **(15 AMP)**
8. Bedroom Receptacles & Lights **(15 AMP)**
9. Bedroom Receptacles & Lights **(15 AMP)**
10. Living Room Receptacles & Lights **(15 AMP)**
11. Living Room Receptacles, Porch light, & Garage Receptacles **(15 AMP)**
12. Garage Receptacles & Lights **(20 AMP)**

✦ AMERISPEC® TIP SERVICE PANEL SAFETY

If you need to remove a service panel's cover, be sure to first turn off the main breaker or remove the main fuse. Keep in mind that this will shut off power to everything in the panel except the thick wires that lead to the main disconnect. Those are still hot, so stay well away from them. While working, wear rubber-soled shoes and stand on a wooden platform. Do not stand on a damp floor.

working with wires

To wire receptacles, switches, light fixtures, and appliances properly, you need to know some basic techniques, including stripping, securing, and splicing wire. This section shows only how to strip and join wires. It does not cover projects that involve running and stripping new cable.

STRIPPING When removing a switch, receptacle, or light fixture that you plan to replace, you could loosen the terminal screws and remove the wires. However, doing so will cause you to unbend and then rebend the stripped wire end, which could cause it to break. As long as the wires are long enough, you are better off cutting them just below where they are stripped. Then you can safely strip and bend a new section of wire.

Buy wire strippers like those shown, with holes in the front of the tool and a spring that automatically opens them. Other types of strippers are more difficult to use.

CONNECTING Screw terminals can accommodate only one wire. If you need to join several wires at a single terminal, connect them to a short length of wire called a pigtail and connect the pigtail to the terminal.

Back-wiring an inexpensive receptacle is not a good idea, as the connection is not as strong as one that joins to a terminal. However, some high-end receptacles and switches grasp the wires securely.

SPLICING Most often, wires are joined, or spliced, with wire nuts or compression sleeves. Wire nuts come in about four sizes to accommodate various wire combinations. Each manufacturer has its own color code to distinguish the sizes. For example, one brand uses a red wire nut to splice four No. 12 or five No. 14 wires. Once you know how many wires of each size you will be splicing, check the wire nut packaging to make sure you get the proper size.

Never use electrician's tape in place of a wire nut or compression sleeve. Tape is useful for emergency repairs, but it is not a substitute for a good mechanical splice.

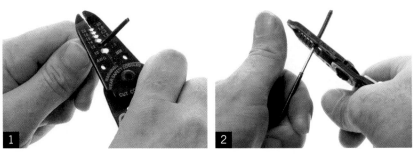

Stripping wire

1 Using wire strippers, insert the wire into the matching hole. Holding the wire firmly, position the strippers on the wire at an angle and then squeeze.

2 Rock the strippers back and forth until the insulation is severed and can be pulled off in one quick motion. With practice, you'll be able to strip wire easily and quickly.

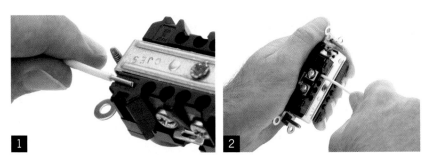

Back-wiring a device

1 When back-wiring, first use the molded strip gauge on the back of the device to measure the amount of insulation to be removed.

2 Poke the stripped wires into their appropriate holes and tug on them to make sure they are secure. Tighten down any unused screw terminals.

AMERISPEC® TIP **DON'T NICK THE WIRE**

Be careful not to nick the wire when stripping off its insulation. A nicked wire will break easily when bent to form a loop for a connection to a screw terminal. If you do nick a wire, snip off the end right below the nick and begin the stripping process again.

WIRING

WORKING WITH STRANDED WIRE

Working with stranded wire, typically used for lamp cords, calls for a slightly different technique than single, solid wire. Begin by stripping about ¾ inch of insulation from the end. Use wire strippers—never a knife, which is likely to cut through some strands. Inspect the strands. If a wire end is damaged, snip off the end and begin again.

Using your thumb and forefinger, twist the wire clockwise until the exposed strands are wound together tightly. To attach the wire to a screw terminal, twist the bare strands into a loop, then hook the loop clockwise around a screw terminal. Tighten the screw, making sure no stray wires are exposed.

✈ AMERISPEC® TIP   SPLICING SOLID AND STRANDED WIRE

If you need to splice a stranded wire to a solid wire, as when installing a new light fixture, do not twist the wires together. Instead, strip about ¾ inch of insulation from each wire. Poke the stranded wire deep into the wire nut, then poke in the solid wire. Twist the wire nut until the connection is secure.

1   **2**

Splicing with a wire nut

1 Strip about 1 inch of insulation from the ends of the wires you are joining. Hold the wires side by side, grab them with a pair of lineman's pliers, and twist the stripped ends together (clockwise) two turns or more. Once the wires are tightly joined, cut them so that the wire nut will completely cover the exposed metal.

2 Screw the wire nut on clockwise until it is tight and no bare wire is exposed. Test the splice by tugging on the wires. If any come loose, redo the splice so it is secure.

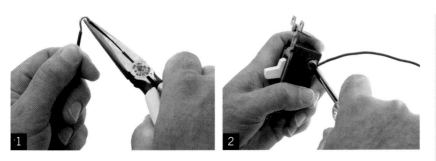

·1   **2**

Joining wires to a screw terminal

1 Strip ½ to ¾ inch of insulation off the wire end. Using long-nose pliers, form a loop in the bare wire. Starting near the insulation, make progressive right-angle bends, moving the pliers toward the wire end until a loop is formed.

2 Hook the wire clockwise around the screw terminal. (If you hook it counterclockwise, it will come loose when you tighten the screw.) Squeeze with the pliers to tighten the stripped wire. Tighten the screw. Wrap electrician's tape around the device to cover the wires and terminals.

SPLICING WITH A COMPRESSION SLEEVE

To put on a compression sleeve, first twist the wire ends clockwise at least 1½ turns. Snip ⅜ to ½ inch off the twisted ends so they are even. Slip a compression sleeve onto the wire ends and crimp the sleeve using a multipurpose tool. If code requires it, put on an insulating cap.

cords and plugs

Cords on lamps and appliances are often pulled and twisted, and an old cord's insulation may become brittle, especially if it is exposed to intense heat. If you see frayed or damaged cord insulation or a cracked or loose plug, fix it right away. Otherwise, people could receive shocks, or a house fire may result.

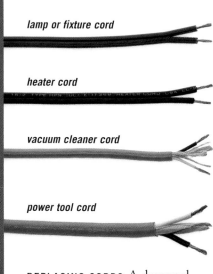

lamp or fixture cord

heater cord

vacuum cleaner cord

power tool cord

REPLACING CORDS A damaged cord should be replaced rather than repaired. However, if the cord threads through a long tube, as with the lamp shown above right, don't pull the old cord out until you have attached its end to the new cord. That way you can pull the new cord through as you pull out the old one.

A lamp cord is typically secured at the base of the socket using a special Underwriter's knot. The wire ends are then stripped and attached to the socket's terminals (see pages 178–179).

Detach or cut a portion of the old cord from the lamp or appliance and take it with you to buy a replacement with the same size wires and the same insulation. Shown at left are some of the most common types of lamp and appliance cords. Replace the plug at the same time as the cord. If possible, buy a cord that has a plug already attached.

REPLACING PLUGS Any plug with a cracked shell or with loose, damaged, or badly bent prongs should be replaced. Plugs that transmit power erratically or get warm when used should also be replaced. If a plug sparks when it's pushed into or pulled out of a receptacle, examine the wires. If they're not firmly attached to the terminal screws, tighten the connections.

At a home center you will find a variety of plugs to fit most any application. In plugs with screw terminals, the wires attach to screws inside the plug body. Self-connecting plugs connect when you poke the

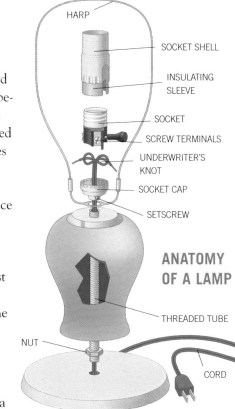

ANATOMY OF A LAMP

HARP
SOCKET SHELL
INSULATING SLEEVE
SOCKET
SCREW TERMINALS
UNDERWRITER'S KNOT
SOCKET CAP
SETSCREW
THREADED TUBE
NUT
CORD

wires into the hole.

Many old-style plugs with screw terminals have a removable insulating disk that covers the terminals and wires. Modern codes now require that plugs have a fixed insulating barrier instead.

ZIPPING A CORD
To separate the strands of a lamp cord, place the cord on a piece of wood. Jab the blade of a utility knife into the groove between the two wires until it digs into the wood. Then pull the cord. If you accidentally expose any bare wire, cut the cord and try again.

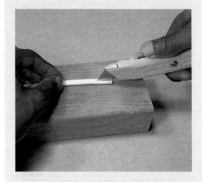

★ AMERISPEC® TIP **WORKING WITH CORDS**

WATCH THOSE RIBS It's important to connect the smooth, hot wire to the brass terminal, and the ribbed, neutral wire to the silver terminal. If you get the wires switched, the lamp or appliance will have power running to it even when it is turned off, creating a safety and fire hazard.

USE TAPE WITH CAUTION If you wrap a damaged cord with electrician's tape, which is at best a temporary repair, be sure to wrap each wire separately so that the two wires will not touch each other.

WIRING

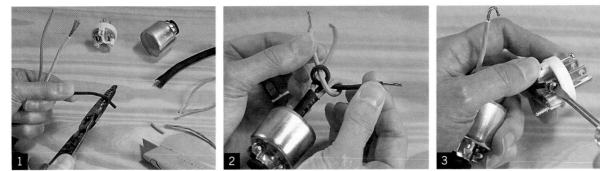
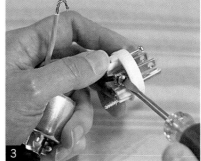

Wiring a plug with screw terminals

1 Unscrew and disassemble the plug. Use a utility knife to strip off the cord's outer sheathing and strip about 1 inch of insulation from the wires.

2 Tie an Underwriter's knot. Make two loops with the wires, pass the loose ends through the loops, and pull.

3 Form loops on the wires and wrap them clockwise around the screw terminals. Tighten the screws, then reassemble the plug.

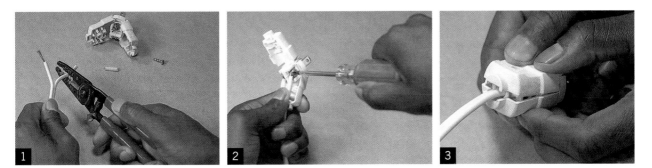

Wiring a snap-shut appliance plug

1 Loosen the screws and open the plug. Use a knife to separate the ends of the wires and then strip about ½ inch of insulation from the wire ends. Twist the wires tight (see page 179). You can also buy a grounded three-prong plug of this type. If you do, strip the sheathing and wires.

2 Loosen the terminal screws and poke the wires in—smooth (black) to the brass terminal, ribbed (white) to the silver terminal, and any ground wire to the remaining terminal. Tighten the screws to clamp the wires.

3 Pull on the wires to make sure the connections are secure. Thread the cord through the groove in the plug body and clamp the body shut. Tighten the plug's screws.

Two more replacement plugs

SELF-CONNECT To attach a self-connecting plug, push the unstripped cord through the shell and into the terminal block. Squeeze the prongs together to grip the cord and slide the shell up until it clicks into place.

self-connecting plug

FEMALE APPLIANCE PLUG First unscrew the plug shell, then feed the cord through the spring guard. Strip the wire ends, wrap them clockwise around the screw terminals, and tighten. Reassemble the plug.

female appliance plug

replacing switches

three-way switch

I f a switch fails to turn on and off or its toggle becomes a bit wobbly, or if it makes a popping sound that may be accompanied by a spark, it's time to replace the switch. You may choose to replace a standard switch with a dimmer or another special-duty switch, as shown on the opposite page.

By far the two most common types of switches are the familiar single-pole variety (as shown in the steps below), which controls one or more lights from one location, and the three-way switch (see left), which allows you to turn lights off and on from two locations. A single-pole switch has two brass terminals and perhaps one green ground terminal, and a three-way has three brass terminals and perhaps a green ground terminal. Most modern switches have back-wiring holes (see page 178) as well as terminals.

Switches are rated for a specific voltage and amperage. Whenever you replace a switch, check the service panel for the correct amperage, and purchase a switch to match.

Unlike receptacles, switches are wired only with hot wires. See page 176 for the two basic ways of wiring a single-pole switch. Three-way-switch wiring is more complicated, so label the wires as you remove them from the old switch so you can replace them in the same configuration.

> **CAUTION** *Always shut off the power to the circuit (page 174) before beginning work. Use a voltage tester to make sure the circuit you're working on is dead before you touch any wires or terminals.*

⚡ AMERISPEC® TIP **MAKE SURE YOU CAN WIRE IT**

Some special switches, such as certain types of timers, can be installed only if power runs to the switch box and there are two cables entering the box (see page 176). If you have only one cable entering the box, check to be sure you can install the switch of your choice. Also, some special switches can be used to replace three-way switches, while others can replace only single-pole switches.

Replacing a single-pole switch

1 Shut off power to the circuit. Remove the switch cover plate, loosen the old switch's mounting screws, and pull the switch gently out of the wall. Test to see that the power is off. If the house wires are very short, loosen the terminal screws and remove the wires. If the wires are long enough to be reused after cutting, snip them as close to the switch as possible.

2 Splice the grounding wires with a short piece that runs to the switch's grounding screw and then join them with a wire nut (see pages 175–176 for various grounding methods). Strip the black wires (there may be one white wire that should be marked black), form loops, and attach them to the terminals (see pages 178–179). Wrap the terminals with electrician's tape.

3 Fold the wires behind the switch. Carefully push the wires into the box and guide the switch's screws into their holes. Then align the box vertically and tighten the screws. Finally, screw the faceplate to the switch. Restore power to the circuit.

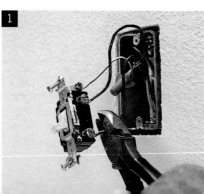

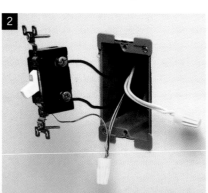

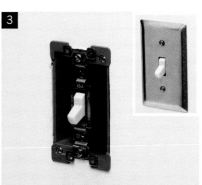

pilot switch

motion-sensor switch

dial timer

preset timer

programmable timer

SPECIAL-DUTY SWITCHES

Today, switches can do more than just turn the lights on and off. Dimmers allow you to control the level of brightness and help save energy. A dimmer switch may have

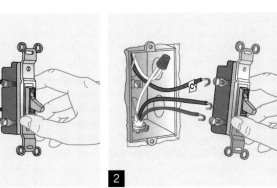

sliding switch dimmer

round dial dimmer

a round dial, a sliding switch, or a toggle that looks just like a standard switch. Some dimmers have separate on-off and dimmer controls, so they retain the level of lighting you chose last time you turned them on. Others have fade controls to turn the light on and off gently.

A pilot switch has a toggle that glows when the fixture or appliance is on but is out of sight and mind. It is useful for basement lights, outdoor lights, and remote appliances such as attic fans.

Some timer switches allow you to set a light, bathroom heater, or other device to turn on and off at predetermined times each day. A programmable timer provides multiple daily settings.

A motion-sensor switch can be used for security, convenience, or energy savings. The switch turns the light on when it detects movement in a room, then shuts off after a predetermined interval.

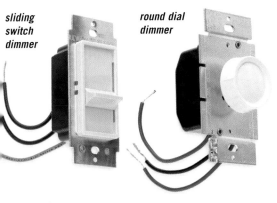

1

Replacing a three-wire switch

1 Shut off the power, remove the cover plate, and test for power. Pull out the switch and use tape to label the wire to the common terminal, which is a different color than the others.

2

2 Cut, strip, and attach the wires as you would for a single-pole switch (see pages 178–179). Attach the labeled wire to the common terminal screw of the new switch. Connect the remaining wires and reattach the box as you would for a single-pole switch.

INSTALLING A DIMMER OR OTHER SPECIAL SWITCH

Wire a dimmer as you would a standard switch, except that most dimmers have short wires (called leads) rather than terminals. Splice the wires to the house's wires using wire nuts. Because a dimmer typically has a thicker body than a single-pole switch, you may need to work with extra care to fold the wires into a smaller space in the box.

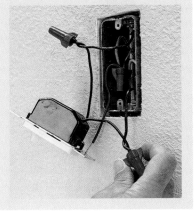

receptacles

The most common household receptacle is the 15- or 20-amp, 120-volt grounded duplex type, which has two outlets. The larger (neutral) slot accepts the wide prong of a three-pronged plug. The smaller (hot) slot is for the narrow prong, and the hole is for the grounding prong. Both amperage and voltage are stamped on the front. Be sure to install 20-amp receptacles only on circuits

15-amp, 120-volt grounded duplex receptacle

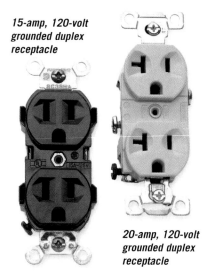

20-amp, 120-volt grounded duplex receptacle

controlled by a 20-amp circuit breaker or fuse. If a receptacle lacks a third hole, it is ungrounded. Consult an electrician to see whether you can provide grounding and install a grounded receptacle.

Use a receptacle analyzer (see page 175) to test whether a receptacle is properly wired and grounded. If it's not, you may need to call in an electrician for an evaluation.

High-voltage 240-volt receptacles have slot configurations to ensure that only the right kind of plug can be inserted. Some combine 120 and 240 voltages to accommodate such appliances as clothes dryers and kitchen ranges, which need higher voltage for motors and lower volt-

age for timers and controls. A three-pole 240-volt receptacle has two hot slots and a grounding slot. Its configuration matches a specific plug and amperage and is not usable with other plugs.

The ground fault circuit interrupter (GFCI) is a device designed to protect you from electric shocks by shutting down when it senses even a tiny change in current. A 120-volt GFCI receptacle takes the place of a standard duplex receptacle and monitors electrical current. Whenever the amounts of incoming and outgoing current are not equal, such as during a ground fault or current leakage, the GFCI opens the circuit instantly, cutting off the electricity. GFCIs are required in

areas such as bathrooms, kitchens, garages, all exterior areas, and in any exposed area where ground faults are most likely to occur. Correctly wired, a single GFCI receptacle can provide protection for other receptacles or lights that are wired down the line.

In general, wire the new receptacle in the same way that the old one was wired. If the wiring is complicated, use tape to label some or all of the wires. See pages 175–176 for different ways receptacles can be grounded and for some common wiring configurations.

ground fault circuit interrupter (GFCI)

A high-quality receptacle can be back-wired (see page 178), but avoid back-wiring an inexpensive receptacle. The connections are usually not as secure as those made by screw terminals.

Replacing a grounded receptacle (middle-of-the-run)

Shut off the power, remove the cover plate, and test to make sure the power is off. As you would for a switch, pull the receptacle out, cut or unhook the wires, strip them, and connect them to the new terminals. Attach the black or colored (hot) wire to the brass terminal and the white (neutral) wire to the silver terminal. Attach the grounds (see pages 175–176). Another way to wire a middle-run switch is to attach

the wires to all four terminals. Screw the receptacle to the box and replace the cover plate.

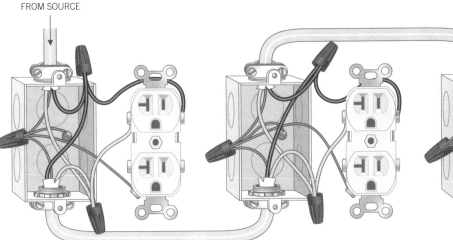

FROM SOURCE

Two switch-controlled receptacles

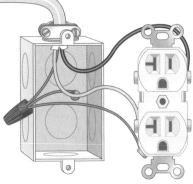

CAUTION *Before working, turn off power to the circuit (see page 174) and test to make sure the power is off. Be extra careful when working on a 240-volt circuit. You may need to shut off two circuit breakers or remove two fuses.*

RECEPTACLE WIRING If a receptacle is in the middle of a cable's run, there will be two cables entering its box, one bringing power in and one sending power down the line. The wires may be connected as shown on the opposite page, or they may be attached to both of the terminals on either side. At the end of the run, only one cable enters the box.

In some cases, a receptacle is split so each of its outlets is wired separately. To do this, first remove the connecting tab joining the two

hot terminals (see below). Sometimes one outlet is wired so it is controlled by a switch, while the other outlet is always hot. Or each outlet may be wired to a different circuit, allowing you to plug in two high-amperage appliances without overloading a circuit.

Two switch-controlled receptacles

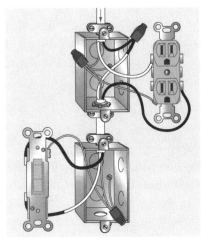

BOTH OUTLETS CONTROLLED BY A SWITCH Here the receptacle is wired much like a light fixture when power runs to the fixture's box (see page 176).

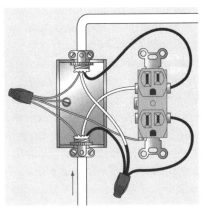

ONLY ONE OUTLET IS SWITCH-CONTROLLED Here the tab between the two brass terminals has been broken off.

FROM SOURCE

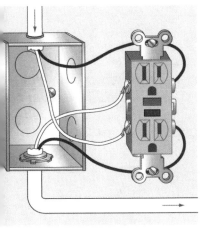

Replacing a GFCI receptacle

To wire a GFCI so it protects other receptacles or lights down the line, as shown, hook the wires that bring power into the box to the LINE terminals and the wires that go out to other receptacles to the LOAD terminals. As with a standard receptacle, hook the hot wires to the brass terminals and the neutral wires to the silver terminals. If the GFCI is at the end of the run, simply hook the wires to the LINE terminals.

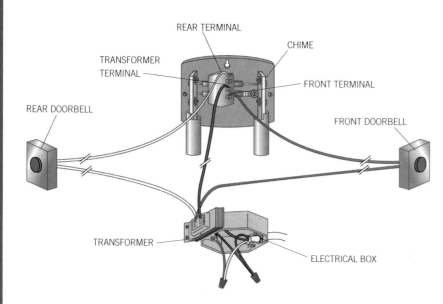

REAR TERMINAL

TRANSFORMER TERMINAL

CHIME

FRONT TERMINAL

REAR DOORBELL

FRONT DOORBELL

TRANSFORMER

ELECTRICAL BOX

doorbell repairs

A doorbell system consists of a push button, the bell or chime, a transformer, and the thin wires that run between the components. The transformer steps power down from 120 volts to a mere 6 to 20 volts, so you can safely work on most of the system while the power is on. The exception is the electrical box to which the transformer is attached. It carries standard voltage, so shut off the power before working on it.

In a system with one button, wires run in a circuit from the transformer to the button, then to the chime, and then back to the transformer. In a two-button system, wires run in circuits through both buttons. (A single wire running from the transformer directly to the chime is used by both circuits.) In a typical chime system, the bell sounds "ding-dong" when the front button is pushed and just "ding" (or "dong") when the rear button is pushed.

A SILENT DOORBELL
One of a variety of problems—a faulty button, chime, transformer,

or wiring—can cause a doorbell not to sound. Start your investigations with the simplest possible repair: the button. If that isn't the problem, move on to the chime, then

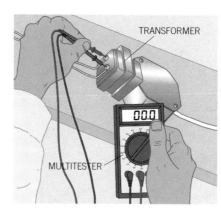

TRANSFORMER

MULTITESTER

The transformer
TEST Touch the probes of a multi-tester or voltmeter to the two terminals of the transformer. If you get a reading that is close to the transformer's voltage rating, and if the button and chime are OK, then the wiring is probably the problem. Otherwise you may need to replace the transformer.

the transformer, then the wiring.

The transformer may be difficult to find. It will be attached to an electrical junction box, perhaps in the basement or attic, on the exterior of the service panel, or in the garage. Follow the wires as best you can, looking for same-colored wires at a transformer.

A CONSTANTLY RINGING DOORBELL
If a doorbell rings constantly (or if a chime is stuck in the chiming mode, indicated by a buzzing sound), either the button is stuck or the wires going to the button are shorted together. To test the button, remove it and disconnect one of the two wires. If the bell does not ring, the button should be replaced. If the bell continues to ring, the problem is a short in the wires. If you can't find the short, you need to replace the wires.

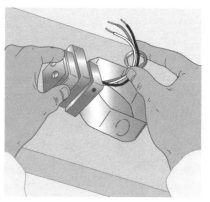

REPLACE Shut off power to the circuit, open the junction box, and test that power is absent. Pull out the wires and remove the wire nuts, restore power, and test to see that power is present in the box. If it is, shut off the power and install a transformer of the same voltage rating as the old one.

REWIRING VS. THE WIRELESS OPTION

REWIRING If the problem is not the transformer, the button, or the chime, the wiring is damaged. You may be able to attach a new wire to the old and pull the new wire through. Otherwise, you will need to sneak the wires through the house.

THE WIRELESS OPTION Installing a wireless chime is a snap. The button is powered by a battery, and the chime plugs into a standard electrical receptacle. On the downside, many people find a wireless chime's tone annoying, and these units sometimes sound when nobody is pushing the button.

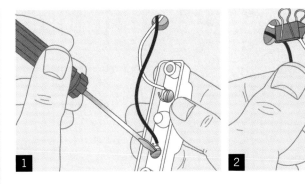

The button

1 Undo the mounting screws (you may need to pry off a cover first) and gently pull the button out. Clean away debris (small cocoons are common). Make sure the terminal screws are tightly fastened. If a wire is rusted or damaged, cut it, strip it, and reattach it to the terminal.

2 If the chime still does not sound, attach a clip to the wires so they cannot slip back into the hole, then remove them from the button. Touch the wires together. If the chime sounds, you simply need to replace the button. If you see a small spark but the chime does not sound, check the chime. If there is no spark, check the transformer.

The chime or bell

1 Remove the cover and then vacuum or gently brush away any dust and debris. See that the wires are tightly joined to the terminal screws. If a wire is damaged, cut it, strip it, and reattach it. Use sandpaper or a soft wire brush to clean any corrosion on the terminals. Check that the moving parts—like the plunger that strikes a chime—move freely, and clean anything that is gumming up the works.

2 Touch the probes of a multitester to the "trans" and "front" terminals. If you get a reading that is close to the chime's voltage rating (usually printed on the cover), the chime probably needs replacing. If you do not have a multitester, disconnect the "trans" and "front" wires and touch them together. A slight spark indicates that the right amount of power is probably getting there, so the chime needs to be replaced. If there is no power, test the transformer (see opposite page).

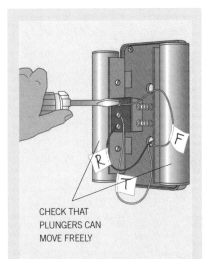

CHECK THAT PLUNGERS CAN MOVE FREELY

REPLACING A CHIME

Purchase a chime that has the same voltage and amp rating as the old one. First label the wires on the old one with tape. Loosen the terminal screws and pull the wires out. Clip the wires so they cannot slip back into the hole in the wall. Remove the chime's mounting screws and pull the chime out. Mount the new chime and attach the wires.

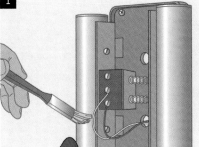

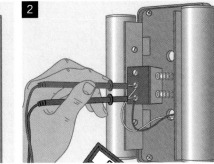

replacing a light fixture

Removing an existing ceiling fixture and installing a new one is usually a straightforward project. In most cases you can reuse the existing attachment hardware in the electrical box or replace it with hardware that comes with the new fixture. If you do need special hardware, it is readily available at a hardware store or home center.

Buy a light with a canopy that is at least as large as the old one or you will probably need to paint the ceiling. Or purchase a decorative medallion to cover ceiling imperfections. Be sure the new fixture will be bright enough. Some can handle only low-wattage bulbs and so may be disappointingly dim. Do not exceed the manufacturer's recommended bulb wattage or the fixture and its wires could overheat, creating a dangerous situation.

Three mounting variations

CENTER MOUNT Some fixtures attach via a single threaded pipe, called a stud or nipple. The stud is typically attached to the center of a metal strap.

PENDANT FIXTURE A pendant light or chandelier usually has a decorative cord that runs up through a chain, then through a center stud and into the electrical box.

HICKEY An older home may have a pancake box that will not take a strap. There may be a ⅛-inch pipe in the center of the box. One solution is to screw a hickey to the pipe and attach a center-mounted fixture.

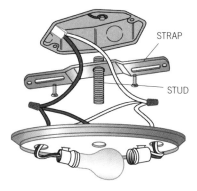

STRAP

STUD

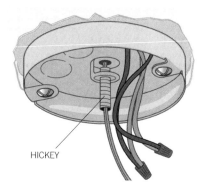

MOUNTING NUT

HICKEY

Installing a surface fixture

1 Shut off power to the circuit and test that the power is off. Screw a strap to the electrical box. Loosely fasten mounting bolts to the bar. Strip the wire ends if necessary.

2 Splice the black fixture wire to the house's hot wire and the white fixture wire to the house's neutral wire. If there is a grounding wire (as shown), secure it and the house's grounding wire to the grounding screw on the strap.

3 Fold wires into the housing box. Push the canopy into place and tighten the bolts (this fixture has keyhole slots that slip over the mounting bolts). Screw in the light bulb and add the globe.

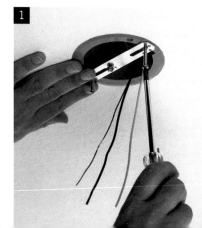

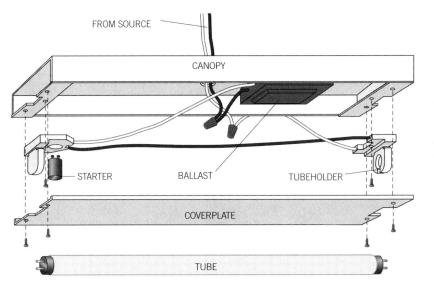

FROM SOURCE

CANOPY

STARTER BALLAST TUBEHOLDER

COVERPLATE

TUBE

tube. Turn on the power. If your new tube holder has push-in connections or terminal screws instead of permanently connected wires, connect the fixture wires to those rather than using wire nuts. A new ballast will have permanently connected wires.

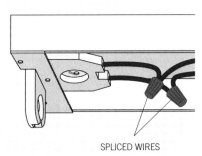

SPLICED WIRES

fluorescent fixtures

Fluorescent lights use less energy than standard incandescent fixtures. You can choose tubes that produce a warm light. Coupled with a diffuser, this can make fluorescent lighting easy on the eyes.

Older fixtures have starters and ballasts that wear out and must be replaced. Newer fixtures have no starters and have electronic ballasts that last a long time. So it often makes sense to replace rather than repair a fixture.

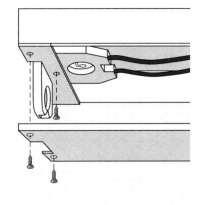

TUBES If a tube flickers, try twisting it tighter into the sockets. If its ends are very dark, replace it.

REPLACING A STARTER Before you replace a starter, shut off the wall switch to the fixture. Remove the tube. Rotate the starter a quarter turn counterclockwise and pull it out of its socket. Place the new starter in the socket and rotate it a quarter turn in either direction.

REPLACING A TUBE HOLDER If a tube holder is cracked or wobbly, it needs to be replaced. Shut off power to the circuit. Remove the tube and the cover plate (see left). Unscrew or unsnap the tube holder from the end of the fixture's canopy. Cut or disconnect the wires connecting the tube holder to the fixture. To connect the wires, strip about ½ inch of insulation from the end of each wire and connect them using wire nuts. Attach the new holder, then install the cover plate and

REPLACING A BALLAST If the fixture hums, the ballast needs to be replaced. Shut off power and test. Remove the coverplate and the

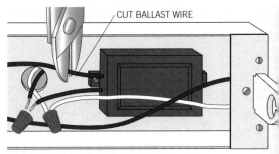

CUT BALLAST WIRE

tube. Cut or disconnect the wires, and remove the ballast. Attach a new ballast, and connect the wires with wire nuts. Install the tubes and test.

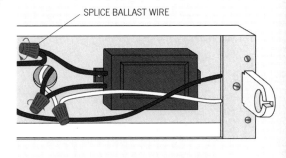

SPLICE BALLAST WIRE

photo credits

PRODUCED BY SUNSET BOOKS

vice president, general manager: Richard A. Smeby

vice president, editorial director: Bob Doyle

production director: Lory Day

operations director: Rosann Sutherland

marketing manager: Linda Barker

art director: Vasken Guiragossian

national account manager/special sales: Brad Moses

STAFF FOR THIS BOOK

writer: Steve Cory

managing editor: Bridget Biscotti Bradley

copy editor: John Edmonds

design and production: Maureen Spuhler

illustrations: Dartmouth Publishing,
    additional illustrations by Anthony Davis

technical consultants: Phil Beaver and Joe Hansa

prepress coordinator: Eligio Hernandez

production specialist: Linda M. Bouchard

proofreader: Meagan C. B. Henderson

indexer: Nanette Cardon

cover: Photography by Jamie Hadley (top left and
    center middle), Frank Gaglione (top middle),
    Mark Rutherford (center left and center
    right), Dan Stultz (top right and bottom
    left), and Christopher Vendetta (bottom
    middle)

10 9 8 7 6 5 4 3
First Printing January 2006

Copyright ©2006 Sunset Publishing Corporation, Menlo Park, CA 94025. First edition. All rights reserved, including the right of reproduction in whole or in part in any form. Library of Congress Control Number 2005936167
ISBN-13: 978-0-376-00180-1
ISBN-10: 0-376-00180-1
Printed in the United States of America

To order Sunset books, visit us at www.sunsetbooks.com.

AmeriSpec® is a registered trademark of AmeriSpec, Inc. For general inquiries, contact AmeriSpec® at 1-800-426-2270, or visit our website at www.amerispec.com.

Courtesy of A.O. Smith WPC (www.hotwater.com): 153 top; **Courtesy of Amerimax (www.amerimax.com):** 87 middle left, 87 middle right; **Scott Atkinson:** 183 bottom right, 64 all, 65 bottom left, 65 top left, 65 top middle, 91 all, 92 all, 93 middle, 182 bottom left; **Courtesy of Belwith (www.belwith.com):** 58 bottom left, 58 bottom middle, 58 bottom right, 61 middle; **Caroline Bureau:** 27 middle center, 27 middle left; **Bruce Burr:** 26 bottom left, 26 top left, 26 top middle, 27 bottom right; **Stephen Carver:** 3 bottom middle, 54 bottom left, 54 bottom middle, 54 bottom right, 54 top left, 54 top middle, 54 top right, 56 bottom left, 56 bottom middle, 56 bottom right, 62 all, 67 top left, 67 top right, 68 middle left, 68 middle right, 75 bottom, 158 left, 158 middle, 158 right, 170 bottom, 170 top; **Steve Cory:** 13, 132 all, 133 right, 154 bottom, 164, 184 top; **Courtesy of DRYLOK (www.ugl.com):** 87 bottom left, 87 bottom middle, 87 bottom right, 88 top left; **Frank Gaglione:** 112 top right, 114 bottom right; **Darrin Haddad:** 128 middle right; **Jamie Hadley:** 26 top right; **Alex Hayden:** 10 right; **Scott Hirko:** 3 top right, 18 all; **Courtesy of ICI Canada, Inc.:** 107 bottom left, 107 top left, 107 top middle; **Steven Mays:** 27 bottom left, 27 middle right, 27 top left, 27 top middle, 27 top right; **Stephen O'Hara:** 12 top; **Courtesy of the Paint Quality Institute:** 107 bottom middle, 107 bottom right, 107 top right; **Norman A. Plate:** 102, 103; **John Reed Forsman:** 117 top left, 117 top middle left, 117 top middle right, 117 top right; **Mark Rutherford:** 2 bottom middle, 3 top middle, 8 top left, 94 all, 133 left, 140 all, 141 all, 145 top, 154 top, 155 left, 172, 174 bottom right, 175 all, 178 all, 179 all, 180 left, 182 bottom middle, 182 bottom right, 182 bottom right inset, 182 top left, 183 middle left, 183 middle right, 183 top left (1), 183 top left (2), 183 top middle, 183 top right (1), 183 top right (2), 184 left, 184 right, 185 middle, 188 all; **Thomas J. Story:** 6; **Dan Stultz:** 2 bottom, 2 top left, 2 top middle, 3 bottom, 38 top, 41 all, 42 all, 43 all, 58 top left, 77 bottom right, 77 top left, 77 top right, 109 all, 111 all, 112 bottom left, 112 bottom middle, 112 bottom right, 112 top middle, 113, 114 bottom left, 114 bottom middle, 114 middle left, 114 middle right, 114 top right, 115 all, 116 all, 117 right (5), 123 all, 124 all, 125 all, 127 all, 129 bottom middle, 129 top left, 129 top middle; **Dave Toht:** 8 bottom, 8 middle, 8 top, 9 all, 10 left, 10 middle, 11, 12 bottom, 23 bottom, 28, 55, 56 top middle, 65 bottom right, 65 middle right, 65 top right, 68 top left, 77 bottom left, 82 top left, 82 top right, 87 middle center, 87 top left, 87 top right, 112 top bottom, 128 top right, 129 middle left, 129 top right, 180 bottom, 181 all; **Courtesy of U.S. Fish and Wildlife Service:** 95; **Christopher Vendetta:** 21 all, 80 all; **Courtesy of Zinsser (www.zinsser.com):** 25 all

index